The
ULTIMATE
PARDON

BILL CORUM

For information write: Prison Power Ministries,
P.O. Box 281
Lone Jack, MO 64070

All Biblical text references are from the
King James Version Bible.

ISBN: 978-0-9895249-0-2

Design: Kevin Williamson Design, LLC

Printed in the United States of America

Please visit our websites for other great articles and information:

www.prisonpowerministries.org

www.theultimatepardon.com

www.afathersblessing.org

For information regarding publicity for author interviews,
email Bill Corum at ppm@theultimatepardon.com or
write to: P.O. Box 281, Lone Jack, MO 64070

23 22 21 20 19 18

11 10 9 8 7 6 5 4

TABLE OF CONTENTS

Introduction

Bright Lights At The End Of The Tunnel

READER, BEWARE

The book you are about to read is the true account of my life; nothing has been added to try to enhance a certain scene or situation. I was first asked in 1989 to write this book; I refused, because the stories were too fresh and painful to talk about. Now, as I write, over thirty years have passed since I lived these stories. This is the first time I am telling some of them.

Writing this has been very difficult for me because I have spent years trying to forget my past. It has been overwhelming at times. To write this book honestly and accurately, I had to go back and relive days of my life I have tried to put behind me. I spent a lot of time crying as I put it all down on paper, and analyzed what I put my family—Debbie, Billy, Larry, Laura, and Richelle—through. Remembering and reliving the details of what I put them through made me almost quit this project several times. But as I wrote I got some insight into why I did the things I did, and I was able to work through some of the pain and get some healing myself. But quite apart from the healing I have experienced, I feel that if only one person reads this book and it saves a family from going through the pain that mine went through, it will be worth it.

If you know me personally or are a family member, you are going to be shocked by some of the things I did in my past. I have always been a private person, keeping many things hidden. I lived a completely double life, sometimes multiple lives. To fully understand the miracles that have taken place in my life, you have to know where I was at and some of the details of the darkness I was immersed in.

I warn you: As you read what I have written in the following pages, some of you are going to be offended or hurt. The things I did were very wrong—sick, even—but I didn't write about them to offend or hurt anyone. I need you to hear and see these stories through my ears and eyes. I want you to get a clear picture of what I lived through and what I should not have lived through. As you read, you will probably think, "This guy is sick and needs help!" I will be the first to admit you are right. I needed—and finally got—that help.

I sincerely hope you will not stop reading until you reach the end, because there is a very bright light at the end of the tunnel.

Bill Corum

Note about Names

Please note that most of the characters in this book—whether people I considered my friends or those I sold drugs to and committed crimes with—are dead. That is the reason I can freely share their stories and use their names. For any of the characters still alive, I did not use their name unless I received permission from them. This is out of respect for them and their families. If I was not able to get their permission, I changed their names.

ACKNOWLEDGEMENTS

First and foremost, I thank Jesus Christ who loved me enough to die for me. YOU changed my life completely and gave me a peace I never knew existed. I love you Jesus.

My wife, and best friend, Debbie. You are the most loving and forgiving human being I know. You could have given up on me long ago, but you chose to wait upon the Lord. Thank you for not giving up on me when most everyone else did. I could have never written this book without you. I love you honey.

My Children: Billy, Larry, Laura, and Richelle. You guys didn't deserve to grow up with a dad like me. You are all winners and needed someone who would tell you that at every turn. That wasn't me, as you grew up. But each of you chose to forgive me and gave me another shot at being a dad. Thanks for the second chance. I will do my best not to disappoint you. I am extremely proud of each one of you and love you with all my heart. Dad.

All of my grandchildren and great-grandchildren—I pray you will never go through any of the garbage I went through. Remember that Jesus loves you and has a plan for your life. He wants you to have life and life more abundant. I love you all.

I can't put into words what my friends at Gospel Tract Society mean to me. Thank you all so much for your help.

Thanks to Kevin Williamson and Chris Manley for sharing the talents God gave them with others, especially me. I pray that God blesses you over and above your expectations.

Special thanks to my dear friend of over forty years, Chuck Hanna, who taught me how to study the Bible, fast, and pray. I love you brother.

Thanks to my three business partners—John, Don, and Jason—who supported my dreams to get back in the prisons.

Thanks to Cord Laws, Doug and Tawnia Loughery, and Ron Fleckal for your special help in this project.

Thanks to my brother-in-law, Lloyd, and sister, Sharon, who prayed more years for me than anyone alive today.

And last, but certainly not least, my father and mother, who loved me unconditionally. No matter what was going on, you never gave up on me. Wait for me by the gate. I love you.

SOLITARY CONFINEMENT

It was 1963. My toilet was a hole in the floor. The concrete was cold. I could hear water running through the bottom of the hole and, although I tried to see it, I never could. It was too far down, and there was not enough light.

I lost all privileges when they sent me to the hole. They took everything away from me, stripping me down to my prison-issued boxers and tee shirt.

It always seemed cold, even in the summer. The screws—prison guards—would leave the windows open at the end of the run even in winter.

This time I was here because I was in the wrong place at the wrong time. A fight broke out and a guy I knew was getting beat by two or three other inmates. I jumped in to help him and didn't see the guards coming to break it up. Everyone fighting got sent to the hole. *Oh well, who cares.* I would do it again to help my friend.

Huh, this may be the exact same cell I was in last time, I thought, looking around me. Every cell looked the same. Nothing had changed since the last time I was here, except for what some lonely inmate scratched on the walls.

There was nothing to sit on—not even a bed. The lousy hacks—guards—would bring me a mattress at two in the morning and take it away at six. Out of twenty-four stinking hours, I was only off that hard, cold concrete for four. The mattress was about three inches thick and it didn't have much padding, but it beat the bare concrete.

The cell was exactly six feet across and nine feet long. I must have measured it fifty times a day, and this time I would be here for twenty days. I did pushups and sit-ups all day to try and stay in shape. I put my feet up against the concrete wall and started doing handstand pushups. I had a reputation in this place, and part of it was my physical strength and the speed of my hands and feet. I shadow-boxed and practiced kicking for hours every day, I could kick a light bulb out of its socket on an eight-foot-high ceiling.

There were six isolation cells back-to-back, two tiers high, twenty-four all together in this section of the prison. If they brought me to the hole at the right time of day and it wasn't cloudy, I could see a little sunlight through the windows at the end of the run. Otherwise there wasn't enough light to see where I was.

When I came here the first time, I had been charged with something worth going to the hole for. I ripped a guy's ear off because he owed me money. I was involved with the men who ran the biggest store in Little Alcatraz—as the guards who transferred from Alcatraz, called our prison—and when someone didn't pay us, we always figured out a way to make them pay. We kept our store customers in line by strict enforcement.

I decided I needed to make an example out of Gray, and that meant doing something he wouldn't forget. I snuck up behind him in the chow hall while he was eating and stole on him—hitting him when he wasn't expecting it. When he hit the ground, I grabbed a whole handful of ear, and jerked with all my might. As strong as I was, he ended up in the infirmary getting most of his ear sewn back on. I earned a lot of respect for that trip to solitary confinement.

This time I was here for trying to help a guy I wasn't even very good friends with. I started thinking back…what led me to be in this God-forsaken place?

AN OUTLAW CHILD

My life of crime and rebellion started when I was about eight years old. My best friend Jesse and I stole things and took them to our hideouts. That's what we called the forts we built in the woods behind our house. Jesse was an American Indian and I thought it was pretty neat having a real Indian for a friend.

We stole cigarettes from his mom and dad and smoked them. When we didn't have cigarettes we made our own. We rolled paper really tight and smoked it. Any kind of paper would work, but the best was something really thin. Sometimes we used paper from telephone books. It was hard to roll, but it worked well. I remember how smoking those paper cigarettes made us choke and cough real badly.

Jesse and I spent whole summers in those woods. We built forts and swung on the vines in the trees, like Tarzan. We had places where we knew no one could find us or the goodies we had stolen. We kept different stolen things in all of our hideouts.

We made bows and arrows, spending hours every day shooting at wasps' nests. We also shot at them with home-made bean shooters; they were real accurate and could destroy a big nest. We would find a small branch on a tree with a good fork in it, and a good straight handle. We notched the top of the fork and tied strips of rubber to it, cut from an old tire inner tube. Out of a piece of thick leather, we made a rock holder—that's what we called it—and tied it to the other end of the rubber strips. We searched for just the right size rock, put it in the leather holder, and pulled it back with all our strength. We used the fork for a sight. Once we got a big wasp nest in the middle of the fork, we'd release the rock, and run as fast as our legs would carry us. The old saying about stirring up a hornet's nest…I know all about it.

We got stung many times every single day and just ran to the pond to put mud on our wasp stings. That was a trick all Indians knew, and Jesse taught me. The next day we headed right back to the woods to do the same thing and got stung all over again. I never told my mom I was getting stung. She probably wouldn't have let me go back to the woods if she had known.

I knew other kids in the neighborhood, but none of them were like me and Jesse. I was afraid they would tell on us, if they knew what we were up to. So I mostly kept to myself and my Indian buddy.

We spent those summers getting into all kinds of mischief. I remember Jesse like it was yesterday, although it has been sixty years.

I was ten years old when we moved away from my friend Jesse. It broke my heart because he and I had some deep, dark secrets. I didn't want to make friends with anyone else; I just wanted to be with my Indian friend.

The secrets we kept were not all that bad, but when I was that young I thought they were the worst things anyone could possibly do. We found some *Playboy* magazines that Jesse's older brother and his friends were hiding. We took them and hid them in our forts.

We were always really careful going to our hideouts, making sure no one followed us or even saw us heading towards the woods. We would have a lot to lose if anyone found our forts. Once inside, we looked at the magazines we stole from the big guys and denied it when they questioned us about what happened to them. We never did it again, because if they caught us, the odds were stacked against us. We could never outrun them and had no chance fighting them.

My mom and dad let me have Jesse over to our new house after we moved in, and the first time he came over we got in big trouble. It seemed to me that we were a hundred miles from where we used to live. In reality it was only five miles farther out of the city, but when you are little and don't drive a car, five miles is an awful long way.

This was at an amusement park. I am on the left and was about 10 years old. A foreshadowing of things to come?

Right across the street from where we lived was an eighty-acre cornfield. They had not harvested it yet, but it was ready. Jesse and I went over in the middle of the cornfield and tore out a bunch of cornstalks. We built ourselves a really cool fort. We made some cigarettes out of corn silks—another thing Indians know how to do—and smoked them in the hideout. We got a little careless and started a fire. After all, this was field corn and it was dry and ready for harvest. We tried to put the fire out, but we had no chance. It was burning out of control. We ran for it and got out . . . but not by much. We burnt up a lot of that hard-working farmer's cornfield that day. No one ever knew it was Jesse and me who started it. If my sister reads this book she will be the first one of my family to know that I did it. I think I am safe now; it has been almost sixty years.

If that wasn't enough excitement for one day, that night we did something that was really serious. We snuck into the house and got one of Mom's big brown grocery sacks—a full-size one. We found a big rock that just barely fit inside the sack and laid it out in the middle of 87th Street. We hid behind some bushes and waited. Most of the cars swerved to avoid it, but just when we were about to give up, a car came along. The driver must have thought it was an empty grocery bag and ran right over it. They lost control, swerved around on the road, and ended up in the ditch. We were hoping they would flip over. Afraid that the driver would come after us, we ran and he never saw us.

I can't remember if Jesse got to come out much after that. No one knew we did that stuff, but my mom and dad probably suspected we were the ones that set the fire.

3

THE REBEL

started kindergarten at Blue Ridge Elementary in Raytown, Missouri in 1949, when I was five years old.

I was very innocent at that age

I hated school from the first day of kindergarten until the day I quit; I do not have one good memory of going to school, although I do have some good memories of things I did when I *skipped* school. If any of my classmates read this book, they will be surprised because I don't think many of them knew how much I hated school. I was good at keeping things from people, and even as a kid in grade school I was honing my skills for when I would live a completely double life as an adult.

When I was eleven years old, for some reason the city sent part of the sixth grade to the high school and the other part to the old Raytown City Hall. I was among those who went to the high school. I got to see Jesse a lot during that time, because he was in the eighth grade and the junior high school was right behind the high school. We often met up and walked over to the store right across the street from Raytown High. It was called EG COLLINS, and all the guys who hung out there were called EG's. I wanted to be an EG, but they wouldn't let any sixth grader be in their gang. It wasn't really a gang like the gangs today; they just called themselves EG's and I thought it was a gang.

It was 1955 and the style was ducktails, cuffed blue jeans, and a pack of cigs rolled up in your tee shirt sleeve. The hit songs were *Rock Around the Clock*, *Mr. Sandman* and *Sixteen Tons*. The EG's would stand around outside the store before school, smoking cigarettes. I would hear one of them telling all about what he did to the girl he was with the previous night. I would listen very intently and sometimes wonder what they were even talking about, because, at age eleven, sex was not something I knew much about. But there was no way I was going to let them think I didn't know. As I listened and watched those guys, I dreamed that one day, I would be an EG and *I* would be telling those stories.

Some of those guys really had cool cars. I remember a nice 1950 Chevrolet in black primer that had a Cadillac engine in it. There was a real big guy named Bob who had a customized car—a chopped and channeled 1949 Mercury. I was so envious of those guys, and wished that someday I could have a Mercury that was chopped.

*When I was only eleven years old and would listen to the EG's
tell stories and watch them in their cars, I dreamed that someday
I would have a chopped 1949 Mercury. It has been fifty-eight years
since I dreamed that, this is my Mercury in 2013
never give up on your dreams.*

I stared at those EG's like most people would stare at a movie star. To me they were greater than any movie star; they represented everything I wanted to be…a rebel.

MY BEST FRIEND'S DEATH

When I was in high school I always listened to WHB on the radio. One morning while getting ready to go to school I heard them report that Jesse Whitestone, sixteen years old, died from drinking a fifth of whiskey on the eve of his seventeenth birthday. My heart almost stopped; I screamed, "NO!" I cried and cried. I was a mess. He had been my closest friend for several years and I would have done anything to bring him back.

The talk around town was that he had been drinking all day, and ran into these drinking-age guys who bought him a fifth of whiskey. They bet him that he couldn't drink all of it in thirty minutes. Word was that Jesse drank it in five minutes. They left him passed out in the backseat of their car and went inside the Raytown bowling alley. When they came back out, he was dead. He choked to death on his own vomit.

That day changed my life.

I didn't care about anything much after that. I managed to get into the EG's and became a total rebel. The EG's were already beginning to break up as a group when I got in. Maybe that's why they let me join. I considered myself a rebel with or without them. They weren't really as bad as I thought they were anyway. They just hung out, smoked a little, drank a little, and tried to lay every girl they could get in their car. I was way more motivated to become a serious rebel than they were.

Not long after Jesse died, I took one of my dad's ice picks; I used his grinder and sharpened it up to a needle point. I went by myself, walking a couple of blocks over from where we lived, and flattened every tire on every car on the whole street. Each time I stuck that ice pick in another tire I cussed and laughed. I was just so angry that Jesse died…I wanted to hurt someone or something.

One night I went through a neighborhood, and if I knew that no one was home, I took their garden hose, broke out their basement window, and put the hose in. I then turned the water on full blast. I did this and other acts of vandalism in neighborhoods that were far enough from mine that I wouldn't be suspected of being involved. I was going to the pool hall the year before Jesse died, but now it became the place I spent most of my time.

Sometimes I wouldn't go to school all day. I would go long enough to be seen and then sneak off. I would go to the pool hall and stay there until it was time to go back to school and catch my bus home. I figured out the school system pretty well and knew when they were looking for me. I would show up and tell them some big lie and be convincing enough to get away with it.

I would hide out in the pipe chases and tunnels where the plumbing and electrical lines for the whole school were. Not even the principal knew how to get in those pipe chases. I would go with a buddy and smoke, and do anything else we weren't supposed to be doing.

I could have made money as a forger back in those days, when the school system sent report cards home to get our parent's signature. I was good at changing any letter on my grade card into anything I wanted it to be. I became an expert at covering my stories and not getting caught. Little did I know, this was my practice for living a life of deception.

I spent more time in the pool hall than I did in school; it seemed that was where all the rebellious guys hung out—and that's what I wanted to be. Jesse was gone and I didn't care about anything.

AN UNFORGETTABLE DAY

When I was fourteen, the pool hall was a much better place to get an education than Consolidated School District Number 2. The classes taught there were not offered at the Raytown schools. Basic classes were: how to pick a straight cue stick, 9-ball, 8-ball, snooker, and how to make a trick shot. If I wanted advance classes, there was: Gambling 101, Drinking, Smoking, Stealing, Advanced Cussing, and Sex Education. I chose the advanced classes and made the honor roll.

Raytown pool hall just like it looked in the late 50's and early 60's. I spent more time here than in school. I started sneaking out of school and going here. I soon learned that what was being taught in here was more fun than school.

At fourteen, I couldn't shoot pool very well yet, and lost more than I won. After I started spending full days in the pool hall I got much better and could hold my own.

The game I was best at was hustling. I could tell when someone couldn't play good, and would draw them into a game for money. I always beat those losers.

When I had been playing for a few years, I always made enough money for dates and gas. I wasn't good enough to beat the best players, but I would play them anyway.

I *was* as good as or better than the best though, when it came to cussing, smoking, and stealing. The best pool players wouldn't even attempt some of the things I did. They were afraid of getting in trouble…trouble was what motivated me.

I have many memories of that dark old pool hall. Except for the lights hanging over the tables it was not well lit. But it was dark in more ways than one. There were a lot of dark characters that hung out there. I am not talking about their skin color, but the color of their hearts. The darkest part of the place though was the evil plans that were devised there.

One day something happened that wasn't evil; it was unforgettable and has been etched in my memory for over fifty years.

There is no way I will ever forget the day I walked out the front door of the pool hall and saw one of the former EG's across 63rd Street getting into his car. I glanced over towards him and heard him say, "Hey kid, wanna go for a ride?"

"Yeah," I hollered back across the street at him, as I ran toward one of my favorite cars. He owned a 1954 Mercury, running an Oldsmobile Rocket engine with 3 deuces. At the top of each back fender were the words *Ramblin' Rose* in Old English lettering. We headed down Blue Ridge and right past the high school. *Oh, I hope somebody sees me riding in this car with Ed. This might be my ticket in with these guys.*

We blasted through the high school speed zone, double the speed limit. I was on cloud nine.

I asked, "Where we going?"

"Does it matter?" Ed asked, with a non-filtered Lucky Strike hanging off his lips.

I shook my head no, as we turned on to Sterling. He really nailed his hot rod. I watched the speedometer as we flew towards 47th Street. We were going over 100 mph before he started slowing for the stop sign.

"She's pretty fast, huh kid." Ed said.

I nodded my head and just grinned at him. We went to 35th and Sterling, then turned around and headed back to the pool hall. We were not going to buy anything or run an errand...he just wanted to take me for a ride. I have no idea why he wanted to take me riding that day—more than likely just to show off his car. But I do know, I have never forgotten that day.

MY FIRST PROSTITUTE

One of my cousins introduced me to prostitution at the age of fourteen. He was two years older than me and when he turned sixteen and could drive he came by my house and picked me up. We headed to downtown Kansas City, where the prostitutes were peddling their goods.

14 years old. Don't look like I should be down at 12th and Vine paying hookers. Things only got darker from this point. Jesse had died and I was mad at the world.

SCHOOL DAYS
1958-59

I have never forgotten the sound of the girl on the corner of 12th Street and Vine, as we slowly cruised by. She would sing out, "Five and two...five for the girl and two for the room." Seven dollars. That was exactly what it cost in 1958 to get a hooker in downtown Kansas City. What a chance we took! But I was all about living on the edge. This was a very dangerous part of town for two young white boys from Raytown. Little did I know that some of the places I found myself in over the next twenty-five years made that place look like a Sunday school picnic.

In Wilbert Harrison's 1959 hit song, *Kansas City*, he sang, "I'm gonna be standing on the corner of 12th Street and Vine, with my Kansas City baby and a bottle of Kansas City wine."

Yep! That was the exact same corner. The first time I heard the words of that song playing on the radio, I wondered if old Wilbert listened to those girls singing their songs on the corner of 12th Street and Vine. I am sure he visited there many times, but he probably didn't have to pay.

My friends and I made a regular habit of going downtown and picking up prostitutes. It wasn't that I couldn't get sex for free; I always had girl friends that would put out. There was just something that really intrigued me about paying for sex and trying to get the hooker to enjoy it. I can't explain it, but I can tell you that the thrill of it never went away for many years.

There were times I would have two or three girlfriends at the same time and be sleeping with all of them. I would be out on a date with one of them and run into one of my buddies. I would take my date home and tell her I had to go help my buddy do something. I would meet him and go downtown to get a hooker.

After I started driving, I drove as far as Junction City, Kansas to pick up hookers. Because of Fort Riley being there and all the soldiers, there was a good variety of prostitutes. The addiction of paying for sex lasted for the next twenty-five years. From the time I was barely a teenager until I was almost forty years old, the thrill of paying a girl for sex had a tight grip on me. It could have cost me my life on more than one occasion.

Right before I left for Marine boot camp, I had a girlfriend, seven years older than me. I didn't know how old she was until one night we were parked in an old rock quarry down on 63rd Street. We were in the backseat having sex when a light flashed through the window, scaring the life out of me. It was a cop. He told me to get dressed and get out of the car. I got out and showed him my driver's license and he asked me how old the girl was. I told him that she told me she was eighteen.

He said, "You'd better hope she's not lying to you."

The thought of her being under age freaked me out more than his badge and flashlight did. I was shaking like a leaf as I walked back to the car. I opened the door and said, "He wants to see some identification."

She handed it to me with fear in her eyes. That *really* made me nervous! I didn't even look at it, I just handed it to him.

"How old did you say she was?" he asked, peering over the top of his glasses.

"Honest, officer, she told me she was eighteen."

"What would you say if I told you she's twenty-five?"

My grin was so big—if I was wearing lipstick, I would have gotten it on both ears. "I don't care how old she is sir, as long as she's not under eighteen."

The nice cop said, "Get your shoes on son and get out of here."

I would take her to drive-in movies, hop in and out of the back seat a couple of times during the night, and then take her home. Then I would go look for one of my friends on the way home, and he and I would high-tail it to 12th and Vine.

I was truly hooked on hookers. I have thought about it for years and I still don't know why. It wasn't because I was ugly and couldn't *get any* on my own. I was good looking and had girls chasing me way before I chased them. I discovered girls about the same time I fell in love with cars. I had a tough time deciding if I wanted to be in the back seat or under the hood. I thought I had to make a choice—but found out I could have both.

After I was old enough to drive, I would go down into some of the worst parts of Kansas City, Missouri; it would be ten or eleven o'clock at night. A hooker would wave me down, and tell me to meet her at the corner. I would park my car and walk with her to an old abandoned building on a dark street. There would be no heat, no lights, and no running water. Most of the windows in the building were broken or missing. She would lead me up a dark stairway to the second or third floor, into a room with nothing but a mattress on the floor, and we would have sex with no type of protection.

It was not something I did once in a while, it was a regular thing. No one can tell me I shouldn't have had my throat cut, been left for dead, or died from some terrible venereal disease. I was a small, skinny kid back then, about five feet, eight inches tall, and weighed about a hundred and thirty-five pounds soaking wet.

I used to park downtown where I could see the hookers flagging down guys. I watched till she got a guy on the line. He would go park his car. Once he got out and took the money out of his wallet to pay her, he would put his wallet under the seat and lock the car. Then he would head off to meet her. I waited until he was in the building with her, and would break into his car. Stealing wallets was easy pickings. Sometimes I got a lot of money and sometimes not much, but whatever I got I used for my next hooker.

FEEDING MY LUSTS

When I was fourteen or fifteen, I would go to my neighbor Charlie's house. He had a mechanic shop in his back yard where he built hot rods. He told me if I would tear down an old barn he had, he would give me a car. It was a 1938 Chevrolet Coupe. I went right to work tearing down that old barn. He even gave me a motor for the car; it was a Studebaker Golden Hawk engine. It was in a basket when he gave it to me and still in the basket when I sold it a couple years later.

The walls and ceilings of that shop were covered with pictures. I'd seen a lot of pictures of naked women, but none like these. These were not regular girlie pictures; the magazines these came out of were from the West Coast. The publications coming from the coasts were years ahead of anything we had here. I spent hours with Charlie in that old garage, working on his hot rods and looking at the pictures—more time looking at the pictures and magazines, than working. I think he got a thrill out of watching me feed my flesh.

Sometimes after helping him in the shop and looking at all his wall paper for hours on end, I started getting in the mood for something more than pictures. I knew what time I needed to leave his garage to find something more fulfilling. I would look at the old hubcap clock on the wall and rush to get whatever project he had me on, done.

I would head for the door and say, "I need to go home, Charlie. I got homework to do."

From under the hood of a hot rod I would hear that unmistakable East Coast accent of his, "Better get your homework done. See you tomorrow, kid." He didn't have kids of his own, and I think he thought of me like his boy.

The homework I referred to was at his home. Charlie's good-looking wife was about ten years younger than him. She always took a shower at the same time every night, and it seemed there was always enough space under the blinds to see her perfectly.

While I watched her, I would think how Charlie was only fifty feet away in his shop and thought I was home doing homework. I would be thinking *I bet nobody has ever done this before.*

A few years later…I was a sexual deviant. As I look back, I think that Charlie and his wife probably knew all along, and it was a big turn on for them.

One thing is for certain, looking at those pictures and watching Charlie's wife fed my sexual appetite. I was a voyeur before I knew the meaning of the word. A lot of you will read this and think I was a Peeping Tom. But let me ask you, have you ever watched a scene in a movie where a couple starts out kissing, and it leads to sex? Or a scene where a woman gets undressed and steps into the shower? Do you turn your eyes away when that happens at the theater? If you don't, then how is that different than what I did at fourteen, except you are paying for it?

HUBCAP BUSINESS

In the late 50's the hubcaps everyone wanted on their custom rides were…Dodge Lancers, Oldsmobile Fiestas or Cadillac Sombreros. If you ever needed any hubcaps, there was one guy who could get them for you—and that was my cousin. This same cousin, who introduced me to hookers, taught me the ropes on stealing hubcaps.

His way of locating requested ones for his customers was unique. He kept a list of everyone he sold to and the particular ones they bought. So if someone wanted a set of Dodge Lancers he took me to where he sold the last set of them and I would steal them back. I was barely fourteen and was glad to be part of his hubcap stealing ring because I just wanted to be out of the house and running around with someone in a car. He never paid me, but I didn't care.

With all the hubcaps we stole, we never got caught, but I am sure if we had, he would not have taken the rap with me. I thought at the time he was a good friend, but found out later I was wrong.

I ended up working with some other guys stealing hubcaps and started getting paid. It was good money considering how easy they were to steal. After a while, I decided to work on my own and not split with anyone. Another advantage to working alone was, I didn't have to worry about someone snitching on me. I became a loner in my illegal activities and that was my pattern for most of my life.

WHEELS OF MY OWN

Just before my sixteenth birthday, I was riding with a friend in his car and we talked about what kind of car I would get. I told him, "I will never own a four door, or a six cylinder...and *never* an automatic."

16 years old. Had wheels of my own and nothing could stop me now. Girls and cars were all I cared about.

My first car was a 1953 Chevrolet four door, automatic with six cylinders. Back in those days everybody put a name on their car. You would paint it on the top of the rear fenders on each side. On my car, I proudly painted *Bona Fide*. It was in Old English, because I wanted it to look like the lettering on Ed's 1954 Mercury, *Ramblin' Rose*.

The definition of *Bona Fide* is: without fraud or deceit, sincere, not counterfeit. I wasn't without fraud or deceit, but I was sincere...about being a hoodlum. I am not sure why I picked that name. I guess it might have something to do with the fact that I didn't pay any attention in school, and didn't know the definition of words. I just thought it sounded cool so I named my car, *Bona Fide*.

I really started getting into trouble once I had my own wheels. I remember the Raytown Police coming into the classroom to get me, and taking me down to the police station for questioning. I don't remember anyone else in school having the cops take them out of class. I had more tickets than would fit in my glove compartment; you name it, and I got a ticket for it. I took the exhaust manifold off the engine and was running it straight out of the block—not too good on valves, I can tell you that—but it was real good for getting me a handful of excessive noise tickets.

I was like a magnet to anyone who was in trouble or headed for trouble. I was close to getting kicked out of school because the principal didn't like the friends I picked, especially one. He actually had the nerve to tell me if I didn't quit running around with Pinky Barnhart, he would kick me out. *Oh really?* He couldn't kick me out if I didn't go there…so I quit. Pinky was my kind of guy; he was transferred from Center High School over in Kansas City for beating up a teacher. Now…that's what I'm talking about!

Pinky had a cool black 50 Ford. We'd drive down the road about 30 or 40 mph and when we saw someone walking; I would stick my arm out the window, double up my fist and keep my arm stiff. Pinky would drive as close to them as he could, so I could hit them in the back of the head. It always knocked them flat. Man, I thought that was fun! It about broke my arm a couple times and probably wouldn't have been as much fun if I was the one walking down the street.

Pinky knew a lot of girls over in Marlboro where he grew up. It was right by Center High School, where he beat up the shop teacher. The girls in that neighborhood were super easy to get in bed. I never figured out the difference between Marlboro and Raytown, but I liked Marlboro better.

Pinky wasn't supposed to be anywhere around his old neighborhood, so we went in my car, and the cops didn't recognize it.

He was only at Raytown High School for three or four months before they threatened to kick him out. I was wishing they would hurry up and do it. I had already quit, and needed someone of his caliber to hang with. He was a good guy and a lot tougher than anybody I ran with... and had girls I didn't know. I really don't know what happened to Pinky, he just sort of disappeared. It's probably a good thing, or he and I might have ended up as the best dressed men in Leavenworth.

RUNNING, ROLLING, AND STEALING

One of my good friends in high school was a guy named Bobby Dolan. He and I stole together; one of our favorite things to do was go to the Liberty Memorial in Kansas City, Missouri and roll homosexuals. We always used Bobby as the decoy, because he was young and good looking. He just walked up and down the sidewalks, and within minutes some guy would pick him up. When he got in the car with the guy, we would rush up and strong arm him of his money. Sometimes we rolled two or three a night. There were occasions when they wanted to fight, but we beat them up and took their money. It seemed liked we always ended back up at the pool hall in Raytown afterward.

My hang out was the pool hall. It was like my office. We talked business there. There was usually something brewing in the pool hall. I would step away for an hour or more to do something illicit. There was always a buddy wanting to share something with me, be it booze, or a girl, or to go on a little stealing spree. It was a place that seemed to breed trouble; my mom nagged me... she even pleaded with me to stay away from the pool hall.

She constantly told me I was going to get in trouble hanging out there and with the people who made it their home. What she didn't know, was that there were really some pretty nice people who went to the pool hall. I was one of the worst guys who hung out there. If anybody was going to lead someone astray, it would be me leading them, not them leading me. I wanted to do wrong; I had a dark side, and it wanted to steal, smoke, drink, and get girls in bed or the back seat of my car.

My dad warned me about getting girls in my car. He told me to never tell a girl I loved her, unless I was sure I did. I loved them all…so I always said it with a clear conscience. I didn't listen to him on most things, and I was sure not listening to him on this. I didn't think he knew very much about life anyway. I could get a girl alone; tell her I loved her, and most of the time it worked. His lessons in life always interfered with my plans. I wasn't about to listen to his or my mom's advice.

My mom always tried to give me advice, telling me things I didn't want to hear—telling me who I should not run around with, and how I would get in trouble with them. She was always telling me things that were in the Bible, and I couldn't possibly see how it pertained to me. It was ancient history, and I didn't like history. History was a subject in school I hated. It was about what already happened, and I didn't really care about what already happened. I cared about what was happening now. I liked living in the moment.

When I was in school I was a runt. I got big and strong in prison lifting weights. Because I am bigger today than the average man, people always ask me if I played sports in high school. I tell them, "I never missed a game." During the school year there was always some kind of sports being played. I didn't play anything, but went to all the games. While everyone else watched the games and the cheerleaders, I was going through their cars in the parking lot and lockers in the gym. I stole anything that wasn't tied down.

MY LAST FIRST DATE

One thing about having a car was that it made it easy to get girls, and I didn't need a room. There were always those girls I knew I could get in the backseat…then there were those I had to work a little harder for. I liked the challenge and I had one in Mary Ann Hopper.

I worked as a fry cook at a drive-in. She kept coming in and we would smile at each other. When I tried to talk to her, she always said she had to go. I knew sooner or later I would get her to go out with me. I asked her out a few times and she kept saying no. That was not a word I liked very well. I usually got my way with girls. Finally, after practically getting on my knees, she said okay. I was so ready and just knew I was going to impress Mary Ann. I decided we would double date with Bob and his girl, that way he could drive and I would have the backseat, where I could use my master's degree. Bob and I decided some booze would make the night a little more interesting and the girls a little looser.

Bob was twenty-one and could buy liquor. He told me what we needed to buy to get the girls going the quickest.

I was getting an education and asked, "What are you going to get?"

"I'll get a pint of sloe gin."

"Why in the world would you want to go slow?"

"Bill, it's not spelled *s-l-o-w* . . . it's spelled *s-l-o-e*."

He came out of the liquor store and put it under his front seat, and we headed out to Lee's Summit to pick up my hard-to-get date. We got Mary Ann and then picked up his girl. I was not going to make any crazy moves with her; it had taken me too long to get her in the car.

After we got to the drive-in theatre we ran to the concession stand to get some cokes. When we got back to Bob's car, a couple of my friends had parked right next to us with their dates. We said hello, introduced our dates, and got back in the car.

"I have something that'll make your Coke better Mary Ann. Hand it here, Bob."

He handed me the gin, I unscrewed the lid and held it out to Mary Ann.

She said, "I don't drink."

I pulled the bottle back and screwed the cap on. I handed it to Bob and his girl. He offered her some and she didn't drink either. Bob said if she wasn't going to drink, then he wasn't either. I was so mad. I thought I was going to get Mary Ann drunk and have my way with her, and she didn't even drink. I was thinking, *The next thing, she will want me to go to church with her!*

I said, "Give that bottle to me, if no one else is drinkin' I am."

Bob handed it to me. I threw my Coke out the window, tipped the gin up, and took a big swig. I kept drinking until the pint was empty…I must have drank that whole pint in less than thirty minutes. That is the last thing I remember. I don't recall getting out of the car. Bob took the girls home. My buddies who were parked next to us took me to Bob's house, put me in my car, and one of them drove me home where he left me passed out in my car. (Kind of reminds me of what happened to my friend Jesse).

The next thing I remember about that night was my mother slapping me in the face, trying to sober me up. My buddies had left me in the car, and somehow I managed to get the front door opened and made it all the way into my bed. I still had all my clothes on, including my shoes. I had thrown up all over Mom's house, and made a mess for her to clean up.

I ran into my buddies a couple days later and they were laughing. What a show I put on at the movie. They told me I got out and urinated all over the side of Bob's car. I then walked to the front of his car and threw up all over the hood. They all had a great view of it. Mary Ann never came back to the drive-in where I worked. I'm not sure why. I am sure I made an impression on her.

There were many more drinking and dating nights after that, but I learned a valuable lesson on that last first date about how not to impress a girl on the first date.

CHANGE AHEAD

I was in the pool hall shooting a game of pool when a guy I wasn't really good friends with walked up to my table and said, "Let's go join the Marines."

I looked up at him and then back down at the ball I was about to sink. "Lemme finish this game first."

That was about as serious as I took life. I figured if I didn't like the Marines, I would just quit. If something was hard or didn't please me, that's how I dealt with it. School made me sick, so I quit. If I didn't like a job, I just quit. Girls didn't put out, I was gone. I quit everything that didn't go my way, so I had nothing to lose.

Dave and I signed up; they gave us a date that we were to leave for boot camp, and we had a party to celebrate. We went back to the pool hall and told all of our friends that we were now United States Marines. I hoped they didn't want me to cut my hair, because that was one thing I wasn't going to do.

I was getting into so much trouble around Raytown I needed to get out of town anyway. The local police harassed me. Not a night went by that I didn't get stopped by the cops. I would have my car completely torn apart and searched—sometimes more than once a night. They didn't need probable cause back then. They gave me tickets some nights and some nights they just tore my back seat out and took everything out of my trunk. I would, of course, have to put it all back.

At the time, I didn't stop to think they were trying to run me out of my own town. Now, looking back, I know without a doubt, that was what it was all about. I caused so much trouble in Raytown; they wanted me gone for good. The cops came to the high school to arrest me all the time. I would run from them in my car and get away; they knew it was me, but couldn't catch me. I was a menace to them. I decided one thing I would do before I left for boot camp. I would go have some fun, and I knew just the guy to do that with.

BURGLARIES AND BOXCARS

Bobby Dolan was one of my closest friends. He liked stealing and chasing girls and nobody enjoyed having fun more than he did. He was definitely the one I needed to have this last party with before the Marines got me. Bobby and I and two other guys left Raytown one night in my old 1953 Chevy. I knew someone in El Paso, Texas, and that's where we headed. We hadn't gone far when we needed gas. We had a little money, but we never paid for gas when we could get it free. We broke into a station, filled up with gas, and got whatever else we could steal. Then we were off again, heading down through Missouri looking for anything easy to steal.

Right after we burglarized a store in the city limits of Joplin, Missouri, we were pulled over by the cops for a curfew law we didn't know about. We had two large brown grocery sacks filled with the stolen goods. There were cartons of cigarettes, candy bars, Brylcreem, and lighter fluid. In those days everyone used grease on their hair; and we had lots of hair. We also all carried Zippo lighters. Later on that lighter fluid would come in handy for more than our lighters.

The cops took us to the police station and began questioning us; none of us were going to tell them anything. I told them we were on our way to my aunt's house in Shreveport, Louisiana. Between the four of us we had about eighteen bucks.

The cop said, "You're going to Shreveport on that amount of money?"

"My car gets good gas mileage, we can make it." I could tell he didn't believe me.

"I think you're all runaways and none of your parents even know you're gone."

I was seventeen and everyone else was fourteen or fifteen. I could tell he wasn't buying any of my lies, so I switched gears. "Sir, you're right. I've been lying. But if you'll let us go…I promise I'll take these guys home, and I'll go straight home."

He leaned back in his chair and laced his fingers together behind his fat head. "I believe you boy…I'm gonna let you go."

"Thank you, sir. You won't be sorry, we'll go straight back to Raytown."

He let us go at six o'clock in the morning.

As we drove away, Bobby started laughing. "Can you believe the ignorant cops let us go? I bet they're gonna go crazy when that store calls in and tells em they got hit."

The store opened at eight a.m. and called in the burglary. The cop hung up and called the police in Raytown, he told them to pick us up; we were on our way home. He had bought my story hook, line, and sinker. But we'd already been on the road for two hours, and were headed for Oklahoma.

When we burglarized gas stations we always got gas, if nothing else. I had worked in enough gas stations to know how the pumps turned on. Once we got inside the building, Bobby started looking for money, or anything of value. I would go into the garage and get the pumps turned on and fill up our car.

There were not many businesses with alarm systems back in the early 60's. The ones that had alarms were easy to beat; they were analog and not digital. We broke into one business in Oklahoma that did have an alarm. It seems like it was a dry cleaners. We got away without getting caught, but it was a close call. I don't think we broke into any more places in Oklahoma after that. We headed on south to El Paso.

My car had some serious problems. The synchronizers were going bad in the transmission and it wouldn't stay in gear. One of the guys had to ride in the middle and keep his foot against the floor shifter to keep it from popping out of gear. The old car threw a rod and started knocking real bad, so we decided we would get rid of it. I pulled into a gas station in Amarillo, Texas, and left it running, because I knew if I shut it off, there would be no way it would ever start again. I told the gas station attendant some outrageous story, and that I needed to sell my car.

"You got a title for it?"

"Yeah, I gottta a title." All I had was the pink slip from registering it. He took that and thought it was the title. "What a moron" I told Bobby.

I sold it to the guy for twenty-five dollars on that pink slip. I guarantee you once he shut it off, it never ran again. We took the money and ate chili at a Mexican restaurant. I remember it being hotter than any I had ever eaten, but we were all starving and would have eaten anything.

We had to figure out a way to get out of Amarillo and get to El Paso. We talked about it, and decided to hop a freight train; somebody remembered passing the rail yard coming into town. We waited till it got dark and went down to the railroad yard. We asked a hobo which train was going to El Paso, he pointed to one and we jumped in a box car. It seemed like we sat there for hours, and then KABOOM! We were thrown around in the car.

"What was that?" Mike asked.

A couple seconds later, KABOOM! We all got thrown to the other end of the boxcar. They were coupling the cars together, getting ready to roll. It wasn't long and we were clanking down the tracks.

It was December and none of us were dressed for winter—it was cold and we were freezing. Once we were out of town and rolling, we broke up a wooden skid and used some of that lighter fluid we stole to start a fire.

We learned a lot about riding box cars. Every time the train stops, the front brakeman goes to the back and the back brakeman to the front. They walk on opposite sides of the train, looking for anything suspicious or out of place. We would be as quiet as we

THE ULTIMATE PARDON

could when they walked by so they wouldn't know that we were there. They never did see us or smell the smoke from the fire.

After we had been riding for a while, that chili we ate started to work on me.

"WHAT DID YOU DO, Bill?" Bobby screamed at me.

"I had to take a dump."

"And you HAD to wipe with my glove? That's not right man, I mean it."

"I'm sorry, man."

"Don't give me that sorry crap, I'm not kidding, I'm really mad."

He told me fifty years later, while I was writing this book, that he stayed mad at me for years over that.

The train finally stopped. It was daylight now, and we sat quietly waiting for it to start moving again. We waited a long time, and finally one of us poked our head out the door...they had unhooked us.

We sat for what seemed like hours, it probably was only minutes. When we hopped down out of that car, we thought for sure we were in El Paso. That was where we wanted to go, and we had taken the train the hobo told us to. That train probably was going there, but they unhooked our boxcar in Tucumcari, New Mexico. To four teenage runaways it seemed like we had been in that box car for days, when in reality it had only been hours. It was a little over a hundred miles from Amarillo to Tucumcari.

We started getting off the train, and when the last one of us hit the ground, the railroad bulls—railroad police—grabbed us and took us to jail. My dad drove over twelve hundred miles roundtrip taking us back to Raytown.

Bobby Dolan ended up going to Boonville; it was a state reformatory back then. He was assigned to a grass-cutting crew, so he told them all his people cut hair. He lied. They put him in the barber shop where it was air conditioned. He always was smarter than the average convict. He cut hair in every prison he ended up in, and has cut hair for over fifty years.

I went on to the Marine Corps. Although I had already joined and they had given me a date to leave for boot camp before our little crime spree, I quit the Marines before I ever got there. If we hadn't been caught I would have faced a court martial with the Marine Corps before I even got to boot camp. Staying out of trouble in the Marines, or anywhere for that matter, didn't last long for any of us. One of the guys I rode the train with died in prison just a few years ago, another one of them got shot and killed robbing a gas station.

Bobby ended up going to prison in Missouri more than once, and today is a legend in Missouri prisons. His reputation as a burglar and safe cracker made him the cover story of a national magazine in 1968. Bobby and his partners were considered by an FBI agent to be the most organized burglary ring in America. He did a bit in Leavenworth for that and was the youngest man on the yard there. He would later legally change his name to Midnight B Dolan. I lost track of him for thirty-two years. I will talk later about Midnight and our relationship today.

MCRD, SAN DIEGO

Those living west of the Mississippi go to boot camp in California, those east of the Mississippi go to South Carolina. MCRD stands for Marine Corps Recruit Depot, and was located in San Diego, California. That was where I went to boot camp. When I stepped off the bus it was unlike anything I had ever dreamed about or maybe I should say, ever had a nightmare about.

The drill instructors were in my face. No teacher or any other human being had ever yelled at me like those guys were yelling.

"WHAT ARE YOU LOOKING AT, BOY?"

"I don't know," I squeaked.

"I DON'T KNOW, SIR, YOU MAGGOT," he screamed at the top of his lungs.

"I don't know, sir," I said a little louder.

He screamed even louder, "I CAN'T HEAR YOU, LITTLE GIRL!"

By now I was so paralyzed with fear, I could hardly breathe. Thank God, he moved down to terrorize another recruit in the line.

The next day, Sergeant Steed screamed at the platoon, "DO YOU LIKE BEING MARINES?"

"Yes, sir," we all said together weakly.

"I CAN'T HEAR YOU GIRLS," our D.I. screamed at the top of his lungs.

"YES, SIR!" we all screamed in unison.

"WELL, YOU MAGGOTS ARE NOT MARINES!" Then he spoke in an almost normal voice. "You have to earn the right to be called Marines. Right now you are recruits. A recruit is the lowest thing on the earth, lower than a worm."

We would be called everything but Marines for the next few weeks. The day they called me a Marine was one of the proudest days of my life, but my actions over the next twenty years wouldn't look like it.

If you are reading this and have been through boot camp, then you understand. If you have never had the pleasure of having a drill instructor calling you every name under the sun, and talking to you like a cur dog, then you won't get a real clear picture.

I won't go into much detail of boot camp; it was just sixteen weeks of physical and mental tearing down and building up. I understand now that all the psychological harassment and physical torture I went through was to prepare me for battle. If I was captured during battle, I wouldn't break down during interrogation. It was for my own good, I just didn't understand it at the time. I have carried some of my training from boot camp through my whole life. It even helped me in some of my criminal endeavors.

At the time, though, I still had the 'quit everything' attitude and did not like what I was experiencing. I didn't plan on staying long. However, I *did* finish boot camp and actually graduated with honors from Regimental Honor Platoon 386

Mom and I right after boot camp graduation.

I was now a full-fledged Marine. I came very close to not graduating because of a fight I got into, and some of the other shenanigans I pulled during boot camp. I still carry a scar from that fight. However, I made it through and the hard part was over. I really had it made. My MOS was 6400, Jet Mechanic. I loved working on engines and tearing stuff apart. I had been a gearhead since I was a little boy. My mom told me after I was grown that when I was two or three, I would take my toys all apart. After I had completely destroyed them, I held them up to my dad and said, "Boke, daddy fix."

I couldn't say broke. I would also pull the heads off grasshoppers and say, "Boke, daddy fix." They would tell me not to tear stuff up and I did it anyway. That should have been a sign to someone that I was headed for a rebellious lifestyle. I never did like people telling me what to do, or when to do it.

CHAPTER

8

ABSENT WITHOUT LEAVE

The first time I went AWOL was when there was a major golf tournament held in Memphis, Tennessee. Memphis was less than twenty miles from the base where I was stationed. (And no, I didn't go AWOL to watch the tournament.)

The PGA notified the Marine Corps that they needed volunteers to act as marshals to keep the crowds back. When they came out to the base I held my hand high in the air, thinking I would get a chance to see some good looking girls, and get away from that stinking base. I didn't care about golf and didn't even know who was playing.

Later on in my life, I looked back and saw that it was a once in a lifetime opportunity, being that close to the best professional golfers in the world. There were times during the days of the tournament that I stood right beside Jack Nicklaus…Gary Player… Arnold Palmer…Chi Chi Rodriguez and other big names. Those guys were the cream of the crop in 1963. Golf was something I knew nothing about, so when I heard a golfer tell his caddy, "Bring me a sand wedge," I expected him to take him a ham and cheese sandwich on rye.

Looking at all the tan, shapely legs out there made me homesick for my girlfriend, who had moved to Florida since I joined the Marines. When the tournament was over, all military personnel were ordered to return to the base in Millington. Everyone did— except me—I had other plans, and started hitchhiking to Florida.

I had a foolproof way of getting rides and covering a lot of ground with each one. I went into a truck stop, got a map of that state, sat down and studied it. I would find a route that was on the way to Winter Haven, Florida where my girlfriend was part of the water skiing show at Cypress Gardens. Then I'd go sit down next to a trucker at the counter, and strike up a conversation.

They would usually look at me and say, "How ya doing, soldier?"

"I'm a Marine, sir."

"Sorry about that, Marine."

I liked being called a Marine...I just didn't like being told what to do.

Then I would ask the truck driver, "Where ya headed?"

If they said a town that was a couple hundred miles in the right direction, I would proceed with my plan.

"My grandmother died and the funerals tomorrow. I'm trying like crazy to get there in time."

"Oh no problem, buddy, I'd be glad to give you a lift. Soon as you're done eatin', we'll get going."

That story hardly ever failed. Back in 1963 the truckers weren't under strict insurance rules like they are today. I rode for one or two hundred miles, concocting my story to these truckers, even pretending to choke up a little, I lied to them and told them how close I was to my grandma. Then I told them about what it was like growing up in the town we were headed for, even talking about some of the little towns around my home that I'd memorized on the map.

When I was running out of money, I waited till late at night, went to a bar, and sat in the parking lot. I stayed in the shadows and watched, until some guy came out by himself stumbling drunk. I watched him stagger around looking for his car, and then I would say, "Hey buddy, you looking for your car? I lost mine too. Let me help you find it."

As soon as he agreed and we started looking, I made sure there was no one else in the parking lot. I would knock him out and steal everything he had on him. I used to hit those drunks with anything I could find to knock them senseless—bricks, two by fours, or whatever. I knew that sometimes I hurt some of them badly, but I didn't care, I knew no one could catch me.

I was so cocky back then, it is a miracle I didn't get caught robbing some of those drunks. Sometimes I would help one find his car, then rob him, and take his car. I wouldn't drive it far, because I knew when he came to, he would call the cops and they would be looking for the car.

While I drove it, though, I would try to blow it up. If it would run 110 mph then I'd go that fast. I loved speed and couldn't get enough of it. I wasn't worried about getting caught by a cop for speeding, because I always got away from them at home. I figured it wouldn't be any different here. I was young and stupid, never stopping to think that at home I knew my way around. This was the cops' home; luckily I never got chased stealing a car from a drunk.

I usually took a stolen car to the next truck stop, and got a ride for a few hundred miles with my dead grandmother story. I never felt bad about lying to those truckers about my grandma dying, because both my grandmothers had been dead for years. As a matter of fact, I didn't feel bad about lying about anything. I was a very polished liar. I had practiced for years and it almost seemed easier to lie than to tell the truth.

I finally arrived in Winter Haven and had a pretty good amount of money on me. I checked into a motel and went to get some new clothes. It had been months since I'd seen Betty Ann and I needed to look real good when she saw me.

"She's not here anymore," the guy behind the ticket counter said.

"WELL, WHERE IS SHE?" I screamed at him, like he was a recruit. The poor guy didn't understand what I had gone through to get there, and how badly I wanted to see her.

He leaned back out of my reach. "She ran off with the world's top Formula One driver, I can't remember his name."

I couldn't believe it! I was so mad I could have killed the guy behind the counter, and the Formula One driver. I knew who he was. I might not know anything about golf, but I knew all about racing. I knew the rotten dog was thirty-five years old, and she was only seventeen. I could never compete with him, he had more money than a show horse could jump over, and was very famous in the racing world. But she had a ring I gave her to go steady with me…and I wanted my ring back.

For a minute I thought about going after them. I could find them and I would get even with him for stealing my girl. As I surveyed all the scenery around me…the bikinis, short shorts, and string bikinis…I forgot about Betty, the race car driver, and my ring. I decided to settle in right there.

I never saw her again. Many years later she gave the ring to her aunt and uncle who lived in Kansas City. They called me and I picked it up. It had been over thirty years since I gave it to her. It was only a few short years later that she died of cancer. Rest in Peace, Betty Ann.

Not too many miles away was the town of Lakeland. I went there and got a job in a gas station. I knew all about working in gas stations. My dad owned a Sinclair station back in Kansas City, Missouri. I helped him around his station when I was a little boy, and fell in love with the smell of oil, and gas. I worked in several different gas stations, and hung around them all the time. I also worked on the pit crew of one of the top dirt car drivers in the Midwest and had no trouble getting a job.

I found a place to stay and settled in. I bought a 650cc Matchless motorcycle for transportation. I got some fake I.D. so I could get into the bars. I worked all day and found girls to party with every night in Tampa. I used to get so drunk, that sometimes I couldn't balance my bike and kick the starter. My bike had a kick starter (this was before electric starters). I would find someone to start it for me. I rode from Tampa to Lakeland, about thirty-five miles away in eighteen or twenty minutes, going well over 120 mph.

I made that ride many times . . . at *that* speed . . . and *that* drunk. But I never had a wreck. Sometimes when I drove into my front yard, I would get off and let the bike just fall over, because I was too drunk to get it up on the kickstand. The next morning I would go out, stand it up to make sure it was still in one piece. Most of the time, I didn't know how I made it home.

One night the cops chased me out of Tampa and I drove off the road into an orange grove. I thought I got away, but when I looked back they were right behind me. It looked like the police car was only missing the trees on each side by a few inches. When I looked at my speedometer, I was going over 80 mph on the dew covered grass. I jumped irrigation ditches, going airborne after every jump. It was a miracle I didn't crash. I flew over a ditch at the end of the grove and lost them.

One day I was on the highway and some guy flew by me on a big Indian motorcycle. I started racing him. I found out later, it was bored and stroked—it was extremely fast. I was running over 130 mph, and wasn't going to catch him, when I went into a high speed wobble. (That is where the front tire starts shaking and the handle bars are going back and forth to where you can barely hang on.) I had never experienced that before, so when I got the bike stopped I sat beside the road for over an hour. I probably smoked a half pack of cigarettes. I was completely freaked out, and realized I could have died.

I shouldn't have been able to do some of the stuff I did. I never once considered that God might have had His hand on me. I just thought I was indestructible and superhuman, and that's why I got away with all my craziness.

THE ULTIMATE PARDON

CHAPTER

HE RATTED ME OUT

After I had lived in Florida for a few weeks, I called my cousin. He was my girl chasing buddy back home in Kansas City, and was my best friend in the whole world at the time.

"You've gotta come down here and see what I've got."

"What do you have?" he asked me.

"I have more girls lined up than you've ever seen."

"Billy...Aunt Martha and Uncle Ebb are really worried about you."

He was one of the few people who still called me Billy. Now he's telling me my folks were worried about me. I was having a blast and didn't want to hear any of that.

"You'd better not tell 'em I called you. Are you coming down here or not?" I asked him, very disgusted.

"Let me call you back."

I hung up the phone in disgust. *Why was he acting so weird?* I wondered.

He was the one who always chased girls and had taught me all about sex, and how important it was to make sure I never let a day go by without getting a girl in bed. He was the one who turned me on to the red light district of Kansas City. *Now I have all these girls at my finger tips and he doesn't want to come down here?* I didn't get it.

About an hour later, my boss hollered at me. "Hey, Gary, it's for you."

That's the alias I was using at the time. I had a cousin named Gary and it was his name I used. I always used names of people I knew something about. That way, if I was questioned about something, I hopefully would know the answer.

"Hello?" It was my cousin.

"I'm coming down, Billy. I'll be there tomorrow."

I was over being mad at him just like that. I still worshipped the ground he walked on and thought he was really something special. I didn't know he was a rat, but was about to find out. Boy was I going to get a rude awakening!

He was two years older than me and had been the one to introduce me to the wild side, girls, drinking, stealing. I considered him my mentor. I thought that the polished con man I had turned into was on account of what he taught me.

I could hardly wait till he arrived. *I* was going to be the big man now and he would look up to me. He had never seen the beaches, and for sure had never seen so many girls in skimpy bikinis. I couldn't sleep very well that night.

I was putting brakes on a car and looked down and saw a pair of polished shoes that just didn't look right in that old gas station garage. My eyes traveled from the shoes, up the pant legs, to the face.

"WOW!!" I said as I jumped up and grabbed my cousin. He looked very serious.

"I didn't come down here by myself."

"You ain't got the lousy cops with you, do you?"

"You can run if you want, but I brought my dad and your dad. They're in the car. I told em I wanted to come in and see you by myself first."

"What in the world did you do that for?" *Now what am I supposed to do?* I couldn't run; my dad had driven twelve hundred miles to see me. "Go get 'em," I said.

My dad walked into the garage and said, "Son, your mom is worried sick. Won't you please come home and see her?" He told me she lost weight and couldn't sleep at night. That's nothing new. She had lost sleep and worried about me all my life...even before I was born.

Our family doctor told dad that mom would die giving birth to me, and that I would die also. My dad went out and bought burial plots for him, my older sister, and my mother and me before she had me. Somebody was trying to kill me before I was born. And they have been trying ever since.

"Yeah, let's go." I was so mad at my cousin. I didn't speak to him for twelve hundred miles. I never talked to him again for many years, and we have never been close since that day. I realized he was the kind of guy who *would not* go to prison for you, and would sing like The Temptations if he got interrogated.

We took turns driving and drove straight through to Kansas City. I stayed with Mom and Dad for a few days. To pacify my mom I agreed to turn myself in. They drove me back to the base in Millington, Tennessee the next day. I was immediately placed on temporary restrictions, and was told I could not leave the base until after my court martial.

At my court martial, I stood before a Marine Corps Colonel, who said, "Son...if you don't straighten up, you will be in the penitentiary before you're twenty-one."

I mocked him by laughing in his face. My laugh should have warned him to do more than just put me on restrictions.

He said, "You are restricted to the perimeter of the base for ninety days. You will not go outside the gates; if you break this rule you will be sent to the brig."

It didn't take me long to decide I wasn't going to stay restricted to the barracks and watch everyone else go to town. They came back half-drunk, bragging about all the fun they had. That wise old Colonel's biggest mistake was not locking me up.

I would have to wait till the perfect time—and take myself off restrictions.

MY MOTHER'S DREAM

My perfect time finally came. But that same night, over five hundred miles away, my mother had a dream. In the dream she saw me come into her living room with mud all over my shoes. I walked around in circles, tracking mud all over her carpet.

She always had dreams about me and it drove me crazy. It was months later that she told me about that specific dream. It really freaked me out. I usually lied to her and told her that her dreams were wrong, but this one was too real…it was exactly what happened the night I went AWOL.

That night really was the perfect time with the thunder and lightning, and a pouring rain that blocked visibility. I waited till I was sure everyone was sleeping, and then quietly dressed, and slipped out of the barracks.

There was a lot of light on the base, so I stayed in the shadows. That came natural for me, because I spent more time in the shadows than in the light most of my life. I made my way to the darkest part of the fence and climbed over in a torrential downpour. I sloshed through the water and mud puddles, until I reached town.

As I walked under the first streetlight I looked down and realized I wore one civilian shoe and one military issue shoe. I certainly couldn't walk around like that! So I climbed back over the fence and snuck back into the barracks. I tracked mud everywhere, but was very careful not to wake anyone. I changed into matching shoes, went back outside, and climbed over the fence. I was on my way again.

I stole a car and hit the highway, listening to some good old rock and roll. I was free again. This was going to be different than the first time I went AWOL.

OFF RESTRICTIONS

The Marine Corps said I was on restrictions and couldn't leave the base. The principal of the Raytown High School said I couldn't run around with Pinky Barnhart. *Is there any other brilliant person that wants to try and tell me what I can or can't do?*

I hadn't planned on climbing the fence three times, but I sure couldn't walk around in two different kinds of shoes. Anyhow, that was all behind me now, as I cruised down the road in the car I had stolen, with music blasting. I headed for St Louis; that town was big enough to get lost and stay lost in.

I had no idea I would run into another guy who was also AWOL from the Marines. He introduced himself as Bill. He had no idea my name was also Bill.

"Gary's the name…nice to meet ya, Bill."

I was still using my cousin's name. Bill and I were together for weeks, and he never knew my real name.

The difference between us was that I was just a private. This guy was a staff sergeant, and had been in the Marines for twelve years. I liked being with him because he was a lot older than me, and I thought he could probably teach me some things. I always hung out with guys older than me…not sure why.

He was originally from Cape Girardeau, Missouri, and had a lot of contacts. He also knew some women there. That sounded good to me. I had never been to Cape Girardeau, so that was reason enough to go. We made a loop from St. Louis to Cape Girardeau to Kansas City.

We would stay one or two days in one town, committing crimes while there, and move on to the next. Sometimes we reversed it.

My thought process at this time was: if *we* don't know where we are going next, then how would the law who chased us know?

I dyed my hair red, so that whenever we hit Kansas City on our circuit no one would recognize me. Each time we got to town, I never called that lousy rat cousin of mine. I figured maybe I would run into him sometime and beat the living tar out of him.

The first time we arrived in Kansas City, we were running low on money.

"Hey Bill, I know where we can get some quick money."

"Where would that be?"

"Do you like queers?" I asked him with a smirk on my face.

"No, and why on earth would you ask me that?"

"I know where we can get paid for beatin' some up."

I was thinking of all the times Bobby Dolan and I went to the Liberty Memorial and rolled them. It had been a while and I wasn't sure that was still their meeting place. We headed up there and sure enough, they were everywhere. It was easy pickings and good money.

Another place we rolled them was Union Station on Main Street. If we went to the bathroom, they always followed us and tried to pick us up.

Bill was a big, tough looking veteran Marine and I knew from my past experiences rolling them, that the best looking guys got hit on quicker. I didn't want to tell Bill he wasn't good looking, so I just told him I would be the bait, and filled him in on what to do when I got picked up. He liked rolling those fags; it was easy. I think he enjoyed beating the life out of them. Every time we came to Kansas City, it was like going to the bank and taking money out of our savings account. We never ran out of money because those guys had been up there for years…and they weren't going anywhere. We ended up hurting some of them pretty bad. Sometimes they tried to fight, but had no chance against two crazy men.

We stole something like seventeen or eighteen cars during that time. We stole one, burglarized a store or rolled a queer, and then headed out on the road again. In those days most store owners kept cash in the store at night. It was before night drops were used. Sometimes we rolled drunks just like I did when I hitchhiked to Florida by myself. It was a lot easier with a partner because one of us kept an eye out for other people. But the best thing about there being two of us was, if we picked a tough guy to roll, he had no chance against us. Sometimes it was hard to tell which of us had the most anger. We took it out on the poor dudes we rolled.

Between rolling homosexuals and drunks, Bill and I had plenty of money during those weeks we were on the run. We drank and smoked a lot, but neither of us did any drugs. We ate good and bought new clothes all the time. Sometimes we just left our old clothes in a motel and bought new ones. Driving a new car, wearing new clothes, having lots of money, we were living it up. When we got what we wanted in one town, we headed to the next on the circuit.

Before we stole a car, I would get a clean license plate the police weren't looking for. I would go to a body shop on Friday night after they closed. In the back lot I would find a badly wrecked car that was going to take a week or more to fix. I'd take the license plate, and steal a car that was the same make and model as the wrecked car. If a cop ran the tags, they wouldn't come up stolen. We partied with chicks Bill knew in Cape Girardeau, some I knew in Kansas City, and ones we met on the road.

MY BLACK CORVETTE

During one of our trips to Cape Girardeau I met this real good looking girl. I told her I would bring my car the next time we came down.

"What kind of car do you have?" she asked.

"I've got a 1962 fuel injected Corvette."

"Oh, wow! What color?"

"What color do you like, baby?"

"Black is my favorite," she replied.

"I'll bring my black Corvette next time I come to see you."

"Are you kidding, it's really black?"

"You think I'd lie to you? Yes, it's black."

She told me she would love to go for a ride in it. I told her I would love to take her for a ride.

We dropped the girls off and Bill said to me, "How are you going to explain not driving a black Corvette?"

"Bill, I'll score with her. Watch me." I was determined to have a black Corvette when I came back. Number one, it was for her, and two, he made me mad, doubting I could get a Corvette.

We were headed back to Kansas City, and I knew exactly where to start looking for a Corvette. I took Bill to Jimmy and Mary's, one of the best steak houses in town. What I didn't tell him was that the restaurant was right across the street from Motor City, a car lot that dealt in new and used Corvettes.

As we pulled up in front of Jimmy and Mary's, I said, "Hey, let's go have a steak; I got somethin' to talk to you about."

"Sounds good to me," he said, licking his lips.

I saw the Corvette while I was parking, but could tell he didn't. He probably wouldn't have, even if I pointed it out to him. He was thinking about eating. He loved eating more than me.

They gave us a table by the window, which was perfect, because I could picture her next to me in that car while he looked at the menu. As we waited on our food, I glanced towards the Corvette and took in a big gulp of air like I had seen a ghost.

"What's wrong, man?" Bill asked.

"Wow, can you believe that?"

Bill looked dumbfounded. "What? Believe what?"

"Look straight across the street at that line of cars. What do you see?"

"I see a line of cars." Bill was not a gearhead and didn't know his cars.

"The one I told her I had, you dummy. It's right on the front line."

It was a black 1962 Corvette with fuel injection. I was determined to get that car and take her in it, no matter what the cost.

"Where are you going to find a wrecked Corvette to get a tag?" he asked.

"I'm not. For her—I'll take the chance driving on a hot tag." I snapped my fingers. "Hurry up, eat that steak, we got work to do."

Cars were so easy to steal back then. You could dump the cigarettes out of a pack, take the tin foil out, and fold it into a little square. Take that little square and reach under the dash, touch the ignition wires together, and it was running. You'd be on your way. Although that was quick and easy, I had a way I liked better. I learned it while working at a Chevrolet dealership doing new car trades.

In the 60's, keys were interchangeable on all GM cars. Any GM key would go all the way into the ignition of another GM car, but wouldn't turn if it was the wrong key. Most car lots left the keys in the cars during the day and pulled them out at closing time. I arrived at a lot close to closing time and pretended to be looking at a car. I would take the keys to the car I wanted and replace them with keys I stole from another lot. At closing time they pulled the keys out of all the cars and locked them up. That night, I would go back to the car lot and get my car.

This was Thursday, and we had two days to get some keys switched and get my Corvette. I was certain I would not find a wrecked Corvette, so I didn't even look for a tag.

With a hot license plate and the shiny black 62 fuelie we headed back to Cape Girardeau. I could hardly wait to get there. Although the road going into the boot heel of Missouri was extremely curvy and dangerous, I figured if any cop made the tags I could outrun them in this car anyway.

DRIVE IT LIKE YOU STOLE IT

We passed a guy hitchhiking and I told Bill I wanted to pick him up and scare the life out of him. Bill argued with me, saying, "We don't have room for him."

I had already gone a mile or so past the guy when I locked the brakes up, cranked the wheel, and made a bat turn at about 50 mph.

Bill said, "You're the craziest dude I know!" I drove back past the hitchhiker, turned around in a driveway, and went back and stopped a ways ahead of him. He ran up to the car, Bill got out, and leaned his seat forward. The guy hesitated because there was barely enough room for a suitcase, but he said, "I really need a ride so I'll try and get back there."

I am not sure how…but he managed to get in.

I was taking turns at crazy speeds, shifting from fourth, grrrrrrr, third, grrrrrrr, second, grrrrrrr . . . sometimes all the way back to first. I'd shift back up through the gears second, third, and accelerating hard to shift into fourth—maybe hitting 130 mph before the next turn—back to third, grrrrrrr, the engine revving to 7,000 rpms, and about to blow. I didn't care. It wasn't my car.

I heard a muffled voice from the cramped hitchhiker folded in behind the seats. "You're driving this thing like you stole it."

I wore a pair of driving gloves and told him I was practicing for a road race. "This road has curves similar to the track I'll be on, and I'm practicing."

After about the second set of turns and all that shifting, downshifting, and speeds over 100 mph, the guy finally screamed from behind me, "LET ME OUT PLEASE!"

I locked the brakes up and we slid sideways. Bill jumped out, pulled the seat forward so the whiner could get out. What a lame punk; we laughed till we thought we would bust a gut.

After the excitement, I almost hoped some dumb copper would try and chase me, because I knew there was no way anyone could catch me in this hot rod. Little did I know, what was about to happen.

Before we went to look for the girls, we went over to McClure, Illinois. It is a little town with a couple hundred people across the bridge about seven miles from Cape Girardeau. I cruised through there just showing off. All those poor farmers and country hicks stared at that new shiny fuel injected Corvette. They had only seen one in pictures. The county Sheriff's car was sitting in front of the local restaurant.

"This should be fun."

"What should be fun?" Bill asked, as I came to a complete stop in front of the eatery's big window, and slipped the Muncie 4-Speed into first gear.

"MAN! Gary, don't!"

I revved the motor to about 4,500 rpm and dumped the clutch. We went sideways for what seemed like a half block. When I hit

6,500 rpms, I slammed second gear, and was fishtailing when I reached for third. I got fourth gear rubber and we were gone. I said, "That was fun, and ought to give 'em something to talk about for a while."

We crossed the bridge back into Missouri that afternoon, going over 120 mph, and went to pick up the girls. We rode around for a little while. It was extremely tight quarters, one girl on Bill's lap and my little honey sitting on me, trying to stay off the shifter. We dropped them at their house and promised to pick them up later that night.

HIGH-SPEED CHASE

I hadn't gone a block when I looked in the rear view mirror and saw the cop.

"Bill, don't look back, but there's a cop on our tail with his lights flashing."

It has been over fifty years…but I will never forget what Bill said.

"What are you going to do?"

I couldn't believe he asked me that. Is there anyone that stupid?

"Not stopping." I clutched and went into first gear, mashing the gas pedal to the floor. We screamed away from that 1961 Chevrolet city police car. *It's probably a six banger*, I thought to myself, *but even if it's not, it's no match for this 360-horsepower monster.*

By now I was in fourth gear and running over 100 mph right through town. I saw a sharp curve coming up, and was sure that the Corvette would handle it okay. As I went into the curve I downshifted to third, to make sure I'd have enough power to pull out of the turn if I needed to. This car handled better than anything I'd ever stolen. *I need to steal these more often*, I thought. The curve was a breeze for me, no problem.

I looked in my rear view mirror just in time to see the police car try to make it through the curve. His car started skipping sideways; just as a car going the other way came into the curve.

KABOOM!! They collided super hard in the middle of the curve; it was a very bad wreck.

Good, now he is out of my way. I didn't care if they were all dead. I was going about 125 mph, when I saw my stop sign up ahead at the intersection of the main highway.

"Bill, look and see if there's anything coming your way."

"It's all clear. Go!"

As I looked to the left, I saw red lights flashing in the distance. I knew that the cops had called in some back up. I went through the stop sign going over 125 mph. The cop wasn't far enough in the distance not to see us blast through the intersection. *He doesn't have them cherries flashing for nothing.* He was definitely after us, and there was no way I was going to stop. He slowed and made the left turn to chase me. I was way ahead of him by the time he slowed to make the turn and build up his speed again.

Bill was silent—maybe he was praying—but he wasn't saying anything. He knew not to try and get me to slow down. I scared the wits out of him in every car we stole, and he had given up trying to slow me down.

We went right through the middle of some little town on a gravel road, with people sitting on their front porch swings enjoying the afternoon. I passed by them running over 130 mph. I crossed into farmland and slowed down on the gravel to try and keep the dust from flying in the air. I didn't see the red lights flashing and my first thought was, *Maybe he wrecked too.*

I saw a cornfield with corn about seven feet tall. I left the road and drove for a quarter mile or so along the edge of the field, then I made a sharp turn and drove into the thick, tall, green corn for probably five or six hundred feet. I didn't want to go into the field at the road because they would see the corn knocked down. By driving so far back off the road before going into the corn, we were now completely hidden.

It was summer and only about three o'clock in the afternoon, so it wouldn't be dark for six hours or more.

We read in the paper later that it was the city police that called the Missouri Highway Patrol. They were the ones chasing us. The highway patrolman, who chased us, claimed he reached speeds of 140 mph, and couldn't get close enough to see my license plate. I don't really know if that's true, and don't really care. All I can tell you is that they didn't catch me. If it *was* true, I needed to steal one of those highway patrol cars that would go 140 mph.

I was glad to have that veteran Marine with me, because he knew a lot of things that saved our tails. He had been in Viet Nam and knew how to survive in rough conditions. The wreck the Cape Girardeau cop had in the curve ended up hurting some people bad. They were in the hospital, in critical condition. The law was bound and determined to catch whoever was responsible. We were just as determined to not get caught. We decided to stay in the cornfield till it got dark.

RUNNING COVERTLY

We found an old abandoned farm house; it was perfect for us to hide out in. We could see real good from the second floor.

We waited till after midnight and snuck back into that little town where I had driven like a maniac down Main Street. We burglarized a little grocery store and got some cigarettes, beer, and sandwich materials. We carefully removed a screen from one of the windows, and with a very thin piece of metal, were able to get the lock open without leaving any trace of forced entry. We were very careful not to tear anything up and only took things we needed, so that nothing would be missed, in case we needed to go back in that same store again.

This really did pay off for us, because we needed to go back in there two more times. The second time was like the first, we made sure they didn't know we had been there.

They set up roadblocks for us and were not going to let us get out. They had identified us as AWOL Marines and linked us to many stolen cars and strong-arm robberies and burglaries. Now with this horrific car wreck, and three people in critical condition, they were determined to catch us.

Around noon the second day we watched them from the second floor window of our hideout as they discovered the corvette in the cornfield. Some crop duster spotted it and called the sheriff. We had to get out of there or they might start going house to house and barn to barn.

That night we burglarized the store again and weren't careful at all, because we were leaving town and were not ever coming back. We destroyed the place so they knew we had been in town the whole time and they weren't good enough to catch us.

We went to the river and made life jackets out of our pants, a trick Bill learned in the Marines. I had not been in long enough to learn that one.

It worked great. We got in the river and floated down stream, right under a bridge they set up a roadblock on. We could hear every word they said, as we covertly glided right beneath them on our backs. It was hard for me not to giggle, listening to them on the bridge talking. I knew they were not going to catch us. When we were safely far enough away from them, we climbed out of the river, put our pants on and stole another car.

Kansas City was the one place I should have stayed away from. I was always running into someone I knew and they told me how bad my mom was doing, and that she just wanted me to call her. I got weak one day and called her; she talked me into coming to see her. I told Bill to wait for me at the hotel we were staying in and I would be back in a couple of hours. I never saw him again.

Seeing my mom look so weak and frail, and knowing I was responsible, was more than I could bear. After hours, that turned into days, of her begging me to turn myself in, I said okay. I knew I was going to be in a lot of trouble for being gone so long, but I didn't realize I was also going to be charged for that wreck that happened while the police chased me.

My mom and dad drove me back to the base in Tennessee. I knew going back this time was not going to be the same. I had been gone a lot longer and was suspected of a lot of criminal activity. I was right; they took me straight to the brig. When you are in the brig you are a disgrace to the United States of America. When *Reveille* was played every morning I had to lay face down on the floor and was not allowed to participate. When we were marching outside and passed by the American flag, I had to turn my head away from it. For the next twenty plus years I was anti-American because of that treatment.

I refused to look towards the flag at ball games. When they played the *Star Spangled Banner* I would talk; sometimes someone would say something to me and I would say I hate this country. I never took my hat off when everyone else did. I hated America and all it stood for.

My folks came to visit me while I was in the brig. They took me over to visitation in leg irons, waist chains, and a chaser—that's what the guards were called—walking behind me with a shotgun at my back. As we approached the room my folks waited in, I could see them both looking out of the window. When we got close enough, I saw the tears streaming down my mother's cheeks. I hated those stinking guards, and the dirty rotten authorities that put me in there. I vowed not to put my mom through that anymore.

I also found out that after I was court-martialed and punished for my military crimes, I was going to have to face charges in Missouri and Illinois. I knew how to get out of that, and knew exactly how to keep Mom from going through the pain of seeing me locked up. I would escape...so with that plan in place, I just had to wait for an opportunity.

ESCAPE FROM THE BRIG

The first few weeks I was in the brig I didn't do anything but stay locked in a cage all day. They treated us like we were animals. They kept all prisoners' cigarettes locked in a big wooden box. Two or three times a day they would unlock it and call our numbers. When I went up, they gave me one cigarette. When everyone had theirs, they would shout out, "The smoking lamp is lit for one cigarette." We might have only taken two or three drags and they would scream, "THE SMOKING LAMP IS OUT," and you had better get it put out fast. It made me so mad…I quit smoking while I was in there.

There was a group of us that did pushups all day, every day. I got in tremendous condition doing thousands of pushups and sit-ups every day. Different varieties of pushups: wide stance, narrow stance, hands back, hands forward, handstand pushups.

One inmate was a French foot fighter, and he was built better than anyone I had ever seen, for someone who didn't even work-out with weights. He had built his entire body doing pushups. He was the one who showed us all the different varieties, and taught me the walking twenty. The walking twenty: We stay down on the ground the whole time, I do one push up then he does one. I do two pushups, he does two. I do three pushups, he does three. We would take that all the way to twenty and then go nineteen, eighteen, and back to one. That may not sound like much, but that is four hundred and eighty-four pushups. We did that several times a day, so you see why I got in shape; when we weren't doing pushups we did sit-ups.

One day they told me I was going to be put on work detail. I told Al, a fellow prisoner who hated the brig more than I did, that I was going to escape.

"Today?" he asked.

"If I don't go today, I might never get another chance," I whispered.

"I wanna go with you."

I didn't care as long as he didn't get in my way. They sent us to paint the inside of a building where they packed parachutes. He and I were sent into the men's restroom to paint. I looked out the window in the bathroom and it was perfect. There was a parking lot full of cars behind the building that couldn't be seen from where the rest of the guards and prisoners worked.

"The first time that chaser comes in to check on us, I'm taking him out and we go out the window," I told Al.

"Okay, man, I'm with you."

In just a few minutes the chaser walked in and when he turned to look at what Al was doing, I hit him in the back of the head with a full can of paint. It knocked him out cold. We went out the window and ran through the lot looking for a car with the keys in it.

"I got one," I hollered. We jumped in and took off. I told Al, "If they try and stop us at the gate, I'm running over the guards."

"No, don't do that."

Before I could respond, we were at the back gate of the base and the guard on duty stepped out and saluted us as we drove through.

I said, "What was that all about?"

I sure wasn't going to stop and ask. We drove through Millington, Tennessee; it would be the last time I ever saw that town.

SOUTHERN HOSPITALITY

We got into Memphis and ran out of gas. As we walked away to find another car, I glanced back and saw why we got saluted. It was the sticker on the front bumper.

"Hey Al, we stole a Colonel's car and that stupid guard at the gate thought I was an officer."

Al snapped to attention and saluted me. We laughed for a while over that one.

We had gone less than a block from where we ran out of gas and there was a maroon 1962 Pontiac Catalina sitting with the keys in the ignition. Don't ask me how I remember the color, cars have always been one of my passions and I just remember certain things.

Back in those days people left their keys in cars more often than you would think. Not a good idea when you have two escaped inmates and they have on prison issue clothing. We wore white tee shirts with BRIG written in huge black letters all the way across the back. We hopped in the Pontiac and took off. I had no idea where we were. I just wanted to put some distance between me and that chaser on the floor with his head caved in.

We hadn't driven very far when I saw a sign. "WELCOME TO MISSISSIPPI." That's what it said, as I flew by at 90 mph. That sign was a little inaccurate, because everyone *wasn't* welcome in Mississippi, as we were about to find out. I had no idea I had just committed "Dyer Act," which is a federal law against taking a stolen motor vehicle across a state line. I had done that dozens of times, just never got caught.

"You'd better slow down, or you're going to get us stopped," Al said.

"You scared, Al?" I mashed the gas pedal to the floor and ran up a little over 100 mph, before I let off.

"No, I'm not scared…I just don't wanna get caught."

We were about a hundred and forty-five miles from Memphis when we drove into the little town of Leland, Mississippi. We cruised around looking for a car we could steal that night, but there was only one car lot. I knew the keys from the stolen Pontiac would fit any GM on the lot.

We noticed a little park just on the edge of town while we drove around that day. I figured it would be a good place to leave the stolen car, so we parked it. We walked back to town; I turned my shirt inside out and went to the car lot, switched the keys, and had a car ready to go that night.

I went to a clothing store and picked out some clothes that fit me, I took them to the counter and told the clerk I forgot my wallet. I asked him if he would leave them at the register, and I would come first thing in the morning to pay. He said that was a good idea. I did that so when I got into the store that night, I wouldn't have to search for my sizes; they would be in a nice pile on the counter.

We went back to the park and waited for all the stores and the car lot to close. When it was dark, we headed back to town. The first thing we did was get our new ride. All I needed was my new clothes. I told Al I would get him some on the road. I had a feeling he wasn't going to be around too long anyway. He was too nervous. While shopping for clothes I had been casing the store, the skylight was the easiest way in, with no alarm. Al was boosting me up on the roof when I saw a flashlight coming down the other end of the alley. I dropped down and pointed to a stack of barrels; he dove in behind them and I took off the opposite direction from the flashlight beam.

I rounded a corner and ran into a revolver barrel longer than Dirty Harry's.

"WHERE YOU GOIN' BOY?" The booming deep southern accent came out of the fattest cop I had ever seen.

"With you sir."

"Where's that feller that was with you?"

"I'm by myself," I lied.

"YOU'RE A LYING SACK OF DIRT."

I was beginning to think I was back in boot camp, or this stupid cop thought I was deaf. I didn't say another word as he was handcuffing me. He led me down the alley and pushed my head down as he put me in the backseat of the squad car.

There were only about twenty-five hundred people in the town of Leland in 1963, and the jail was small, and really old. As he took me into the decrepit, falling down building they called a jail, I checked out everything we walked past, planning my escape. It was simple. It looked like there were only six or eight inmates in the whole jail. From the cell I was in I could hear everything going on. I had been there for way over an hour, and they still had not brought Al in. That was good. Maybe he got away. Now I wouldn't have to worry about what he might tell them.

My thoughts were interrupted as the old steel outside door slammed. I listened carefully, and heard Al's voice.

"Can I have something to eat?"

My heart sank. *Where has he been all this time?* I thought to myself. I fell asleep on the steel bunk. I had been awake for many hours. I hadn't slept well the night before we escaped; I couldn't shut my mind off. Sleep finally came, even though I was lying on a steel bunk with no mattress or any kind of padding. Suddenly I was awakened by the rattling keys in the cell door. It was the sheriff.

"You wanna tell me what you're a doin' in my town, boy? Your buddy already took us out to the car ya'll stole in Tennessee. He even showed us the car ya'll stole here. We know you are the two Marines that escaped from the brig in Millington, Tennessee, and we already notified 'em."

I thought to myself, *this guy must have been vaccinated with a phonograph needle...he never shuts up.*

I didn't say anything, but I wished like everything I could get my hands on that rat Al. They must have known what I was thinking, because I never saw Al again. It would be many years before I quit thinking about getting even with that dirty snitch.

The deputy took me back to my cell, and I saw a couple more weaknesses in that tin can they called a jail. I would just wait for my chance. The chance never came, however, because I fell asleep and when they woke me up, it was to transfer me. They took me about an hour up the road to Coahoma County Jail in Clarksdale, Mississippi.

This was a lot different than the jail I had just come from; it was very secure. I would need to study a while to get out of there. Out of one hundred and forty-three prisoners, only thirteen were white.

This was around the time that James Meredith was attempting to be the first black man to go to the University of Mississippi. It was an hour away in Oxford, Mississippi. Boy was I glad I wasn't there. I had enough trouble of my own without getting in the middle of those riots. There was more prejudice in those southern states than I had ever been around in my life. The atmosphere was tense. All gas stations had restrooms marked men, women, and colored. Drinking fountains everywhere were marked white and colored. In Kansas City, where I grew up, there was some prejudice, but nothing close to this.

MISSISSIPPI JAILS

I thought that escaping from the brig would keep my mom from experiencing the pain of seeing me locked up. Boy, was I ever stupid. After a couple of weeks in Clarksdale, she and my dad came to see me. There was no visiting room. They had to walk down catwalks and upstairs to whatever cell I was in. My mother had never been exposed to the language and gestures she heard and saw that day. I told them never to come back there again. They wouldn't have a chance to anyway, because I was transferred the next week to exactly where I didn't want to go— Oxford, Mississippi.

A deputy picked me up, and even though we were only traveling sixty some miles, he handcuffed and shackled me. The leg shackles had a chain that came up and ran through waist chains, as well as the handcuffs. The chains were covered with a black box at my waist. I had never been in those kinds of chains. I thought it was crazy. I wondered if once I became a federal prisoner these chains would be standard procedure. He took me to a jail near the federal courthouse, where I would officially be charged with "Dyer Act."

Oxford really felt the effects of the riots caused by James Meredith, because it was the town the university was in. I didn't want to be here. The first night I was there, they brought in twenty or thirty men who were involved in rioting. They put them all in our cell, which was already overcrowded. The rioters slept on the floor and were released the next morning.

A few nights after I arrived, a new guy came in. When he took his shirt off, I saw big scars all over his back. I asked him, "What happened to your back?"

"Black Annie," he said.

"What's Black Annie?"

"Thas the whip theys use on ya up at Parchman, son."

"What's Parchman?"

"Thas da Missippi State Pen, ones tha most evil prisons they is. You better hopes you neva goes dere. You know what mens say when da up dere?"

"No, what do they say?"

"I's gonna come back and kills me a guard or two."

"Do they go back?"

"When da gets out a Parchman, da gits as fah away from Missippi as da can git."

I fell asleep after talking with him and dreamed of being beaten with a whip at Parchman. I woke up with a great idea . . . I would escape. Funny, how that was always on my mind.

Back in the early sixties you could buy a candy bar for a dime. But you could get a gigantic Baby Ruth for a quarter. I wrote a friend of mine and told him to buy a giant Baby Ruth and send it to me. But before he sent it, I wanted him to put half of a hacksaw blade inside. I was determined to get out of Mississippi.

"That stupid punk took the letter I wrote him and showed it to my dad and mom," I said to one of the guys locked up with me. "First my cousin rats me out, now a guy I thought was my friend."

I was learning the hard way that I couldn't trust anyone. It is a lesson anyone who has plans to live and do the things I did needs to learn.

I was only five feet ten inches tall and weighed about one hundred and sixty pounds. I felt like a little boy among those guys who had been in prisons like Parchman. I might not have been able to compete physically with some of them, but I could compete mentally with any of them. None seemed very bright to me. It was probably just the deep southern drawl and they moved too slow to suit me.

All of those guys just accepted being in jail as their lot in life. I was already thinking of ways to escape and constantly worked on a plan. *If I could get out of here, they won't ever catch me again*, I thought. I was there for a few weeks before I went before a federal judge for the first time. I thought maybe when they took me to court I could escape. The federal courthouse was directly across the street from the jail and they escorted me across, completely chained up. I could hardly move. You would have thought I was a serial killer.

Before I was done, I traveled over twenty-five hundred miles in handcuffs, waist chains, leg irons, and that black box.

BIG TED

The first time I traveled any distance with the US Marshals, it was to the Federal Correctional Institution in Ashland, Kentucky. It took us quite a while to get there, because the Marshals had business along the way and they stopped in little towns. They left me in jails overnight and sometimes longer. The first day we traveled north to Springfield, Missouri, and they dropped me at the Greene County Jail. This old jail had bars in between the two-man cells and you could see from one end of the jail to the other.

There was a guy named Ted in the cell right next to mine. He was the biggest man I'd ever seen up to that point in my life. I was told he had been in Alcatraz for over twelve years. He looked like he'd been lifting weights the whole time.

They were closing the infamous "Rock" in California down, and the most dangerous and incorrigible inmates were being transferred to a brand new maximum security federal prison in Marion, Illinois. "Big" Ted was one of those inmates.

I was suddenly awakened by the guard screaming, "Get that man down; get him down!"

"You get him down! I didn't hang him up there," said Big Ted, the dead man's cellmate.

I was wide awake now and I knew I wouldn't be going back to sleep for a while. As I watched all the activity going on in the cell right next to mine, I wondered how *anyone* could be as coldhearted as Big Ted.

As a five-foot-ten-inch, one-hundred-sixty-pound, eighteen-year-old kid, I was terrified of him. Even though there were bars between his cell and mine, he looked like he could just rip them out and come over and get me. I thought to myself, *What am I doing here with this madman?* I never dreamed that twenty years later, I would be physically bigger than him, and just as coldhearted. I once saw a man with his wrists slit, bleeding to death under a stairway in a prison; he looked up at me as if to say, "Please help me." I walked away and never told anyone about it for years.

101st AIRBORNE

A few days later some different Marshals came to get me. I was very glad to get out of there alive. I wondered where we were going now. These US Marshals drove me all over the place. They claimed they were going to pick up an inmate at Scott County Jail in Huntsville, Tennessee. I sometimes wondered if they were just messing with my mind, because it took an awfully long time to get to where we were supposed to be going. When we got to Huntsville, the inmate wasn't ready, so they said I would have to stay in the jail overnight.

It was a filthy dump—cockroaches, rats, and I later found out, crabs. I got a real bad case of them. I also got into a fight with an Airborne Ranger, 101st Airborne—that's what his tattoo said. I thought, *I am a Marine and he's a punk army dude*, but he whipped me like a four-year old at Walmart.

When the US Marshals picked me up the next day to continue on our trip, my lip was cut. I think my nose was broken, and my crotch was itching like crazy. I didn't have any idea why. All I knew was that it was impossible to scratch with that miserable black box locked over the chains. A few more dirty county jails and we finally arrived at what was to be my home for the next sixty days. The federal judge sent me there on what they called a Sixty-Day Observation.

I spent the first week in the Fish Tank—that is what they called the area where they kept all the new "fish." They made me strip and shower. They knew immediately what was up, and gave me some A200 to put on my crotch. It quickly took care of the critters.

When a new inmate gets to prison, they are kept in isolation for orientation, and completely separated from the rest of the population for the first week or two. They brought my meals to my cell; I was not allowed to go in the chow hall or out on the yard with everyone else. They did that to see if there were any glaring problems that would cause disruptions when I was released into general population.

It was very different being locked in a cell all alone; I had been in county jails for the last few months, where I was around other inmates day and night. Now, I was in a cell where I couldn't see or talk to anyone. I remember I was mad at God. I found something sharp and cut a cross in my leg. That scar is still there. It seems a little strange to be mad at God and cut a cross in your leg. I hear people today say they wrestle with God, and I always wonder who wins that one.

Finally the day came; I was assigned to a cell house. Escaping was still in the forefront of mind because I knew when I went back before that judge he would give me more time. The first day I was allowed to go on the yard, I planned to run and hit the fence.

I will never forget that day; it was sunny and warm. I had been locked in cells for months and it felt so good to get in the fresh air, see grass, and walk around without any chains. While I soaked it all in, an inmate ran and jumped up on the fence; he started to climb, and was about ten feet off the ground.

A single shot came from one of the gun towers and the inmate fell backwards off the fence. I thought to myself, *I think I am going to stay here and forget about escaping.*

I began lifting weights and my body responded immediately. I grew like I was on steroids. I gained over two inches on my arms, and I am not sure how much weight, but when I went back before the judge in Oxford, the guys I had been in jail with couldn't believe I changed that much in sixty days. They hardly recognized me.

THE ULTIMATE PARDON

CHAPTER

14

THE SENTENCING

I didn't do well in the testing and counseling I had to go through at Ashland in my sixty day observation. I hated the psychiatrist they forced me to see as part of my sentence. Everything he said always lead back to—it's entirely your mom and dad's fault. According to him everything I did wrong was because of the way they raised me. He would say, "If your mother hadn't done such and such, you wouldn't have done this or that."

I would look at his beady little eyes and say, "drop dead!"

I don't think my sessions with him got very high scores. When I went back before the judge he gave me a zip six, which was six months to six years. I was so mad, I couldn't see straight. It wasn't supposed to go this way.

After sentencing, I stayed in the jail in Oxford, Mississippi till the US Marshals got around to coming after me. I did a lot of waiting on those Marshals. Altogether, I was there for about four months.

In Oxford, I only got to eat twice a day—six o'clock in the morning and six o'clock at night. It was the same thing morning and evening—cornbread and greens with a cup of water. Day after day, week after week, month after month I ate this slop. It was years before I would eat cornbread, and I am not too crazy about it today. It's been over fifty years.

When the US Marshals finally came to get me, it was a very long trip to the Federal Correctional Institution in Englewood, Colorado. On the way there, *again*, the Marshals had business to attend to in several towns. *Again*, they left me in different jails overnight. The last stop before Englewood was in El Reno, Oklahoma, where I spent one night at that federal prison in one of their holding cells.

Finally we arrived at the sally port of the prison which would be my home for a while. Little Alcatraz is what some of the inmates, and even some of the guards called it, because it was laid out just like Alcatraz inside the walls. The only difference was it wasn't surrounded by water, but mountains. One of the guards there had been a guard at Alcatraz.

One day I asked him, "Did you know Big Ted?"

"Everybody knew Big Ted," he said.

When I got to Englewood an inmate told me that some guys wanted me to sit with them at lunch my first day in population. I asked him who they were; he told me they were some of the most powerful men in the prison. I had mixed feelings about meeting with those guys. I wondered, *What could they want from me? I just got here, they don't even know me.* If I didn't show up, I was being disrespectful. If I did show up, what was I supposed to say to them, and how should I act? I am not going to tell you I wasn't real nervous.

Finally, the day came for me to get released into the population. All I could think about was the meeting I was supposed to go to. I will never forget that day in the chow hall, not because of my meeting, but because of the fight that happened right in front of me.

I heard a fight was going to happen and who the guys were. I was warned to keep some distance between me and the stupid new inmate in front of me in the chow line. The other inmate's name was Jim Wagner, by far the toughest dude in the whole joint. He worked in the chow hall on the serving line.

PUNCH THE TOUGH GUY

Someone told this new inmate that when he got to prison, he needed to find out who the toughest guy in the place was. He was told to go up at the first opportunity and hit him right in the mouth. That would let everyone know how tough *he* was.

I lagged behind on purpose when the new inmate got directly in front of Wagner. The new guy telegraphed his punch; Wagner blocked it, and hit him with a right cross that nearly took his head off. He was out on his feet, but before he could hit the floor, Wagner jumped over the counter and hit him at least a dozen more times before the guards could get there. He was a bloody, unconscious mess.

The hacks rushed in, handcuffed them both, and took Wagner to the hole. The new guy went to the hospital. Jim looked at me and just shook his head. "Won't they ever learn?" As they took him away, although we had never met, he knew I was okay, or he wouldn't have spoken to me.

When he got out of the hole, I was one of the first guys he looked up. He and I became good friends. Believe me, he was a good guy to have as a friend.

Wow, quite an introduction to my first day in general population. After all that excitement, I forgot about the meeting I was supposed to be in. I found a spot to eat and was interrupted by an inmate who quickly reminded me I was to join him and his friends. It was the meeting I was supposed to be in.

Between the weight lifting at Ashland, Kentucky and all the pushups and sit-ups I did over the last several months, I got pretty big. I figured that might be why they were interested in having me be a part of their crew. I found out sometime later that they knew everything about me. I guess they liked some of the things they heard, and believed I could bring something extra to the organization they ran. I felt proud that I was being considered a potential member of their group.

I found out in that meeting the reason Wagner the tough guy had acknowledged me as they were taking him to the hole. He was one of the leaders of this crew and was one of the guys who wanted me in. We became like family and were closer than brothers.

Many times I proved I was what they expected me to be. I would not snitch if it meant me taking all the heat. That is the type of man they were looking for in members. I backed them up when they needed me, and was willing to die in the process. These guys all had connections in different cities around the US. The one I was closest to was from St. Louis, Missouri, so we were homeys.

Back in the early sixties, prisons were a lot more inhumane than they are today. There were no pay phones and you were not allowed to make phone calls at all. You were only allowed to write and receive letters from six people and they had to be approved by the Feds.

When you were sent to the hole, it was serious punishment. No writing materials and no reading materials. They didn't feed you much. You were stripped down to your underwear and that was it. No furniture, no toilet or sink. There was just a hole in the concrete floor for a toilet. They still used the whip in some prisons—Parchman, Mississippi, and Tucker Farm, Arkansas among others. It was real hard time.

I will never forget some of the guys I did time with. It was like being at war; you didn't forget the guys you fought with. This was our battleground. While I was there, there were riots and murders and we survived them all.

I remember exactly where I was walking in the prison the day John F. Kennedy was killed. They broadcast it over the intercom. I didn't have any compassion for him or his family, because I was locked up and felt like he hadn't done anything to help me. I was self-centered and anti-American. I really thought the world owed *me* something. I was still full of anger, which increased over the next twenty years.

During my time there I got to know some career criminals. They taught me skills that allowed me to commit crimes for the next twenty years. I only got caught one time and I beat that case with a crooked lawyer—a fact that I was proud of.

There were about twelve hundred inmates at Englewood, and though I never knew many of them personally, almost all knew who I was, or at least they knew I was a part of a crew that controlled nearly everything inside the walls of "Little Alcatraz."

RUNNING A STORE

We ran it like a business on the street. There were meetings held to discuss details of the financials within our organization. Making money was what drove the business, and of course, the power that comes with having more money than anyone else in the joint.

We ran the biggest store in the whole prison; our store was almost bigger than the commissary. We may even have had *more* of some items than the commissary. Our rates were two for one if we liked you, a whole lot more if we didn't, sometimes as high as ten for one, for the lames. That meant if a prisoner ran out of Oreo cookies in the middle of the week and wanted a pack before it was his day to go to commissary, we sold him a pack, and when he made commissary he paid us back two packs or whatever we decided the rate was.

No inmate was allowed to have over one carton or ten packs of cigarettes in their possession at one time. There were times we had between fifty and a hundred cartons of cigarettes. We made weak inmates who didn't smoke keep them for us. We also stashed them in different places in the prison.

We had lots of power and money, and with those two things, I could get anything I wanted done in prison. Other contraband items I sold were called sweats (pictures of nude women). If the prison guards caught you with a picture of a naked woman the size of a postage stamp, it was ten days in the hole. I could get big money for those pictures. Now inmates in prison can subscribe to *Playboy* and *Penthouse*. Bob Dylan said it well…The Times They Are A-Changin'.

There were times business got interrupted by a trip to the hole, because of a fight or getting caught with contraband. I always lost twenty pounds or more in the hole, because they didn't feed men in the hole the same as general population—portions were much smaller.

When the guards came to the end of the run of six cells, they brought a regular tray from the chow hall. If the general population ate meatloaf, I got one sixth of a piece of meatloaf, one sixth of a slice of bread, one sixth of a helping of mashed potatoes, and a cup of water. I was used to eating my portion in the chow hall and maybe someone else's. Now I got one sixth of a normal portion.

When I got out of the hole it would take me a while to gain back the weight I lost. The party was on—with the best food and plenty of home brew when one of our crew got out of the hole. It was like the prodigal son returning home. One of my partners would watch my interests while I was away or vice versa.

I walked over to Jim Wagner, and said, "There's something I have to do today, watch my business if anything happens"

"Is it Gray?" Jim asked.

"Yep, he's a couple weeks late today and told one of the guy's he's not too worried about it."

I'd given Gray two packs of cigarettes on a rate of four for one, he owed me eight packs. I was going to see to it he paid today. I walked into the chow hall and saw him sitting in his normal spot. He didn't see me as I walked up and stole on him. When he went to the floor I grabbed him by the ear and took off running. I pulled his fat butt up off the floor. He weighed a lot more than me, but I was one of the strongest guys in the whole joint. When I stopped he went to the infirmary to get half of his ear sewn back on—I went to the hole. I made my point. When I got out of the hole, they told me he paid the debt. That trip to the hole was worth it, and earned me more respect.

I was young and didn't really care if I got caught being an enforcer. I made sure people who didn't want to pay us back on time knew there would always be repercussions. I was also getting a reputation as a man who wouldn't let the fear of punishment stop me. After a couple trips to the hole and some counsel from some of my partners, I learned how to take care of those situations without getting caught. I never went back to the hole again, except for helping a friend out of a jam one time.

We controlled the card games when there was money involved. One of the games we played a lot of was bridge. I know that doesn't sound like a tough guy card game, but it was one we played, and there was always money involved. It takes a sharp mind and deep thinking to play it…and cheat like we did. We had codes and signals with our cigarettes, the way we held them in our mouth, the way we blew the smoke—direction, smoke rings, coughing, etc. It was foolproof. We studied it like NFL players study their playbooks. Everyone in our crew had it down pat. We never got caught and made lots of money.

From the time I got involved with that power circle, till the day I left, I always had my trousers creased, my shirts starched and pressed, and my shoes always sparkling. I had inmates under me that I took care of and they made sure I was taken care of. I didn't get involved in any sex play, because that could get time added to my sentence, plus God made me *really* like females. However, with all that said, I *did* have two or three sweet boys I walked for.

To walk for someone meant they were spoken for, and no one else would mess with them. I told those punks up front that I would have nothing to do with them sexually. They could get into relationships with each other or someone else, but I would walk for them and protect them. One of them did my laundry; another did my shoes, and so on.

I had been into weight lifting since I was twelve or thirteen. I was never in one place long enough to make much progress, but in prison I really got into it. My body blew up quickly. Before I escaped from the brig, I learned how to kick from a savate expert—French foot fighting. I only learned one kick—the front kick. I taught some of my buddies how to kick and we became lethal with our hands and feet.

Today martial artists and kick boxers are so much better than we were, but at that time and in that place we were the best. I continued lifting weights for the rest of my time in prison. When I got out I was big and strong, and my heart was harder than Big Ted's. I hurt people in prison, watched men die, and I didn't give it a second thought.

15

THE REBEL MAKES PAROLE

After my release from prison I returned to Kansas City to start my parole.

Around the time I was released from prison in 1964

I didn't plan on becoming a law-abiding citizen, or never breaking the law again. I was just going to be careful and never go back to prison. I succeeded with my plans for eighteen years committing crimes, promoting prostitution, pornography, and dealing drugs without going back.

I was only home a few days when one of my friends who was in the crew with me in the joint came to visit. I didn't want my folks to know he was in town, because it was a parole violation to associate with a known felon. I got him a motel room and we started planning a heist we would do together.

I told him one day, "You stay here; I'll go get us a girl."

I didn't even have anyone in mind, but I knew I could get one quick. I drove up to the high school and picked up a girl I had never seen before. I took her down to the Elm Cliff Motel where Bob was waiting. We got a couple of fifths of whiskey and got her drunk. We ended up keeping her there for two days until the Raytown cops showed up at my mom and dad's house.

Someone had seen her get into the car with me and wrote down the license number. When she didn't show up at home that night, her parents called the police. They went to the high school and started questioning people and came up with the license plate number of my dad's car.

I went home to get some clothes and walked into a beehive.

Dad said, "Let's go for a drive."

I still didn't know what it was all about, but could tell he was very disturbed and I wasn't going to argue with him.

We started driving and he said, "Do you want to tell me where the girl is that you picked up at the high school?"

"I don't know what you're talking about."

"Bill, they have witnesses that saw her get in the car with you, and someone took the license plate number. That little girl is only fifteen years old."

"Oh wow, I didn't know that," I said. I told him that I had taken her to a motel and that I got her drunk.

"Did you s_ _ _w that little girl?" he asked me angrily.

"No," I lied.

My dad had no idea that Bob was in town, and that we had both been with her for two days.

I told my dad, "I'll get her back to the school."

I got her back to the school and told her to dummy up (prison language, to not talk). When I told Bob the cops had been to my house looking for me, and they knew I had taken her, and that she was only fifteen years old, he freaked out.

He said, "Get me to the Greyhound station."

I put him on a bus for San Jose, California and never heard from him again.

Now I am going to tell a part of the story that you are not going to believe, but it's the truth.

"Get some clothes packed, Bill; out of sight, out of mind," Dad said.

"Where are we going?" I questioned him, while he and I packed some bags for the trip. He wanted to get me away from this situation for a while. I didn't have to report to my P.O. for another three weeks.

Dad said, "We are going to stay gone and see what happens."

I cannot explain how it happened; all I can tell you is that my mom and dad were good Christians. They prayed the whole time Dad and I were gone. When we got back, we never heard another thing from the parents of that girl, or from the Raytown Police. Bada Bing, Bada Boom. It was finished.

THE MARRIED YEARS

Not too long after that happened I met another fifteen-year-old girl, but the difference with this one was that her parents didn't mind us being together. I fell in love with her. She was the sweetest girl I had ever been with and by far the best looking. She looked like Marlo Thomas of the TV show *That Girl*. We would walk into a restaurant and you could hear people all over the room whispering, "Look, there's that girl." I loved the fact that everyone looked at her. What I didn't love were all the guys looking. I got into a fight almost every time we went somewhere. Some guy would be staring at her. I would bust him in the mouth. That happened more times than I could count. I was very jealous and didn't want anyone to even look at her.

One time a guy she went to high school with got smart with us on the road and wanted me to pull over. We pulled off the road and stopped. I was at his car before he got his door opened. He had his window down and started to smart off to me. I busted him in the mouth. His lip was split wide open and bleeding bad. I told him to get out, but he was too scared. I got back into my car and drove away. I see that guy sometimes now and he still has a terrible scar from smarting off to the wrong guy.

Marsha's dad owned a plumbing company. I worked as a rough-in carpenter. He would come out on jobs to check on his men and see me working. He liked what he saw, because I never walked, I ran everywhere. He decided he needed someone like me at his plumbing shop and persuaded me to work for him.

Her mom and dad were in agreement when we told them we wanted to get married. Marsha and I got married five days after she turned sixteen. We moved into a house on her mom and dad's property. The relationship we had with her parents was highly volatile and we moved off their property within months after being married.

I think altogether we moved five times the first year of our marriage. It was hard on a young marriage. Our first son was born in 1966; we named him after me and her dad. Our marriage was filled with lies and deception. I still had darkness in me that drove me. Pornography had a hold on me and I didn't know how to escape. Also, I didn't want to lose the burglary skills I had honed in prison. So with my wife and now my baby boy at stake, I continued living a secret, double life.

I worked construction jobs during the day and lied to my wife, telling her that I had side construction jobs to do at night. I would go out and burglarize, or run around with the other crowd she knew nothing about. I brought part of the money home and gave it to her. I told her it was from the side jobs.

Our second son was born in 1969. He won the cutest baby contest at the church my wife and I attended. Yes, I was going to church and putting on a front for my family and friends.

One time my wife was going somewhere and my truck was parked behind her car. I told her I would move it because there were things in it I didn't want her to see. I must have made too big a deal out of moving it so she could take her own car, because she insisted on taking the truck. When she came back home she had found a lot of money I had hidden in the glove compartment. I lied to her and said I had saved it to buy her a present. Since I told her that, I ended up buying her something with the money.

I learned a valuable lesson that night and never left money where she could find it again. I continued to do burglaries throughout our marriage, and my fence bought anything I stole.

CONSTRUCTION CON MAN

I was working one time on two big high-rise apartments next door to each other. People had already occupied the first building and we were working on the second. You could access either building from the parking garages connecting the two buildings.

On my lunch break I would go to my car in the parking garage and change out of my construction clothes and put on dress clothes. I went to the lobby of the occupied apartments and waited till I saw someone getting into the elevator with their keys in their hand. You had to have a room key to access the elevator. I acted like I was reaching for my keys, but would let them put theirs in first and punch in the floor number.

I would say, "Thanks."

I pushed a floor number several floors from the one they were getting off on. Once I was on my floor, I would knock on a door to make sure no one was home, and then I would go in. I had learned from working on that building that if I put my knee against the steel door jamb and pushed hard, the jamb would give and the bolt would back away enough that I could open the door. There were no deadbolts on those doors.

I only stole things that I could get into my pockets, or under my coat. Then I would return to my car, change into my work clothes, and go back up on the job. Thirty minutes was all I had to change, burglarize, change back, and get back to work. I probably did one a week for over a year, never got caught. I never kept anything that came out of those apartments…only the cash.

I worked for a company for several years and I broke into their jobsites and stole tools and equipment. I always had my key for the jobsites I worked on. I used them to get into construction fences and trailers, and would always make it appear as a forced entry.

I remember one jobsite in particular. It was a brand new high rise and we had geared up to start and had many thousands of dollars in tools. I let myself in and got a whole truckload of new tools. The last thing I loaded was a big generator. Before I loaded up the cutting torch outfit, I used it to cut the locks off the door.

I was the first one on the job each day, so the next morning when I arrived, I pretended to discover the burglary, and called my boss.

"John, we had a break in last night. They got all our new tools, looks like they used a torch on the locks."

"What all did they get?"

"It looks like almost everything," I sighed.

"Call the police, and I'll be there in a minute."

The police came out and John gave them a list of what was gone. The cops told him that it had to have been at least two men and possibly three, because no one man could carry that generator by himself.

"Except for Superman," John said, as he nodded towards me. They all laughed; I guess they never suspected me and didn't know how strong I was.

On a different jobsite, the superintendent of the company showed up one day. He told the foreman, "I know for sure that Bill Corum is stealing from us, but I can't catch him." The foreman was one of my close Italian friends so he came straight to me and told me word for word what Leo said. He knew I was stealing, but he wasn't about to rat me out because we did some things together, and he wasn't a snitch. He told me about it because he didn't want me to get caught.

When he told me, I said, "Go tell him I said he never will catch me, because it takes a thief to catch a thief, and he's not a good enough thief to catch me."

Of course, I knew he wouldn't tell Leo, I was just being cocky. The truth was, I stole from that company for a long time after that, and he never caught me, but I was a little more careful.

THEY KILLED MY FENCE

I lived a completely double life; I was married, going to church, and stealing almost every day. I fenced everything I stole to a guy who owned a junk yard. When I first met Sol, I introduced myself as Jim Gardner. He was a guy I had been in prison with. I knew all about him, where he was born, and raised, where he went to grade school and high school, his parents' names, etc. I figured if I was ever questioned about anything, I knew the answers.

Not long after I was fencing stolen goods to Sol, I found out he was involved with the top names in the Kansas City underworld. I figured if they trusted him, I should. I finally told him who I really was. After that, he would have me meet him in some of the places the mob bosses hung out. They had ways of finding out who I really was, so I was glad I told him the truth. It would have been real embarrassing if he introduced me to any of them as Jim Gardner, and they exposed me as a liar.

Although I was around those bosses only a short time, it gave me credibility for the contract work Kenny and I would do years later. I must have made the right impression, because I am still alive and Sol's not.

There was one construction job I was on for over a year. It was a huge shopping center and there were multiple trailers with material and tools. They kept security guards on duty nights and weekends to make sure no one stole anything.

Almost every Saturday I told my wife I had a side job. I would go to that jobsite. I got a couple magnetic signs with my company's name on them. A block from the job, I would pull over and stick them on each door of my personal truck. When I pulled up to the gate, I just drove right in. I put on my hardhat and would sit in the guard's car with him and drink a cup of coffee.

After a few minutes I'd say, "They got me working again this weekend...I can't ever get a day off. I had better get to work before they fire me."

He would just laugh, and say, "They would never fire a guy like you who's always willing to work weekends."

Time and time again, I sat in that security guard's car, drank a little coffee, and then stole something to take to Sol. When the job was almost over, they realized they were missing a lot of material and tools. All my neighbors and coworkers thought I was this honest, hard-working guy. There were times I thought about what a rotten man I was, but something kept driving me.

I remember one day, I was with a guy that my wife and I were very good friends with. I was driving him home. When we got close, he pointed to his neighbor's house and said, "See that house? That guy has more guns than you've ever seen—pistols, rifles, and shotguns galore. He doesn't even keep them locked up."

A couple of months later when I was with him again, he said, "Bill, remember my neighbor I told you had all those guns?"

"I think so . . . what about him?"

"Somebody robbed him, and got all his guns."

"No way! Are you kidding?"

My neighbors, friends, and relatives all thought I was an honest, hard-working, good father and husband. In reality, I was involved with some real serious people.

Sol would often have me meet him in a River Quay bar and restaurant and we'd talk like we were at Denny's.

"You look excited, Bill, what have you got for me?"

"I've got pistols, rifles, and shotguns galore."

"Bring them by my place. I'll take them."

I have no idea what he did with all those guns, but he bought every gun I stole from my friend's neighbor.

La Costa Nostra (this thing of ours) was still going strong in 1970. Willie Cammisano was trying to move the go-go dancing and pornography from 12th Street, where they planned to build a new hotel, down to the River Quay. He faced a lot of opposition from another strong force in the mob. The River Quay was a time bomb over parking lot disputes and other battles between mob families. It exploded in a series of fires, bombings and contract murders. I was spending more and more time in the Quay, and sometimes I didn't know if I might be in the wrong place at the wrong time. I just knew that when Sol told me to meet him there, I did.

At this time I was deeply involved in criminal activity.

When they murdered Sol, it was really bad news for me, not because he was a good friend, but because he was the only fence in town I trusted. The feds were giving him immunity for testifying before a Federal Grand Jury. The problem was who he was testifying against…Nick Civella, the kingpin of the Kansas City Crime Family. It was over some sports gambling deal. I told him it was not a good thing to be testifying against Civella, or for that matter, against anyone. Even though Civella was accused of his murder, they were never able to convict him. They said it was a mob hit…I don't know. I just know it interfered with my life, and that wasn't a good thing either.

When I was around my wife or our friends I couldn't act like I knew or cared anything about Sol's death, although it was on every news channel. They had raped his wife while they made him watch and then murdered him. I saw people die in prison, so it wasn't that big a deal to me. Besides, I knew what happened to rats.

Not too long after Sol was killed, I started doing business with his associate, Frank, who Sol told me never to trust. I didn't take his advice, and started working with Frank, because I knew he was a fence like Sol who would buy anything. I knew him already, because I had been with Sol quite a few times when he came around. I had some stuff to unload one day and thought what the heck, so I walked into his office. "What's up Jim?"

I thought, *There are as many people who know me as Jim in Kansas City, as there are who know my real name*. When Sol told me to not trust Frank, I asked him to never tell him my real name. He at least did that for me.

Frank totally trusted me, because he knew Sol did, so I was automatically in. I found out pretty quick why Sol told me not to trust him. The money was never right and he screwed me around on a lot of deals. He would send me to get certain things for him and when I came back with them, he told me it wasn't the right thing or something was wrong with it.

One time, he wanted a computer out of a crane that was down at the old General Motors plant in Leeds. It was in a highly guarded area and was a very hard place to get into. I had to pick a certain spot on the fence, out of the sight of the guards. This would have been a job I could have used some help on, but it was a lot safer this way. I always worked by myself doing any kind of stealing. That way, if I had to run I didn't have to worry about a partner getting caught and worry about what he might say.

I managed to get the computer he wanted out of this big old crane and took it to him. He said there was another piece he needed, and it was worthless without it. He put it under his desk and refused to pay me till I brought the other piece.

I told him, "I will not go back there, and if I ever come in here and see that thing gone, I am going to blow your brains all over this room.

I think he believed me, because that computer was under his desk for the next couple years. I took him a lot of stolen merchandise and he always paid me just like Sol. The money was just as green, just not as much.

We had many arguments and disagreements but our relationship ended when I told him about a big Lull forklift. The bricklayers were using it on the construction site I was on, and he said he would pay me ten thousand dollars for it. I arrived early one Saturday morning and went in through the main gate. I fired it up and drove it across the jobsite. On the way through, I picked up a big Lincoln pipeline welder and drove it right through the gate on the back side of the job site. The site had a front gate on State Ave. in Kansas City, Kansas and a back gate on Parallel. I drove the forklift a few blocks on Parallel and jumped over to State Ave. because it was faster. I drove it from 72nd to 38th, which is a long way on a piece of stolen equipment early Saturday morning.

I wore a hooded sweatshirt with a snub nose .38 in the pouch. When I got to where I was going to show it to Frank, I pulled into a gas station and told the clerk I was waiting for a truck and trailer to pick up my machine. I asked him if I could leave it there an hour or so. He said, "Sure."

I called Frank. He said he would pick me up at the corner of 36th and State. I walked the two blocks and he was there in less than five minutes in his big brown Cadillac. I got into the back seat and we took a ride. I was real nervous because he had a guy with him I had never seen before.

He said, "Jim, don't worry about this guy. He's cool."

"I don't care, you know how I feel about strangers."

"Calm down, where is this forklift?" Frank asked.

"It's just up ahead, at that gas station on the right." We drove by, slowing just a bit.

The stranger in the front seat spoke for the first time. "You can't buy that, Frank."

"Why can't I?" Frank asked, surprised.

"There are only a few of that particular model around. You could hide it for ten years and the day you bring it out, they will arrest you."

Frank looked at me in the rear view mirror. "If he says I can't buy it, Jim, I can't buy it."

"Give me five thousand then," I said.

The stranger spoke again, "It's not the price, Jim…your price of ten thousand dollars was good. It's just too hot."

"Shut up...you don't even know me!" I said angrily to the stranger.

I pulled the .38 caliber revolver out of the pouch on my sweat-shirt, cocked it, and put it to the back of Frank's head.

"I ought to blow your stinkin' brains out just like they did Sol. Take me to my truck."

"Sure, Jim. Where is it?" he asked with a shaky voice.

"It's at the gas station at 71st and State Ave."

When we got to the station where my truck was, I got out. I never said another word to Frank, and I never saw him again.

THE BEGINNING OF THE END

My wife and I grew further and further apart. I was getting so involved with the other "family" that I didn't take care of my own. It was getting harder and harder to hide my involvement with those other people. I used aliases when away from home, and keeping all my lies straight was a job in itself.

An eighty-five-year-old lady told me one day, "You know if you never tell a lie, you don't have to remember what you said."

Boy, is that the truth. I wish I had met her and got that in my heart when I was about eight years old. My life would have turned out a lot different.

I was not spending much time with my wife and was getting angrier all the time. I will never forget one time while spanking my oldest son; he looked at me and said, "Why are you being so mean, Daddy?"

He was only seven at the time, so he probably doesn't remember it. But I sure do. He saw a difference in me from spanking to spanking. I believe the double life, mixed with pornography, and the fear of the people I associated with, caused my anger to grow.

In 1971 our baby girl was born, and I was out committing crimes and pretending to be this good Christian father. I always wanted a girl, but didn't know how to walk away from what I was doing. I let it destroy my family. Although I really desired to be a good husband and father, this dark, evil side of me, that no one knew existed, is what I kept on obeying. This secret life I was living tore me apart inside. I wanted to get out, but was afraid to.

One of the blackest sides I had was pornography. I kept it completely secret. I was involved in pornography since I was friends with Jesse. We had little cartoon books between the ages of eight and ten. If you flipped the pages real fast, it was like watching a movie. By the time I was twelve or thirteen years old I was deep into porno. At fourteen I was working in Charlie's garage staring for hours at the pictures he had his walls and ceiling plastered with. Then I would go watch his wife in real live shows. I went into the first adult book store that opened in Kansas City. At one time in my life I spent as much as one hundred dollars a day watching porno. It is a progressive habit just like crack cocaine or meth.

Add all that to my cousin taking me downtown to pick up a hooker once or twice a week and I was being groomed and mentally set up for it to be an obsession. Try bringing that into a brand new marriage. For a sixteen-year-old, innocent and good girl—it was a recipe for disaster. It is a miracle we stayed together for ten years, through my lies, unfaithfulness, stealing, and being a complete fraud.

It was more than any marriage could survive. Our divorce was almost forty years ago, but I still see and feel the ripple effects of it. It doesn't just hurt the husband and wife, it hurts everyone.

In the ten years Marsha and I were married, I never drank or used drugs. I was doing burglaries and telling too many lies to let alcohol be in the mix. I knew that if I was drinking, I wouldn't be able to keep my lies straight. If I needed to run from a burglary, I wanted to be alert. I thought people who did drugs were stupid. That was why they called it dope—you were a dope if you did it.

LIVING WITH A WILD MAN

When my wife and I were first separated and waiting on our divorce, I moved in with a buddy of mine and started partying with him every night. He drank heavily and I started drinking and found it helped mask the pain of losing my family. I was truly sorry I put other things before them, and wanted them back. I just didn't know how to undo all the terrible things I had done. Because I knew of no other formula for disassociating myself with the people I was involved with, I stayed drunk and high. I was scared and confused.

Eddy lived in an old farm house on the edge of Kansas City, and was all man. This was thirty years before people started using the term, "MAN CAVE." Eddy had a B/Gas drag bike that would go 150 mph in the quarter mile. That was world-class speed back in those days. He kept his bike on a stand in the living room.

One of the bedrooms had a Snap-On tool chest full of tools with a parts washer, an engine stand with a 427 C.I. big block on it, and a workbench on the adjacent wall. Eddy's bedroom was painted black—floor, walls, ceiling, and windows. When you turned the lights out it was dark. On his bed post was a holster hanging with a long-barrel .44 Magnum. There were guns in every room and in every corner of every room. This was a bona fide Man Cave.

Eddy was short, about five feet five inches tall, and weighed about two hundred and fifty pounds. His hairline was receding, but the rest of the hair on his head had no intentions of surrendering and had grown in length to the middle of his back.

His scraggly beard grew almost as long as his hair and reached toward his belly button.

We would take the drag bike out in front of his house, Eddy would climb on, and I'd push him to get it started. He would ride down the street and come flying back by me going 140 mph. When he finished, his hair and beard looked like he'd combed it with the north wind and a barbed wire fence.

All the cops in Riverside knew to call backup when attempting to arrest him. I think most every cop there had broken a night stick over his head. He was like a bowling ball—have you ever tried to knock a bowling ball down?

Eddy was a serious car guy! The summer I lived with him, he owned five different Corvettes, two or three different pickup trucks, a real Yenko Camaro, and a 1923 Bucket T.

One day after riding around all afternoon, we decided to see which was the fastest, Eddy's T or my built up 900 Kawasaki. My girlfriend Candy was with me on the bike and her three year old son rode with Eddy in the bucket T. We went out on the highway and took off. I was going 130 mph when he flew by me. I looked over and the kingpin was almost out of the front end on the T. When he looked back and smiled, I motioned for him to stop. When he did, it was almost completely out. He would have lost a front wheel, and at that speed in a car weighing only 1250 pounds, and with no seat belts, there would have been nothing left of either of them. It was just one of our many close calls. He was one of the craziest people I ever knew in my life and one of the best friends I ever had.

Essie Ray my wild partner for many years. He was a man who truly should have lived in the Wild West days. I miss him so much, but will see him again . . . he's also a light at the end of the tunnel.

I have been in over twenty-five car and motorcycle wrecks, and Eddy is the only guy I knew who had been in more than me. He once flipped a Corvette on the Paseo Bridge in Kansas City going over 100 mph. Some of the things he lived through were amazing.

He was infamous for walking into restaurants, sitting down at a table with strangers, and eating off of one of their plates. I was with him one night when we both ordered steak and eggs. He took one bite out of his steak and sailed it like a Frisbee across the restaurant towards a waitress, yelling, "This piece of meat ain't cooked right."

He might go over to a corner in a busy restaurant, light a cigar, and stand on his head and smoke it. He would go with Kenny, another of our buddies, into a restaurant at two or three o'clock in the morning after they had been out drinking all night. They would order a big breakfast and then gag themselves and throw up in their plates. They would then switch plates and eat it. Everyone who saw them do it would get sick. That was the idea. We got kicked out of every restaurant in town before it was over. He did other things that are too gross for me to put in print. Your imagination couldn't take you there, so don't even try.

Eddy wasn't afraid to fight anybody, anytime. Nobody really wanted to fight him, because even if they won, they wouldn't get out of it without some damage.

Once, he rode his Harley Davidson into Daddy's Money, a night club in Riverside, and parked it in front of the bar. He got off, sat down at the bar beside me, and ordered a drink. The owner came out and said, "Hey, your bike is leaking oil on my carpet."

Eddy got off the barstool, took off his shirt, laid it under the bike and climbed back up on the barstool.

The bouncer was about six-five and weighed two-seventy. He came over to me and said, "Superman, please get Eddy out of here, I don't want to fight him."

Another thing Eddy and I did for fun was go into a business where there were "No Smoking" signs posted. Eddy would wait till he saw the manager, then he'd light a cigarette. The manager would rush over and point to the sign and say, "Don't you see that? You can't smoke in here.""

Eddy would look up at the sign like he was trying to focus, look real stupid, and act like he couldn't read. He would then look the guy right in the face, shake his head all funny, and say, "I ain't huntin."

Even though Eddy did stupid stuff and acted ignorant, he was a very bright and successful business man. He just liked having fun.

LIVING ON THE EDGE

Eddy introduced me to a girl I ended up living with off and on for quite a few years. One night after I told him how much I missed my wife, he said, "I got just the thing for you."

We hopped in his brand new Chevy pickup and didn't run under 90 mph all the way from Raytown to Riverside, Missouri. We drove into the trailer park Eddy grew up in. He pulled up in front of the only house and honked his horn. Three girls ran out. Eddy said, "I want Candy."

She jumped in the truck between us, as the other two girls ran back into the house.

"This is Jim," Eddy said.

I told him I wanted to use my alias, because I didn't know if I might get back with my wife. She immediately started playing with my arms, and feeling my biceps.

"I like you," she said.

I wore a tank top and was built a lot better than the average guy.

About that time, one of her sisters yelled out, "Leo wants you back in here, Candy."

She kissed me and said, "I'll see you tomorrow. I will call S Hog.

With that, she jumped out of the truck, and ran back into the house.

My head was spinning. I had lots of questions for Eddy on the way back home.

"Who's S Hog?" I asked.

"That be one of my nicknames, dad. They also call me Essie Ray."

I never heard such strange language before. From that day on, Eddy called me dad, and I called him son.

"My name is Eddy Ray, so they call me Essie Ray," he explained.

"Oh, I get it," I said. I questioned Eddy about the other girls, who they were, and who was Leo? Whose house were we just at?

That house belonged to those three girls' parents, and they owned the trailer court. Candy was nineteen and Leo was her boyfriend. They lived together there with her mom and dad. One of the girls was her little sister who was sixteen; she and her boyfriend also lived there (he is now doing sixty-plus years in the Missouri prison system). The other sister living there was married and her husband was out of town. Their twenty-one year old brother and his girlfriend also lived with mom and dad.

Oh my God, is this real or is it Memorex? Essie Ray went on to tell me that Leo had seven brothers and was pretty jealous of Candy. Did I really want to get mixed up in all this?

Yes, without a doubt, I was all about adventure and living on the edge. My motto was: *If you're not living on the edge, you're taking up too much space.*

Candy called the next day and Eddy handed me the phone, "Here ya go, Jim."

We set a spot to meet and I don't remember what happened, but she changed it for some reason and came out to Eddy's house. We found out later Leo and several of his brothers were waiting for me at the spot where we originally were going to meet. A couple of years later Leo and I became friends and did some drug deals.

Essie Ray and I remained friends for over thirty-five years. I spent a lot of time with him before he died.

WILLIE, WHISKEY AND DISCO

My choice of alcohol never stayed the same very long. I went through stages where I drank 151 Rum only, there were times I only drank Wild Turkey, then Jack Daniels, and so on. There were particular songs I drank to. I went into a bar, put several dollars in the juke box, and selected the same song over and over. During one of those periods, my best friend was Willie Nelson. The words to his 1973 hit song, *Whiskey River*, fit me perfectly. I tried to cover the pain of losing my wife with a river of whiskey. The song says, "Whiskey river take my mind, you're all I've got, take care of me."

I went through spells where I liked wine, drinking five or six bottles of wine every night. I was able to consume a lot of alcohol. It wasn't uncommon for me to drink a case of beer and some hard liquor back to back, and still drive and function. In all the years of drinking and driving I never got a DUI. I still don't understand that. I went through seasons of my life where I woke up in the middle of the night to pee, and would get a beer out of the fridge and drink it before going back to bed.

When I got up in the morning, I took however many beers were left in the fridge and drank them on the way to work. I would stop and get a half pint of Wild Turkey, and drink the whole thing between the time the whistle blew at 8:00 a.m. and noon. I usually drank two or three beers in a bar over my lunch hour and bought a half pint of Wild Turkey to last till 4:30 p.m.

At quitting time I would head home, take a short nap, get up and shower, then go out again and party till closing time. Some nights I left Missouri and headed to a private club in Kansas that stayed opened till 3:30 a.m. I would maybe get an hour or two of sleep before going to work. I never missed a day, until I started making so much money dealing cocaine.

One of my party spots was the Country Club Plaza, in Kansas City. I frequented it for several years. It was high class and the women were high class. The drugs and booze were high class. At least that is how the Plaza made you feel. I'd dress in my bright, tailored, long sleeve polyester shirt, my tight fitting bell bottoms, and find plenty of distractions to drown the constant thoughts of losing my wife and children.

My goal every night was to not go home alone. There were, I'm sure, a lot of people who were just there to dance, but that was the last thing on my mind. Disco was in its prime; the words from KC & the Sunshine Band fueled my nightly goal. Do a little dance…make a little love…get down tonight.

I was polished at going to a club, picking a girl within an hour or so, and getting her to leave with me. I would take her to her apartment and afterwards would leave her in bed, telling her I couldn't stay the night. I'd then head back to the club and try to pick up another girl before closing time. That was called a double header. One of my buddies was known for dumping girls and making them walk, or kicking them out of his car if they wouldn't put out.

One night, a guy asked Alex, the bartender, "Is that Nasty Nick standing over there?"

"Yeah, that's him," Alex said.

"Take a good look at him, because he won't look like that, the next time you see him."

I guess Nick had left one too many girls stranded or kicked out in the rain. For quite a while, he had me or someone walk him to his car at night. All the years I ran the Plaza with Nick, I was either living with or split up with Candy. She and I had this understanding—do what you want.

CHAPTER

19

HOOKERS FOR FREE

Eddy introduced me to Kenny when I was thirty years old. He became my closest friend, and then my most dangerous enemy. Kenny and I got so crazy at the end that Eddy and many of our other friends didn't want to be around us.

I had been caught in the web of paying hookers since I was fourteen. Kenny soon introduced me to a new way of dealing with them.

The first time He and I picked a prostitute up together we were out repossessing cars. She flagged us down at 27th and Prospect. It was early evening and still light out when I stopped and she got in my car. We would need to get a room.

"You know someplace we could go, Superman?" Kenny asked.

"Yeah, down to the Broadway Hotel, 13th and Broadway."

I knew Mousey and a lot of the regulars who hung out there—it was a whorehouse I frequented. We walked into the lobby of the dilapidated old hotel; the wallpaper was falling off and you could see the crusty walls underneath it. I glanced at Mousey and winked as I headed up the stairs with the hooker. He yelled out a room number to me as I neared the second floor. I had an arrangement with him and a running tab no one ever asked me to pay. He knew who I associated with and just wanted me on his side.

When he knew who the prostitutes were, he got a cut from them, and that cut covered most of my tab. He didn't know this girl so that wouldn't be the case today. While I was upstairs with her,

Kenny entertained Mousey and the others with some of his wild and gory stories. His stories sounded like tall tales, but they were all true. Not many people had the stomach to handle them.

"It's your turn, buddy…the room at the top of the stairs," I said to Kenny, as I entered the lobby.

Kenny disappeared up the shaky old stairway. After a while I heard him and the whore laughing as they came down the stairs. I said goodbye to Mousey and the guys, and headed out the front door. When we got to the parking lot, Kenny said, "Superman, I'm gonna lay down in the back seat. I feel like throwin' up."

"Sure, buddy. Do whatever you need to; just don't throw up in my car." I didn't want him getting sick in my brand new 1976 Ford Thunderbird with Leather seats. The whore got in the front seat with me and Kenny stretched out in the back.

Kenny and I in our prime and most dangerous times of our lives. We are in front of his parking garage in downtown Kansas City, Missouri. There were a lot of illegal activities that took place in that garage.

"How you doing back there?" I asked, after we drove a few blocks.

"I think I'll be okay as long as I stay down."

By now it was dark, and as we approached 27th and Prospect where we picked her up, Kenny said, "Hey Superman, turn before we get to 27th and drive around the block. Let her out a little ways down from the corner so we won't be right under that streetlight."

"That's a good idea," she said.

"Put ALL the money on the dash, every cent of it."

I looked over to see Kenny's buck knife with its six inch blade pressed hard against her neck. It was dark and maybe it was just my imagination, but it actually looked like she was bleeding a little. I knew Kenny kept his knives like razors. She pulled the cash we gave her out of her garter belt and laid it on the dash.

"Count it, Superman, every last penny better be there," he growled.

"How much did you give her?" I asked him.

"I gave her forty dollars."

It's all there," I said.

"Stop right here, Superman." He pointed to the curb.

I eased over and came to a stop about a half block from the corner.

"Do you see those houses right there?" Kenny said through clenched teeth.

"Yes, sir I do."

"Get out of the car and walk straight between those houses. Don't look back. If you look back, I'll get out, and will cut your scrawny throat from ear to ear."

She got out and walked toward the houses as I drove off. At the corner, we turned on to Prospect and headed back out to repo some more cars.

"Now, *that* is how you do that, Superman."

"Wow, I was really feeling sorry for you! I thought you were sick."

That night started years of a new thing for me. Paying prostitutes would never be the same again. I still experienced the insatiable thrill of paying for sex, and now was introduced to something that made it even more exciting. If they charged forty dollars, I might give them a hundred, and they would treat me real special. But it didn't matter what I gave them. I always got my money back, no exceptions.

I took a lot of my buddies with me on those free hooker adventures; they didn't always like what happened. I lost some friends because of it. They thought I was completely out of control when it came to getting our money back. I did whatever was necessary to get it back and it wasn't always a pretty picture. Many times it ended in bloodshed, but not our blood.

KENNY'S BEEN STABBED

Only once in all the years Kenny and I took our money back did we shed any of our own blood.

"Can you stay for supper, Bill?" Mom asked when I stopped by their house one evening.

"Sure, I don't have to be anywhere for a while."

We had just sat down to eat when the phone rang. Mom answered it.

"Hello…yes, just a minute," she said as she handed me the phone.

It was my girlfriend, Candy. She said she was at Kenny's house and he had been stabbed. He needed me to get over there as fast as I could.

"Tell him I'm on the way," I said while hanging up the phone.

"I gotta go, Mom. I'll explain later."

I ran out of the front door and hopped in my car. Kenny's house was in Parkville, Missouri and I knew the absolute fastest route to get there. I had no idea who had stabbed him, I just knew he was my best friend and I had to get to him as quick as I could.

I flew down Highway 50 in my new 1977 Mustang, equipped with a high-performance engine, four-speed manual tranny and lots of ground effects and headed towards I-435. I took 435 to I-70 and headed downtown. I headed for the Broadway Bridge—that route could cut about ten minutes off the next fastest route to Kenny's house. I didn't stop at the toll gate on the Broadway Bridge, and was running well over 100 mph.

I wasn't worried about getting stopped; Kenny and I had raced across this bridge dozens of times and knew there was no place for cops to set up radar. The little grove of trees towards the beginning of the bridge where they used to run radar was gone. Kenny took his chainsaw and cut them all down.

I got to Kenny's in record time. Candy was trying to clean the blood out of his brand new truck so his wife wouldn't see it. He had picked up a hooker downtown in broad daylight, took her to the Crown Center parking garage. After she gave him oral sex, he told her he needed the money back.

She reached in her purse and came at him with a knife. She stabbed him in the neck, thigh, and cut off the end of his finger. Kenny grabbed her hand with the knife and bit down on her knuckle until he said he heard bone crush. He still couldn't get her to let go of the knife, so he beat her closed fist on the dash until she dropped it.

When I arrived at his house, he was picking the meat from her hand out from between his teeth with a toothpick. After she dropped the knife, she scrambled across the seat, opened the passenger door and fell out. It was a long fall because Kenny had installed on his truck the biggest lift kit you could buy. He practically needed a stepladder to get in. When she landed on the ground he was right on top of her.

He looked at me with those wild eyes of his and said, "I kicked her in the head until there was blood coming out of every hole— eyes, ears, nose and mouth. Then I got in her purse and got every last cent of my money."

"We got to get you sewed up, buddy." I was trying to calm him down.

Kenny only had his new truck a few days. He didn't even have a license on it yet. That was probably the only thing that saved him, because he said there were some people in the parking lot who saw him kicking her.

I knew I couldn't take him to any hospital around because they might be looking for him. That is, if the hooker had even made it to the hospital. He found the end of his finger on the floorboard of the truck and kept it in his mouth till he drove home. I ended up taking him to an old crooked veterinarian we knew. He would not say anything. He sewed Kenny's finger back on and stitched up his neck and leg, and we were off again.

Most prostitutes gave the money back without a fight. The ones who wouldn't, always lost because we didn't care anything about our own lives, much less theirs. I was extremely dangerous. The pain of losing my family made me not care if I lived or died.

CHAPTER

20

DRUGS AND BEATDOWNS

Candy ended up being like a partner in crime. She knew about things Kenny and I had done that could have put us away for good. She backed me up whenever I needed back up. She was with us at times we took our money back from hookers; she was tight lipped and would go to prison for me.

Kenny and I went to back up a guy buying a quarter million dollars' worth of cocaine. We brought Uzi's and all kinds of artillery with us. Guess who else we used as one of our most capable shooters? You guessed it, my girlfriend Candy. She would just as soon shoot you or beat the life out of you, as to look at you.

Candy's sister stole two bags of weed from me once, and I told her to get the pot or the money back, I didn't care which.

"Beat her down if she doesn't give it up," I told Candy.

"I'll get *something* out of her," she said, grinning.

She rolled us a joint and I got us a beer out of her folk's refrigerator. We sat down at the kitchen table and waited. When we heard her sister and her friend drive in the driveway in her friend's new Jeep, Candy went out to meet them. I followed her outside. They had the doors off, it was hot and they were in tank tops and shorts.

"Where's Jim's pot?"

"I don't know."

"Don't you lie to me, he knows you took it."

Candy pulled her out of the Jeep by her hair and threw her in the gravel. Her legs and arms were not protected and the tiny bits of gravel tore her up. Candy, at this point, positioned herself on top of her sister.

"Where are the two ounces of weed?"

"You and Jim can drop dead! Even if I knew I wouldn't tell you."

"Beat her bad, Candy."

Candy had her hand balled into a fist, and as soon as I said that, she hit her right in the mouth. She started pounding the life out of her. It was over quick. In the end, her sister had cut lips, a cut over her eye, and black eyes. I never got my weed back, but she ended up in the hospital and never stole anything from me again.

We were living at her mom and dad's place when it happened, and I don't think they even took sides. They probably knew she stole it, and thought she got what she deserved. They were pretty cool; the old lady smoked weed with us, and stayed up partying with us half the night.

GETTING EVEN

One thing about me was…I always got revenge. When I got into a fight in boot camp and the guy beat me up, one of my friends told him, "You better sleep with one eye open. Bill Corum doesn't get mad, he gets even. He will get you."

Another time Candy and I were Christmas shopping together, and the lines in the store were crazy long. Our cashier was overwhelmed by the crowds, so she rung up our bill of a little over two hundred dollars and forgot to get our money. We hurried putting our purchases into the basket, trying to get out of there without paying, when a lady in the next aisle over said, "You forgot to get their money."

The cashier was shocked and gasped, "Oh, thank you so much."

She looked at me and, of course, I went back like a nice guy and paid her.

We loaded our packages and I started the car. After sitting there a few minutes she asked, "What are you doing?"

I glared at her, and she knew what I was thinking. We waited till the lady who told on us came out, so I could see which car she got in. I followed her out of the parking lot and Candy wrote her license number down.

My connection ran the plate and got me an address. I drove by, and sure enough, her car was there. I waited for several months and made sure she still lived there before I got even. She may have had fire insurance, but what she went through wasn't worth her opening her big mouth in that store.

Back when Kenny and I repossessed cars, a guy got real tough with us and ran us off his property. Fast forward a year and a half and we were in downtown Kansas City on some business. It was January and the temperature was about two degrees above zero. I started driving towards south Kansas City, the opposite direction we were supposed to be going.

Kenny looked over at me with that look only he could give a person. "Where you goin, Superman?"

"You're gonna like where I am going."

I stopped by a construction site and jumped out. I grabbed a concrete block and set it on the floorboard of my car, and drove off. The suspense was killing Kenny.

"I got to know, where are we going?"

I approached the neighborhood where the tough guy had run us off, Kenny started laughing. Before we turned onto his street, I pulled over, and slammed the car in park.

"You drive." By the time I got the passenger door closed, we were rolling.

It was a little past midnight and I could see the flickering light from their TV set, through the sheer curtains behind the large picture window. I jumped out and ran as Kenny pulled forward a few houses. I threw the concrete block through the middle of the window, ran across a couple of front yards and jumped back into the car.

"Kenny, I wonder if he's got any plywood…it sure is cold out."

"We could go back and burn his house down. That would keep 'em warm." Kenny laughed hysterically.

I always figured out a way to get even. Even though sometimes I waited years. Between me and a couple of the guys I ran with, no one was safe if they crossed us.

I'LL HAVE TO KILL HER TOO

Bill H, a friend of mine, was making some trips to Bogota and brought back the most pure cocaine we'd ever seen. He was also working on several other projects at the same time. He and I became close and he trusted me completely. One day, I found out just how much he really trusted me. He brought one of his latest projects out to my house to show me.

He was in the process of perfecting a homemade silencer. It was necessary that every single piece be made from material that could be purchased at hundreds of locations. That way, if the silencer was ever found, it would be impossible to trace where the material came from. I'll always remember the day he brought it to my house to demonstrate.

The reason it is etched in my memory so well is because a Raytown cop was running radar about 200 feet away from where he decided to try his experimental silencer. We stepped into my garage and opened the back door. The cop sat right across the street in plain view. I said, "Are you sure?"

Bill had a big grin on his face as he pointed the .22 caliber rifle toward the ground in my backyard, and said, "I'm very sure."

It literally sounded like someone typing on an electric typewriter, tick, tick, tick, tick, tick. He'd fired five shots as fast as he could pull the trigger. His new invention was a total success. Boy! Was I ever relieved.

Bill left me some of his killer cocaine that day. That coke turned into a nightmare for me. Before it was all over, I thought I would be a candidate for death row.

Candy knew a girl named Cricket, but didn't know her boyfriend. I broke the cardinal rule and let someone I didn't know come to my house to buy drugs. Bill's Bogota cocaine was as close to 100% pure as I'd ever seen—it was yellow. Cricket brought her boyfriend over to score some. Although I had never met Cricket, I totally trusted Candy, and she said she was cool. Cricket looked like a movie star. The guy she was with was a stone junkie—skin and bones, dark circles under his eyes, and rotten teeth. I was checking his girlfriend out, trying to figure out how to get rid of him while he fixed himself at my kitchen table. A few seconds passed, and he was on my kitchen floor heavily overdosed. I put him in the bathtub, ran cold water on him, and slapped the snot out of him.

After almost an hour, he opened his eyes. I took him back into the kitchen and sat him in a chair where he looked at his gorgeous girlfriend and said, "Only do half of it, Cricket."

"SHE'S NOT DOING ANY OF IT HERE, YOU STUPID IDIOT" I screamed at the top of my voice.

They were both fully alert now, seeing a side of me most people didn't want to see. What they didn't realize was that for the last fifty minutes my mind was about to blow up, thinking...

Where am I going to put his body?

I'll have to kill her too . . . but I don't want to kill that beautiful thing.

Cricket would forget that punk, if I could get her alone.

What am I going to do with that old van he's driving? She is so good looking!

I can't let her leave here if he dies. I have to kill her, but not before . . .

Him saying 'only do half' put my mind on overload. I had done some real serious things, but not on such short notice. That is what had me so stressed out; I didn't have enough time to think. I didn't know if they'd told someone they were coming to my house. Anyway, he was awake and well enough for me to beat him half to death.

"Get out of my house, and don't ever come back in my neighborhood!"

I trusted Candy. She knew enough things to put me away for life. If I'd had to kill them and get rid of their bodies, she wouldn't tell. She would have helped. One thing for sure, she wasn't a rat. I believe she would have gone to prison for me, and those kind of friends are hard to find.

NEVER STEAL FROM FRIENDS

One of my buddies got drunk one night, wrecked his car, and it caught on fire. When the cops arrived they couldn't get the doors opened, so they broke out the window. That was just enough air to cause the small fire to burst into flames. He was burnt to death. The next day I decided to go get all the good stuff out of his house before anyone else did. I figured I had as much right to it as anybody; after all, he was one of my friends. You might think that it was a pretty low down thing to do, robbing a good friend, but I knew he wouldn't care . . . he was dead.

I parked my car down the street and walked to his house. It was winter so I wore a hooded sweatshirt with the hood pulled up tight. I jimmied the lock on his front door and grabbed the cash and drugs I knew was there. I was in the bedroom filling up a pillow case full of pistols, watches, rings, and some other jewelry that must have belonged to one of his girlfriends or his estranged wife, and was ready to leave. *What was that?* I thought someone was at the front door; it didn't get latched when I came in. Another knock, and the door swung open a little.

A guy poked his head in and said, "TV repair man."

I took my hood off and unzipped the sweatshirt. When I walked out of the bedroom he looked embarrassed and kind of scared because he was standing in the living room.

"Your wife called."

"I know, it's over there," I said, pointing to the TV on the opposite side of the room.

As he walked towards it, he said, "Let me take a look."

He pulled it out from the wall, and I returned to the bedroom, got my pillow case, stepped back through into the kitchen without him ever looking up. I quietly opened the back door, stepped out, pulled up my hood and went to my car. One of Dick's girlfriends must have called the TV repair company a day or two before he was killed. I have no idea how long the guy worked behind that TV, but I bet the bill never got paid.

I walked in my front door and said, "Come here, Candy, I have something for you."

"Where did you get this?" She picked up a watch. "I like this one, is it for me?"

"Dick Barber left you, me, and Kenny something in his will," I laughed.

"You robbed a dead guy?" she asked, as she slipped the watch on her wrist and started laughing.

CHAPTER

AN EIGHTY-YEAR-OLD HOOKER

Sal one of my Italian friends said to me one day, "Hey, Crazy Bill, you want to be a chauffeur and bodyguard for an eighty-year-old madam?"

"What?" I asked.

A key mafia figure gave me that nickname, Crazy Bill. He had heard the story about when I first came home from prison and went to a hotel that had hookers. After I paid for one's services, she said I hadn't paid her. I was alone and she had dudes in there to protect her, so I paid again. She must have thought I was stupid and didn't know all hookers got their money up front. I was so mad, that the next day I returned with a double-sided axe and ran down the hall, chopping every door on that floor.

Fifteen years later I ran through a bar on Main Street with a running chainsaw. That probably added some validity to my nickname. I had my reasons for doing that though. I got mad at Candy when she took a job tending bar at a joint on 36th and Main in Kansas City. Kenny took me there one night and dropped me in the back parking lot. I told him to pick me up at the front door. I fired up the McCullough chainsaw and went in the back door. I was going to cut the bar in half and walk out the front door. When I saw how dark it was, I changed my mind. I could just imagine some off-duty cop shooting me in the back while I bent over sawing the bar in half. *I'll probably never make it to the front door and won't take that chance.* So I just walked through the bar with the saw idling and walked out the front door. I shut it off, got in Kenny's car, and rode off. For no more than that, they continued calling me Crazy Bill.

"So, do you want the job or not?" Sal asked again.

"What do I have to do? Tell me about it."

"I'll have to take you up to meet her."

Her name was May; she was eighty years old, and had run this cathouse for twelve years. She was a former hooker, and had run whorehouses in Chicago for forty years. This old gal really knew the business and was very sharp for her age. Every whorehouse I knew of was operated out of someone's house, hotel, or an old apartment. Hers was located in a business district in Englewood a small community in Independence, Missouri. There were quite a few other businesses there. A friend of mine had his business right next door to hers.

Mr. T was what everyone called him. He named his store Mr. Records. It was one of the biggest head shops in the whole city and he was one of the groundbreakers when it came to drug paraphernalia. He was a standup guy I trusted and we would ultimately do a lot of business together.

May's business was located next door to his shop. The entrance was a glass door with a steep set of stairs covered with red carpet. May was a very good business woman; she always kept five or six girls working for her. Most of her clientele were high-class men, there was no one walking in off the streets. She only allowed men who were white-collar workers and executives making good money; they, more than likely, would keep their mouths shut.

Her little business operation in Englewood proved to me that the authorities in Independence could be bought. There was no possible way she could have operated that many years without getting busted. This wasn't the State of Nevada…prostitution was not legal here.

During my interview with May, she told me she had been robbed a couple of times and was really in fear for her life. She asked me, "Do you carry a gun?"

I pulled out my .9mm and my .357, and said, "No, I carry two of them, and sometimes a sawed-off shotgun in my trench coat."

"You're hired. I'm going to feel real safe with you." She said, with a huge smile.

May was amazing looking for her age. She was very elegant and hardly had any wrinkles on her face. I would have guessed her age at sixty, not eighty. I could tell she liked me and this would be a fun job. "When do you want me to start?" I asked her.

"I want you to take me home tonight. I close at five." She smiled.

This job had some excellent perks. She lived in an apartment on the Country Club Plaza that cost her over two thousand dollars a month. In 1977 that was very expensive. I picked her up at her door every day at eight a.m., and took her to the whorehouse. I then picked her up at five p.m. and took her back to her apartment on the Plaza. I'd walk her in, make sure she was safe inside, and not leave until I heard her set all the locks on her door.

On Tuesdays, she went to the beauty shop. I waited outside the salon till she was done and took her to work. Sometimes I would take her to lunch or shopping. I think she enjoyed being seen with me. I watched her like a hawk when I was with her and wouldn't think twice about killing anyone who tried to hurt her.

On Thursdays, I took her to get her facial and then to work. She was open from nine to five and only open Monday through Friday; she ran it like a business. I never did ask her if she paid taxes, but it wouldn't have surprised me if she did.

One of my fringe benefits was...I had access to her girls, providing they didn't have a scheduled appointment. All the girls working for May were not streetwalkers; they were pretty and she made them carry themselves with class. She did that because of the customers she catered to. She thought a lot of me and paid me good, tipped me well, and gave me perks. My girlfriend at the time was Candy, and she rode with me sometimes.

May would kid her and say, "I would give you a run for your money for this guy if I was forty years younger."

Candy would just laugh. She didn't care if I dated some of May's employees because we were swingers and that was part of our agreement.

May's was one of the really good jobs Sal landed me over the years. Some of the other things he had me do were not so colorful and rewarding. Some of the good times we had together were sharing women and drugs. He and I partied a lot over the years and remain friends today.

SWINGING MAY BE HAZARDOUS

Candy and I got involved in swinging, way before the reality show *Wife Swap* was on television. Everything was okay as long as we played by my rules. I only let her sleep with guys I picked. The wars began when she tried to see somebody I didn't know.

She would tell me she didn't want to date anyone, she just needed some space. We split up and I would catch her out with some guy that same night. I'd beat the poor guy senseless, sometimes leaving him for dead, when all he wanted was to get laid.

One time I called her mom's and she told me Candy had gone out with some guy. I drank for a while and then went over there, but she wasn't home yet. I went back to the bar, and drank some more, and checked back again about midnight. There was a car sitting in front of her mom and dad's house, running. I didn't recognize it, but I was sure it was them.

I parked in back, snuck around the side of the house, and came up on the passenger side of the car. I jerked the door open, and this poor guy was in the passenger seat with his pants down around his ankles. She slid over behind the steering wheel, dropped the gearshift into drive and floored the car. I held onto the door handle and wasn't letting go. We flew up the gravel driveway, heading for the highway. I managed to climb in and was sitting on this naked guy's lap. I reached over and slammed the car into park going about 25 mph.

She started screaming as I wore this guy out. With my left hand gripping his throat, I pounded my right fist into his face, cutting him up bad. I probably hit him four or five times after he was unconscious. I was out of control.

Candy was beating on me the whole time, telling me to stop. After all I had done for her, she acted like she was in love with this low life dude whom she'd just met that day. I dragged her out of his car and left him there naked and unconscious, sitting in the middle of the road at the entrance of the trailer court.

Here I was full of cocaine, steroids and overdosed on crazy.
I was strong and took it out on my victims.

To say our relationship was tumultuous would be an understatement. This went on for several years; it was hard on my hands and her wannabe boyfriends.

We got into a fight another day and broke up—she started the fight, so I knew she met someone she wanted to lay. I laid on a hill with a rifle all night waiting for them to come back. When it was starting to get light out, I got up and left for fear of someone seeing me. If she had come home that night, I would have shot one or both of them, and I might be writing this from death row.

GUNS, DRUGS AND FIRES

One of mine and Kenny's passions was guns. I couldn't legally have a gun because of my felony conviction, but that didn't stop me from owning them illegally. I was just super careful. I had throwaways and always wiped them down. Kenny owned one of every model Smith and Wesson they came out with. Whenever a new model came out, Kenny ordered it before it was even available. He didn't have a record and would buy and register guns like any law-abiding citizen. He also owned about as many midnight specials as legal guns. Anytime anyone on the streets sold a gun, Kenny or I was there with the money to buy it.

When we got real big into dealing drugs, we upped the ante and started buying fully automatic weapons. We owned a couple of Uzis and some Mac10s, hand grenades, and any other illegal weapon we could get. We both carried at least two pistols on us everywhere we went. We never hesitated to buy guns, because one of our friends bought cocaine in Colombia and could smuggle them in. Guns were illegal in Colombia and ones we paid a hundred bucks for on the streets of Kansas City, he sold for ten times that. One thousand dollars for a Midnight Special seems insane, but that's what they paid. I can't imagine what the authorities would have done to him if they had caught him bringing in guns. It was easy money though, because they never searched his bags going out of the United States or going into Colombia, only when he came back into the States.

Kenny and I cultivated and grew our relationship so that we became as close as brothers. We trusted each other enough to do things together that could have put us away forever. We were freelance contractors and were not a part of the organization or any family. We just did what we were hired to do and everyone was happy.

Without using any names, I will just say we worked for a very well-organized group. We always carried out the many different jobs they gave us and gained their highest approval After we carried out two or three jobs for them, we were asked if we wanted to get more involved. I was ecstatic, but Kenny said no. I didn't have any idea what they wanted us to do, I just wanted to be more involved. We argued over it. I thought to be given that opportunity was the pinnacle. I will never forget the things Kenny said to me that day.

"Bill, these people will put you in the trunk of a car with a bullet in your head! You mean nothing to them! What are you thinking? I am not going to let any grease-ball put you or me in a box."

"I understand." I said.

I really did and I never forgot . . . Kenny probably saved my life that day.

Either they must have not cared, or they respected us for our decision, because we were asked to do other jobs after that. We did what they asked, got paid, and the subject of getting more involved never came up again.

Kenny was one of the people I associated with in those days that most people were deathly afraid of, and probably with good reason. The day we picked up that first hooker together and he put his knife to her throat, I knew he was unlike anyone I had ever known in my life. One night he shot a guy with a 12-gauge shotgun. Kenny shot that man because he didn't like the color of his skin. He was the kind of guy who would even kill his own family if they crossed him. I nearly saw that happen.

After we buried Kenny's dad, we went over to his mom's and had dinner with some of the family. A few days later he and his mom had a falling out over a ring his dad promised him. She refused to give it to him. Sometimes he opened his eyes real wide and made them look huge and wild; he looked at me like that and said, "Superman, if I knew where that old lady hid that ring, I would take a rusty butter knife and go cut her throat."

"That's your mom."

His eyes got bigger than ever. "I know, that's why I would enjoy slicing her throat from ear to ear."

He made sure his mom never got to see his son. When she was on her death bed begging, Kenny said he would kill anyone who took the baby to see her.

Kenny and I dealt drugs and did contract work for unions and other organizations. Although our job assignments were always completed and they paid us well, we started repossessing cars strictly for the thrill of it. Kenny owned a parking garage at 9th and Locust in downtown Kansas City. When we would repo a car, we always took it to the parking garage instead of taking it back to the car lot. If we didn't, the owners would go to the lot and steal their cars back before it opened in the morning. Some of the owners of the cars we popped shot at us. That was a big mistake, because however crazy they were, we were ten times crazier. If they wanted to have a shootout, we always gladly accommodated them. The difference between us was we actually knew how to shoot the guns we carried. We went to the range and practiced every week. Most of the people shooting at us couldn't hit anything fifteen feet away.

Kenny raced and built drag racing bikes. In the early years there were only five different keys that fit Kawasaki motorcycles. Since he was an authorized repair shop, he owned all five of the keys. So on some of the nights we were repossessing cars, we stole motorcycles for him to use in his race bike builds. It was so simple. If we saw a bike sitting in a side yard or a garage with the door open, I dropped him off and he rolled it away. Down the street a little ways, he tried the five keys till he hit the right one and off we went to the parking garage. He had hiding places in that big old parking garage his customers never knew about. He would take the bike in and hide it for a few days until he got it torn apart.

We could take it apart in a few hours. He would then build a custom race motor to send to California. He owned his own boring machines and milling machines, so he could build custom stuff that couldn't be traced. We never got caught on any of those bike thefts and there were many of them.

We did a lot of insurance fires. Many were so much fun we probably would have done them for free, because we were both pyromaniacs. Only one time did we have a really close call. We had our way of burning houses down, but my friend wanted the fire done his way. Since he was paying the bill, we agreed. The customer should always be satisfied. Bill H wanted us to put a tire in every room of his Overland Park house, soak it with gasoline, and set it on fire.

The investigators would know it was arson, but if they couldn't pin it on the homeowner, the insurance company had to pay. He wanted it done this way because even if the fire department got it put out before it was burned completely down, there would be enough smoke damage to get one hundred percent loss payout. We picked up Candy, headed to downtown Kansas City, and filled the back of my Chevy Suburban full of old tires. I had the garage door opener to Bill's house.

We pulled in the driveway, hit the door opener, and drove in. We started carrying tires throughout the house, putting them in every room.

"Wow! Can you believe it, Superman? They just remodeled… new everything! They even bought all brand new furniture. Oh well, it ain't my house."

After the last tire was in place, we each grabbed a five-gallon can of gas and started through the house pouring a little in each tire. We figured four five-gallon cans would be enough.

"Splash some on the clothes in the closets," I yelled to him.

I poured some all over the new couch and chairs in the living room. We put the four empty cans in the back of the Suburban; I hit the garage door opener. Candy backed the truck out and headed for the spot where she was to pick us up. I closed the garage door and asked Kenny, "Do you want to do it, or do you want me to?"

"You did the last thing, it's my turn," he said.

There was a door at the front of the garage going into the kitchen and a walkout door at the back that went into the backyard. I walked across the garage and out the back door. Kenny lit a flare and threw it in the kitchen where we had soaked the floor.

KABOOM!!!

The door I'd just stepped through blew shut and Kenny was hurled through the closed door. He jumped up off the ground and we ran through the back yard, heading for the fence. We jumped the fence and were now really moving through the neighbor's yard. We saw the next fence and both jumped it. Afterward, we slowed down to a walk. We casually walked down the sidewalk on 87th Street headed for Antioch where Candy was waiting— just about the time we heard the siren of a fire truck.

"I'll bet the roof doesn't even leak," Kenny said.

We jumped in the truck and Candy took off, headed back to Parkville.

THE ULTIMATE PARDON

CHAPTER

FUN IN THE FLORIDA SUN

I wouldn't see Bill H, who paid Kenny and me to burn his Overland Park home, for several months. I didn't know anyone else as cautious as him, but he was also one of the slickest guys I knew. He wanted to make sure enough time passed so we wouldn't get caught. There was no one I would rather do illegal activities with, because there was so much planning that went into anything he was involved in. He was just as careful if you did something you could receive a slap on the wrist for, or something you could get the electric chair for.

He refused to talk illegal business if there was any chance of someone overhearing. When he hired me to burn his house down, we went for a ride in his airplane. He figured no one would hear us talking over the roar of the engine. Now, several months after the fire, he felt safe enough to talk while we drifted around on his sailboat just off the coast of Florida. We drank his favorite, Johnny Walker Red, and smoked some quality hash. Then he said, "The fire marshal knew without a doubt it was arson. They figured everything out, but there was one detail they couldn't figure out. They could never come up with a solution as to how that walkout door in the back of the garage got splintered. They said it looked like someone took an axe to it. Do you know what happened?"

I laughed out loud. "Yeah...I know exactly what happened. Kenny got blown through it. We spread that gas a long time before we lit it and the fumes had taken over. When he threw the flare in, it exploded and blew his whole body across the length of the garage and through the door."

We both got a good laugh out of that.

"Hey, Bill, I got a question for you. How did that fire department get there so quick?"

"Some old busy body across the street was on the phone and saw the flash in the house. She hung up and called the fire department."

Bill told me that Kenny was right, the roof never leaked. But it blew the studs through the sheetrock walls, and the smoke damage was bad enough to get them a huge settlement. That Bill was a smart one. He got the money, even though it was obvious arson. They couldn't prove he knew anything about it.

I stayed on the sunny Florida beaches with Bill H for another two weeks. Jimmy Buffet's song, *Margaritaville*, was a year old and was still hot on the charts. I went daily to a beach bar where there was a juke box outside. I'd load it up with change or dollar bills and select that song to play over and over. That song and the beverage took me to another place. I changed the words to *Margaritaville* to fit me. One thing I knew for certain about the situation I was in…some people might claim there's a woman to blame, but I knew it was my own fault.

I never got a tattoo and some people thought my reasons were crazy. But I was dead serious. I thought I might be on the FBI's most wanted list one day and didn't want any identifying marks on me, making me easy to spot. I listened to that song over and over and actually thought about getting a Mexican cutie tattoo; it is amazing how powerfully music can affect us.

I partied every night. Bill had a brand-new black Cadillac and he let me use it while I was there. I thought this was what life was all about; sex, drugs, and rock and roll. About a week or two after I arrived back in Kansas City, an FBI agent came by my mother's house looking for me. The guy left her a card to give to me, and said I was to call him. I figured I may as well call, because they knew how to find me anyway.

When I called the guy, he said, "What do you know about the whereabouts of Bill H_ _ _ _?"

I said, "I don't have any idea where he is."

Which was the truth...I had not seen him since I left Florida. I never heard from the FBI on that case again. We will get back to Bill H later.

CHAPTER

24

COCAINE AND DIAMONDS

Kenny and I used a philosophy in our drug business similar to that of legitimate businesses. We noticed some of the most successful business plans were based on volume, like the ones that advertised they had sold a gazillion hamburgers. We decided we needed to go for volume in our sales if we were going to make big money. We went from selling a few ounces of pot a week to one hundred pounds a week.

When we started selling cocaine it wasn't long before our suppliers couldn't keep up with our demand. We gave them an ultimatum—either supply us with what we need or introduce us to their connection. They had no choice and we took over the market. Kenny was married to a Greek gal and her father was a pharmacist. He soon got us pharmaceutical products to use as cut on our cocaine.

This was back in the late seventies and early eighties when everyone went to head shops to get cut for their cocaine. In those head shops you could buy inositol, mannitol, and mannite. We figured out pretty quickly that it wasn't real inositol, mannitol, and mannite. We used to joke about it and say everyone was buying cut that was cut. We got Kenny's father-in-law to start getting us pharmaceutical inositol and mannitol. This stuff had more crystals and more shine to it than some of the coke you could buy on the streets. We got him to get us some pharmaceutical speed that lasted about twenty minutes. We got anesthetic ether from someone who stole it from a hospital.

You could take our cut and make bad cocaine into good cocaine. To experiment, we took it to mainliners, who shot it and said it was better than some of the coke on the streets. A machine shop made us a cylinder and a piston out of aluminum. Kenny and I built an angle iron frame and put the piston and cylinder in it with a ten-ton jack. We mixed up our cut, mixed that with the cocaine, sprayed it with anesthetic ether, and pressed it for three or four hours.

It took a cold chisel and hammer to break it apart. When we took orders for cocaine we asked them what percent rock they wanted—the more rock, the more expensive. We could give them solid rock if that was what they wanted.

Four friends at a car show? Not really. The couple in the middle . . . well . . . they were just caught in the middle. Joe, the Italian guy on the right, was one of my biggest cocaine customers. In a few months I would be implicated as being one of the leading cocaine dealers in Kansas City. I attended Joe's funeral several years ago; he died a drug addict in a nursing home.

We started teaching our customers how to make it. I started selling them presses and cut, and convinced them they were better off to buy it in powder form. They could grind it up, mix the cut, and make their own rocks. Those who bought it in powder form saved me a lot of work.

Probably one of the most colorful sales we ever made was to a professional musician. He was in town for a concert. I didn't try to get permission to use his name, so I will just tell you he has sold over a hundred million albums. He bought six ounces of coke from us one night for a party. He didn't come personally, but had it delivered to him by a mule (a person who transports drugs). We were invited to the after party since we were supplying the coke. We turned down the invitation. When the mule made the delivery, the singer's bodyguards were a little arrogant about it.

One of them told our delivery boy, "You mean they don't want to meet him?"

Our guy came back and told us he said to them, "I don't think they want to meet anybody new."

And that was exactly what he should have said. We didn't care if it was a rock star or the Queen of England. We were not interested. The more people who saw us and knew what we did, the better chance of us getting busted.

All the time this was going on we were involved in many other types of illegal activities with the organization. We always used stolen cars when we did something for them that could get us a week in jail, or a death sentence.

We never knew when we were going to get a call to do something, and wouldn't have time to go out and steal a car, so we always kept cars handy. Kenny and I thought just alike, if we saw a tip on a table in a restaurant and no one was looking, whoever saw it first got it.

It seemed he and I were on the same wave length at all times. If we pulled into a Quik Trip or a 7-Eleven to get a pack of cigarettes, and there was a car sitting there with the motor running, we never said a word. Whoever was the passenger would jump in the running car and drive off. The one driving our car would go on into the store, buy something, and then go pick the other one up. We already knew where the stolen car was going; we had a prearranged apartment complex picked out. That way, when we needed a car we would just go pick it up. We never used a car more than once.

We stole countless cars over the years and never got caught. We obviously didn't use every car we stole, but we always checked to see if it was still there before we needed it. One car was in an apartment complex parking lot for seven months before it was discovered.

One of the times we used a stolen car was when we went to see some diamonds taken in the JC Sloan Company robbery in Kansas City. We were the first ones to see the stones, worth seven hundred and eighty thousand dollars. We saw them less than two hours after the holdup. They were all wrapped and priced, and we were supposed to pay twelve percent and have them sold in Chicago for fifteen percent. Not a lot of money, but we were going to pick up about twenty-three grand driving them five hundred miles.

Actually, we planned to make a lot more than that, because we were going to trade cocaine for the diamonds. We would give them about one hundred thousand bucks worth of cocaine, which we had only about fifty grand in. I guess they were smarter than we thought. When we arrived, they only wanted a couple of ounces of coke and the rest in cash. We gave them a couple ounces of coke and got a few really nice stones.

Kenny had a ring made out of one of them, with a band to match his gold and platinum Rolex band. His ring appraised for forty-five thousand dollars. The other nice stone I gave to a good friend of mine, who still has it to this day and is afraid to do anything with it. It's been over thirty years. I think he's safe.

CHAPTER

LITTLE DEBBIE

had just come back from being with my buddy, Bill, in Florida, and was sitting in my Italian friend's bar one night when Mike, another friend of mine, came in.

He said, "Bill, you've got to meet this girl I'm going with, she's really good looking and so nice."

"Some other time, buddy, it's getting late."

He talked me into going to meet her that night. It was about ten o'clock, and she was already in bed since she had to work the next day. Driving from the bar to Grandview where she lived was another half hour. On the way out, I stuck my Colt .45 automatic across Mike's face and fired a couple of shots out his window.

"What's wrong with you?" he asked.

"Just making sure it still works."

"You're crazy, Bill."

"That's what they call me."

It was late when we got to Debbie's apartment, about 10:30 p.m., and she had gotten dressed and put her makeup back on.

WOW! I thought when I saw her. *I have to have this gal.* We had small talk and then headed back to Sal's bar where Mike left his car. He reached in his pocket to get a cigarette and pulled out a .45 casing. When I'd fired the .45, one of those casings went right into his pocket.

I dropped him off and started plotting on how I was going to get Debbie away from him. I called him the next day and said, "Mike, why don't you see if Debbie has any girlfriends I can go out with and we could double date."

He went for it, "Okay, I'll call her."

She fixed me up with Linda, a girl she worked with. I took Linda out, spent the night with her, and had no interest in seeing her anymore. She called me and tried to get me to go out again, but I always made an excuse. One night she called me down at Sal's bar.

She said, "Do you want to come over to my house for a barbeque tomorrow?"

"I can't tomorrow."

"Oh, that's too bad; Debbie and her daughter Richelle are coming over."

I said, "Well...let me check. I might be able to make it."

I was there the next day. After the barbeque I told the girls I could try to get in touch with Mike and we could all go out. I called his house and his mom said he was out on a date. I didn't want to tell Debbie, so I took them both out. Linda's oldest daughter babysat the little ones.

We went to a bar and ran into a guy I hardly knew, he latched onto Debbie and we made it a foursome the rest of the evening. When we got back to Linda's the kids were all sleeping. Linda went to the bathroom and was really sick. I slipped my phone number to Debbie before she went in to help her and I passed out.

When she finally called a week later, I asked her out. She said no. Getting turned down wasn't something I was used to. She said Linda really liked me, and she couldn't do that to her friend. I told her I didn't like Linda and was never planning to see her again. I started calling Debbie and called her every day for thirty days. I would be on a date and tell my date I had some business to take care. I would stop at a pay phone and call Debbie to talk for ten or fifteen minutes.

I called her several times a day. Then one night I called her and said, "What are you doing?"

"I was just getting ready to take my daughter and a little friend of hers out for ice cream. Do you want to go?"

"Where are you going for that?"

"We're going to Baskin Robbins down the street."

Did I ever want to go! I had never in my life worked this hard to go out with someone. I drove like mad to get there; I didn't want to mess this up.

Finally, the elusive Debbie, her daughter, and some other little kid, went on our first date. I had to start somewhere. We have been married now for over thirty-three years, but the road we traveled wasn't a smooth one.

Debbie and I were both alcoholics when we started dating in October of 1979. I was also a drug addict, drug dealer, and contractor for the underworld, and did a pretty good job of keeping her in the dark on the dealing and contracting part. She really had no idea what kind of character she was getting involved with.

One night I took her to a dance and as we were walking in to the building, a guy I knew came out and said, "Hey, Jim."

Debbie looked at me with the most surprised look and said, "Jim? I thought your name was Bill."

I blew it off with some comment about how he must have had me mixed up with someone else, but she was a little suspicious. Later on that night, she asked me if I had ever beaten women, or killed anyone. I told her of course not, and convinced her she was safe with me. She and her four-year-old daughter moved in with me the following January.

We decided to get married in March, and the day before I was supposed to pick up our license, I left town with Big John on a drug deal. I didn't come home that night. I called her from out of town the next day and she said, "Maybe we need to just call this whole thing off and forget about getting married. I can't live this way."

"No baby, I'll be back tonight and I promise I'll get the license tomorrow."

March 28, 1980. Debbie and I getting married at my parents' house. She had no idea that the next years of her life would be filled with guns, drugs, and violence.

We got married on the twenty-eighth of March, 1980. Debbie and her daughter and my three kids would have their lives turned inside out in a few short years. By then she had figured out I was dealing, but had no idea the level of dealer I was. She and I were partying every night, with a house full of people. We lived next door to a liquor store, so didn't have to go far when we ran out of drinks. We put in a real nice above-ground pool the first summer we were together and literally partied every single night of the week. I got falling down drunk and high every day because of the abundance of drugs and booze. Our marriage was about over after six months of drinking and drugging.

We had both been through the pain of divorce before and neither of us wanted to go through it again. We talked about it and decided it was the drinking that was causing all the problems. So we agreed to quit. She did, but I continued to sneak around and drink. Debbie was having panic attacks before she met me, but they got worse now that she didn't have booze to fall back on. She held a full-time job, but struggled because of these attacks.

One day she came home early to find the kitchen table piled full of money, cocaine, and guns.

It was enough to push her over the edge...she quit her job on account of the panic attacks she was having. She starting seeing a counselor and that counselor sent her to a psychiatrist who put her on Thorazine. Her dad gave her some of his Valium to help.

On another occasion she came home to find our garage full of bales of marijuana. She fell apart and thought she was going to lose her mind. I had a great idea—I was moving five or ten thousand Quaaludes a month, so I would just set some aside for her each month and she would be fine.

NO HUSBAND OR FATHER

My kids from my first marriage were also suffering. On the weekends, they were supposed to come see their daddy, but I wasn't always there. Debbie would go get them and bring them over to play with Richelle, and tried her best to help fill the void. You know, a mom trying to be a dad somehow never works out. I have a friend who wrote a book about prisons. He says, "We don't have a prison problem, we don't have an inmate problem, we have a father problem."

My own kids saw Debbie more than they saw me. When I was there, I wasn't really there. I never gave them my undivided attention. My friend who wrote the book also says, "When you are where you are, *BE* there." How many times have we been with someone and knew they weren't there?

My oldest son decided he wanted to come and live with his dad. My mother knew my lifestyle was not one she wanted her grandson around. Mommas have a way of knowing what we are doing even when they can't see us. Billy told her he had his mind made up. He wanted to come.

He moved in with us when he was fifteen years old. I tried to be a good dad and thought buying him stuff would show him I loved him. I paid to have a 1969 Camaro built for him...Essie Ray put together a motor that was bad to the bone. All my son really needed was to have me spend time with him, but I had turned a corner in the cocaine world and started not coming home for weeks at a time.

Larry and Laura would come over to see me and their brother on weekends and I wouldn't be there. That was thirty-three years ago and it is still painful to me. Laura just recently wrote Debbie a letter telling her how much it meant to her when Debbie would pick her up and bring her to spend the weekend with us, though I wasn't there. I felt so bad when I read what she wrote. I was a terrible father.

Every time I walked out the door of our house I carried two pistols, and sometimes a briefcase with an Uzi in it. There were times I had another briefcase with forty or fifty thousand dollars in it. Debbie never knew when I left if she would see me again. I would kiss her goodbye and say, "I'll see you tonight, honey," and might not come home for two or three weeks.

I bought her a couple of guns, took her to the Bullet Hole, and taught her how to shoot. It was amazing and kind of made me mad that she was better than I was, and I was good. She never used those guns, but on one occasion she came very close.

I had a little run in with a guy who was pretty notorious and one day he showed up at my house unannounced with a guy we didn't know. No one came to my house without calling first, and never brought someone we didn't know. Debbie knew the rules and it totally freaked her out. This particular guy was known for shooting people and she was afraid he might try and shoot me. I was in the gym in the backyard when she hollered at me. "Ted Hall is at the front door."

I came around the corner of the house and met him in the driveway. I had been working out, and didn't have a gun on me, but I wasn't afraid of this punk. Debbie told me later that she got her .357 Magnum out and stood at the front window with a bead drawn on him till he and his friend were back in his car leaving. I am glad he didn't make a funny move that day, or she might be writing this book from death row.

SOMETHING HAPPENED TODAY

My marriage to Debbie was turning out just like my first one. It was filled with lies, pornography, unfaithfulness, and much more criminal activity. Again, it was more than any woman should have to put up with.

One night Debbie said, "Something happened to me today, Bill."

"What happened?" I shot back at her.

"I asked Jesus to come into my heart. I'm a Christian now," she said.

"So?" I replied.

"You mean you aren't mad at me?"

"I don't care what you do."

She then asked me what she should do. I told her I didn't know. Maybe she should read the Bible. I had a friend named Chuck Hanna who was a Bible thumper. I told her Chuck would be glad to talk to her. When Chuck came over to talk Bible with her, I left. I didn't want anything to do with God.

Debbie continued to go with me to parties and deliver drugs after she became a Christian. I was heavy into pornography, and would take her with me to deliver drugs. On the way, I would stop at an adult bookstore and pull into the parking lot. "I'm going in and watch some movies, you want to go?"

I knew she wouldn't go in with me, I guess I was just doing it to torment her. She sat in the parking lot of those adult bookstores and read her Bible. Then one day, God told her she couldn't go with me anymore. That is when she and I really started drifting apart. I had gone up a rung or two in the drug world. I kissed her good bye and didn't come home for weeks at a time. I spent more time with Charlie and my cocaine customers than with my own family. It was just like I had done with my first marriage.

26

A ROAD TRIP

Charlie and I continued as business partners without Kenny involved, and we took over a large part of the cocaine business being done in Kansas City. I came up with some ideas that trumped the ones Kenny and I used, that made us so successful. Sometimes Charlie and I, and a couple of friends, would take off and party for a week or more at a time.

It's funny how music played such a big part in my drinking, drugging, and partying days. One song became my favorite right after I met Charlie in 1975. Whenever I did cocaine I loved listening to JJ Cale's hit song, *Cocaine*. When I heard it I would enter another world.

While you are doing "toot" you believe every word of that song. The line that says, *she don't lie*, is especially encouraging while you are doing it.

I had *Cocaine* blasting over the stereo when I got the phone call in the middle of my party. I hung up the phone and yelled, "Charlie, this miserable little punk has the nerve to call me while I'm partying and tell me to hurry up and get something done for him. I may go down there and kill this scum bag. Do you wanna to go with me?"

"I want to go too," yelled Mark from the hot tub.

"If we go down there, we can't let him go with us," Charlie said, nodding towards Mark, who was now climbing out of the hot tub heading for the table lined with cocaine.

"Well, I'm goin' with or without you, or him or anyone else," I snarled at Charlie.

It was about 3:30 Sunday morning and we were at the Racket Club, a private club that some friend of Mark's got us into. We had been partying for several days when we came there after midnight to finish the party in style. I had not slept for seventy-two hours or more. We'd checked into a room at the Embassy on the Park about two days before. It was five hundred dollars a night and I don't think we had stayed there since we checked in. I was driving a friend's car and knew he wasn't worried if I didn't get it back right away.

"We can drop the girls at the hotel, and then go down there and take care of this. You follow me downtown and we'll take this car," I said to Charlie.

We headed down Rainbow to 47th St. and then east through the Plaza to Main. The Embassy on the Park was in downtown Kansas City, Missouri on Wyandotte between 12th and 13th Street. It didn't take us to long to get there at 4:00 a.m. It was September 5th, 1982—a day we would never forget.

We took the girls into the hotel and told them to rest up, we would be back. We had one briefcase with six or eight ounces of uncut cocaine and another with over sixty thousand dollars in it. We also had some pot, guns, scales, and other paraphernalia. The girls went to bed and passed out; we did a little more coke and got really wired. I took a couple of downers to try and settle down a little, and to keep my heart from jumping out of my chest.

We spent a long time trying to figure out where to hide those two briefcases from the girls we didn't know. Finally, after searching that monstrous place, we found that in each of the two bedrooms there were these big dressers. They were hollow underneath, and it took two people to move them. So we put the briefcase with the cocaine under one, and put the briefcase with the money under the other.

The girls were passed out by now; we cut them off on the coke several hours earlier because we had plans. We had been loading them up on downers and pot to get them in the mood. They were so jacked up, they fell asleep and had no idea what was going on. I was so mad at this little punk in Holden, I could only think of killing him.

We decided I would drive and take the Smoky and the Bandit Trans Am belonging to my buddy, Ron. It was brand new and ran super. I drove it like it was stolen.

We ended up taking Mark with us, although I am not sure how that happened because Charlie was so against it. Mark was a really good friend of mine, and he and Charlie had been friends for thirty years. He wanted to protect Mark in case something went wrong. What could possibly go wrong? Three guys who hadn't been to sleep for days, wired out of their minds on cocaine, and going fifty or sixty miles out of town to kill a guy?

I was going down I-70 towards Highway 131, running over 100 mph, and I realized I better slow down. Charlie was a felon, I was a felon, and Mark...well let's just say he had some history also. I carried a brand new Model 59 Smith and Wesson .9mm automatic—a gun that had never been registered. It was going to be thrown into the river as soon as I killed that punk and drove back across a bridge. We stopped at a truck stop on the way and I bought some coffee and cigarettes. Charlie bought a couple of tire knockers—those are little baseball bats truckers use to check the air in their tires.

Once we were headed south on 131 towards our target, we did some more cocaine. This punk was living in a little town thinking he was safe, but we were about to rock his world. He was trying to get me to move some gems for him. He had a couple pounds of rubies, emeralds, and a few other stones, I didn't really have a market for that kind of merchandise, and he acted mad because I wasn't moving them fast enough. I had returned them to him a few days earlier and knew exactly what else he had in the house. I was going to kill him and take everything he had.

We reached Holden about one or two in the afternoon on September 5th. It was a beautiful Sunday afternoon. People were already home from church, had eaten dinner and were sitting in lawn chairs out in their yards. We were so blind we could not see them.

We were snow blind. If you remember Black Sabbath's song, *Snowblind*, it was about doing so much coke you are blinded by it. I had been there many times. I just had never gone to do a major crime or kill someone while blind on cocaine. We couldn't see anything as I backed into his front yard, got out, and kicked his front door open.

The punk was passed out on his bed from doing Quaaludes all night; he didn't even know we were in his house. We got everything together that we were going to take with us. After getting a couple of grocery sacks out of the kitchen I started filling them. One was filled with about five pounds of pot and two or three pounds of hashish, and another with bags of precious gems. I counted out and stuffed fifty-two bundles, with one thousand dollars in each bundle, into the bag with the gems. I also inventoried a twelve-gauge shotgun, a few thousand Quaaludes, and other pills.

At the last minute I decided it was better to beat him almost to death and tell him to never come back in our state again, than to kill him. So with that, we proceeded to beat him with the tire knockers. I didn't know if he even felt it, he was so jacked up on the downers. After the first hit or two he was unconscious.

He was lying face down on the bed stark naked and bleeding like a stuck hog when we heard a loud speaker outside.

"COME OUT WITH YOUR HANDS UP."

WE WERE SURROUNDED

"**W**hat was that?" Charlie yelled. I ran and peeked out the venetian blinds.

"You're not going to believe this," I quietly said to Charlie.

"Mark, you and Charlie block that back door and I'll block the door going into the garage."

They threw the washer and dryer against the back door, while I dragged the couch over and turned it up on end against the door going into the garage. By now we were all three at the windows peeking out.

"Oh my God, there must be twenty of them," Mark screamed.

"Be quiet, they'll hear us," I whispered.

"Bill, they're all the way around the entire house," Charlie whispered from the bedroom.

Some of them had on city police uniforms. Some were sheriff's deputies and some were farmers and country boys carrying rifles and shotguns. It was broad daylight and no way could we run. We had a bunch of vigilantes in the yard.

"COME OUT NOW!" There it was again, but it seemed louder this time.

I was not used to being caught. I had been out of prison for eighteen years, committing crimes, promoting prostitution and pornography, dealing drugs, and had never been caught. I was not prepared for this. I had to think.

"I'll go out and talk to them," Mark said.

"Shut up, you aren't going anywhere," Charlie said.

Charlie and I ran into the bedroom where the punk was bleeding to death. We each went to a different window to see if we could get a better view. They had the house completely surrounded.

"If it was dark out we might have a chance," I whispered to Charlie.

Just then, I thought I heard the front door open and ran back into the living room. The door was wide open and Mark was walking down the sidewalk with his hands in the air. I jumped and my body was completely horizontal with outstretched arms. I slammed the front door and threw a couple of big easy chairs against it.

"That's crazy, what's he doing?" I said loud enough for everybody outside to hear me.

"What in the world is he thinking?" Charlie said, very disappointed.

I immediately ejected the round out of the chamber of the .9mm in my hand. I dropped the clip out and started wiping fingerprints off all fifteen rounds, the clip, and the gun. I threw the clip under the television set. I threw the bullets all over the house and took the gun itself, and dropped it behind the stove. I wiped all the fingerprints off the shotgun and put it behind one of the beds.

All that time, Charlie was watching as they slammed Mark's face into the gravel, handcuffed him, put him in a car, and drove away.

"What do you think he'll say?" Charlie asked me.

"Your guess is as good as mine."

"COME OUT OR WE ARE COMING IN AFTER YOU," the cops said again.

Was it louder every time they said it, or was it just me? We got the punk up off the bed and took him to the front door. We told him to go out and tell them there was no one else in the house. We were definitely snow blind and snow stupid.

He stumbled out without a stitch of clothes on, and his back was red with blood from the top of his head to his heels. They put him in an ambulance and rushed him to a hospital. It took over one hundred stitches to close those cuts.

He hadn't been out there a minute when we heard, "THIS IS YOUR LAST CHANCE."

We walked out of that house around three o'clock in the afternoon on September 5, 1982. As we rode beside each other in the backseat of the patrol car, I could tell those country cops were scared to death. I looked in the rearview mirror and saw that my nostrils were caked with white rings from days of snorting cocaine. I looked over at Charlie and his were too. I thought to myself, *They could get enough coke out of our noses to charge us with 'possession with intent to distribute'*. I stuck my tongue out trying to reach my nostrils to lick some of it off. He saw me and tried to do the same. When they booked us into the jail it was Sunday afternoon. Normally, that means you aren't going anywhere till Monday morning when a judge arraigns you and sets your bond. We were not the average guys they were used to booking.

MONEY, POWER, AND INFLUENCE

The three things I always wanted in life were money, power, and influence. I had two of them already. If I wanted to do something that cost ten thousand dollars I did it, because tomorrow I had another ten thousand. I rode in limousines, stayed in five-hundred-dollar-a-night hotels, and once bought twenty thousand dollars' worth of cocaine for a one-night party. So I had the money I'd always wanted.

I had enough power to make a phone call and have somebody killed. So I had the power I'd always wanted.

I was about to find out that I also had the influence I'd always wanted.

Our one phone call was to a city councilwoman in Kansas City who we sold cocaine to and partied with. "You know who you need to call?" Charlie asked her.

"Yes, I do," was her reply.

She called the judge who we were also selling coke to and partying with. When you are selling cocaine to a judge, he doesn't want you in jail. In less than twelve hours, at 1:30 a.m. on September 6th, we walked out of jail without ever seeing a judge. They originally were going to book us on an attempted murder charge. Now, less than twelve hours later, through the influence of this powerful judge, attorneys, and bondsmen, our bond was set at fifty thousand dollars each. We were able to give a bondsman fifteen thousand dollars and walk out of the jail.

I walked out of there, thinking, *Now I have all three—money, power, and influence.*

Kind of a funny thing happened in all that fiasco. We called Jimmy, a friend of ours, to go down to the Embassy and get the money to pay the bondsman. We told him to take someone with him because he couldn't move that furniture we put it under by himself. He got the briefcase and was on the way to get us, and for some reason he looked inside and saw the uncut cocaine. He stopped and called the jail. They actually let him talk to Charlie.

"I can't come down and get you with this!"

"You went to the wrong bedroom. It's under the other dresser." Charlie laughed.

Jimmy had to go get his friend again, go to the Embassy, and put the briefcase with the cocaine back and get the one with the cash in it.

You think we trusted Jimmy? They don't come any more trustworthy. He would have done anything for us. The lawyer told us to come down and see him on Tuesday morning. He said to bring ten thousand dollars each and he would start the case. Before it was over, we paid him nearly one hundred thousand dollars.

I have had many mug shots taken of me, but this would be the last one. This was September 5th, 1982

When we finally got arraigned, we were charged with first-degree assault with intent to kill, which carried fifteen years to life. We were also charged with first-degree burglary, which carried five to fifteen years.

CHAPTER

27

I'M A GOOD DRIVER

One time, not too long after Debbie became a Christian, I showed up at home on a motorcycle. She was always so glad to see me and would go almost anywhere I asked her to.

I asked her, "You wanna go for a ride with me?"

Of course, she jumped at the chance to just be with me for a while. It was early evening, but not dark yet, so we took off and went across the winding Little Blue River Road down to Noland Road. We then headed south towards Highway 50. When we got to 50 we went west up a hill; I was going about fifty-five miles an hour in fifth gear, and I saw a deer standing on the south side of the road. I thought to myself, *I can get by her before she can get across.*

I downshifted to third and nailed the bike. I was probably running about seventy and thought I made it when I felt the impact. We went from the middle lane into the gravel shoulder. I swerved and fishtailed in the gravel, but somehow managed to keep the bike up and get back on the road. I was in shock, I didn't really know what had happened, and Debbie started screaming and crying, "Stop, please stop!"

"What's wrong with you? That stupid thing almost killed us!"

I thought she wanted me to stop because we hit a deer, and she is real sensitive about animals getting hit by cars and such. She kept asking me to stop. I was getting ready to cuss her out when I looked back and her leg was sticking straight out. That deer had tried to jump over the bike and kicked her in the knee, knocking us off the highway. I took her to the hospital and she was just bruised up badly, but nothing was broken.

The next day I told Charlie and Mark about it. They couldn't believe we were going seventy miles per hour and a deer knocked us into the gravel, and we didn't turn over.

"How could you possibly do that Bill?"

I said, "I'm a good bike rider."

No matter how bad the wreck was, I always took the credit. I flipped a van six times end over end and rolled down a big hill into a creek. Every piece of glass was gone, three of the wheels and tires were ripped off, and only the lug nuts were still on. It looked like it had been hit by a train. I didn't have on a seat belt and ended up with a few stitches in my elbow.

I took my seventy-five-year-old mother down to see that van, and she said, "Bill, don't you see? God has His hand on you, son."

"God had nothin' to do with it. I'm a good driver."

That is how big my ego was. I had overdosed a few times—on two occasions my heart stopped. I got run over on a motorcycle by a pickup truck, and only got my pants ripped. I survived a riot in prison, shootings and knife fights, and over twenty-five car and motorcycle wrecks. There were eight specific times I knew I should have died and didn't. When I powerlifted, I took anabolic steroids in doses big enough to kill an elephant. I began to believe my nickname, "SUPERMAN," was not just a nickname. I thought I really was bullet proof. I didn't ever think I was alive for any reason other than I was tough; I was bad and indestructible.

NO PLEA BARGAINS

The lawyers called us one day in a panic. They said the guy we beat up had given a twenty-page typewritten statement to the narcotics division. He gave the names of everyone he had ever had any drug dealings with in the past eight or ten years.

The most serious part of the whole statement was that he listed us as being some of the leading cocaine dealers in Kansas City. He gave amounts he bought from us. He even gave amounts of cocaine he heard we'd sold to other dealers.

The reason he gave this statement was because they promised that if he cooperated, they would return all his property to him, including all the money. We couldn't believe he really thought the cops were going to give him back his money.

He named everyone in the statement—the judge we were selling to, and the city councilwoman. It wasn't long before we began seeing people going down.

A few short months after the punk ratted on us, we saw Kenny Weld get busted. He was named in that statement. They got him in Blue Springs, Missouri with twenty-nine pounds of cocaine. If you stepped on it six times, it was five million dollars' worth. Kenny got a sentence of twenty-five years. We couldn't pick up a paper without seeing a name that was also in the statement.

Our attorneys freaked out. They told us to quit dealing. When we saw them the morning after they bonded us out, I turned a white bank bag upside down over the attorney's desk. Thirty thousand dollars in cash tumbled out. They knew where the money came from. "This is an assault and burglary case. If you get arrested selling drugs, it is really going to complicate things," they told us.

I went ballistic; I jumped up and screamed at them, "We don't tell you how to practice law. And you don't tell us how we should make money!"

They reluctantly agreed, but told us we should be aware that, without a doubt, our phones would be tapped. We needed to be very careful so we didn't complicate the case. They would continue on as we planned.

I had gone off on them like a roman candle in the very beginning when they asked if we would each consider getting a different attorney. When I asked why, they said, "In case one of you decides to plea bargain."

I screamed like a drill instructor, "THERE WILL BE NO PLEA!" And I meant it with all my being at the time.

We began using codes on the phone. I taught my wife how to talk using code. We developed a code and carried on conversations without any suspicion. It was a very fearful time in our lives, constantly under surveillance and knowing we were only the slightest slip away from possible drug charges.

TROUBLE IN MIAMI

Kenny got involved with a guy in Florida who owed him forty-five grand. He was down there babysitting him, trying to collect his money. The trouble was, that this guy had been on the cover of *Time* magazine a few years earlier as being one of the leading cocaine dealers in the whole country. Now Kenny was there partying with him. Supposedly, his money was all in a bank in the Cayman Islands, so they rented a private jet in Miami, and flew to the Caymans. When they landed, they were too late—the bank was closed and wouldn't open back up till Monday morning. They flew back to Miami, got some clothes, and flew back to the Cayman Islands to party all weekend.

When the weekend was over and they were supposed to be able to get his money, they ended up in jail because they didn't have money to pay the hotel bill or the bar tab. The guy who flew them over told Kenny they owed him seventeen thousand, five hundred dollars.

Kenny took off his ring and handed it to him. "This ring is worth forty-five grand. I'm going to let you hold it till we get this figured out. Whatever you do, you'd better be here when we get ready to leave."

They called home and Kenny's brother wired them the money to pay the bills. They got out of jail. The guy went to the bank, and the bank had frozen his account. The private jet was gone, and they had to get more money wired and take a commercial airliner back to Miami. As soon as they got back, Kenny went to get his ring.

The guy said, "Somebody has to pay me the seventeen thousand, five hundred dollars I'm owed."

Kenny borrowed the money against his Porsche and took a check for seventeen thousand, five hundred dollars to the guy, who handed him back his ring. Kenny put the ring on his finger as the guy looked at the check, and said, "This check is made out to you, and you need to endorse it."

"Oh, sure, give it here."

The guy handed it back to him to sign. Kenny took the check, put it in his pocket, and walked out the door. The next day Kenny was on the seventy-foot cruiser that belonged to the guy he was down there babysitting when a black Cadillac pulled up at the dock. Two big Italian-looking guys got out and started across the dock towards the boat. Kenny stepped out of the cabin with his silver Colt 45 and said, "Don't even come near this boat if you wanna live."

They got back in the Caddy and left. Kenny called me and said, "Superman, I'm afraid for the very first time in my life. These guys know where my Porsche is parked and there's no way I can get it."

"Do you want me to come down there and get your car?"

"No," he said and hung up. I didn't know what to make of that.

POWER TO KILL

Since Kenny was temporarily out of the picture, my new cocaine partner Charlie and I were on a fast roll. I was staying out of the night life and clubs at this point, because I didn't need the exposure. I conducted my business from hotel rooms or stash houses we had around the city. I refused to talk to anyone who didn't have at least seventy-eight hundred dollars to buy a quarter pound.

I had given up selling grams and ounces a long time ago. There were too many people to see and too much traffic for the small profit to be made. Not only did I have a real serious cocaine habit, but I was becoming more paranoid every day. I didn't trust anyone, and was certain everyone I saw was undercover. It got so bad I didn't trust my wife or cocaine partner.

If you've ever done much coke, you know exactly what I'm talking about. I thought my partner was ripping me off, I thought my customers were out to get me. Kenny's older brother, Willard, taught us how to deal with people who couldn't be trusted. I started thinking about whacking some of those guys who were out to get me. Cocaine was definitely doing my thinking.

Our whole operation was set up to be pretty portable. I had the press that Kenny and I built; Charlie had the hot boxes, scales and chemicals. I still got cut from Kenny's father-in-law. We could get it all in a couple of big suitcases and set up shop wherever we landed. I sawed and jack-hammered Charlie's basement floor and put a safe in the concrete. It was beneath a carpet, under a pool table. We also buried igloo coolers in the ground in a couple different locations with cocaine and money in them.

One day I got a phone call from Kenny. Hey said, "Hey man, I wanna see you. I'm back in town."

I was so excited to hear from my friend and I said, "Where you at? I'll come get ya." I picked him up and headed to the airport.

"Where we goin, Superman?"

"You're gonna like where we're goin. Charlie is due in from the coast, he has a big load and I'm supposed to pick him up. Did you ever get here at the perfect time! It will be the best snow you've ever seen,"

"Better than Bill H was bringing in from Bogotá?" Kenny asked.

"No, I don't think there's ever been anything that good. Speaking of Bill, I wonder where he is?"

When we got to the airport to pick up Charlie, he spotted Kenny and me just as he was coming off the plane. I could see it in his eyes—he was very upset.

I told Kenny, "Wait here a minute, let me go talk to Charlie."

Charlie and I stepped outside and he went completely berserk. "What's wrong with you, bringing him here?"

"Charlie, Kenny's been my best friend. He'd never tell anyone about our operation."

"That's not the point, he's blazing hot. He's been in Florida for four months with a guy who's been labeled as one of the biggest dealers in the entire country. Do you think for a minute they're not watching everyone connected to that guy?" Charlie's veins in his neck were about to come through his skin.

"I'm sorry, I just know he's my best friend, I'd die for him and he would for me."

After a minute or so, Charlie said, "It's okay; let's go get the product."

We went to the baggage claim and picked up the bags with the coke. (This was before they scanned your bags.) Kenny's house was close to the airport and he assured us he wasn't hot. He said if we would be more comfortable, we could go to Charlie's instead. Charlie told me to make sure we weren't being followed and go to his house.

At Charlie's, we took a look at what he just brought in—very high quality. We could step on it six times; that meant for every kilo we had, we could make six kilos out of it.

Charlie also had visited our friends up in Mendocino County, who had the best pot I ever smoked—and I had smoked every kind there was. Whenever we went to get our shipment of cocaine, we always brought back a little of that good pot. It was never for sale, it was just for our own pleasure and sometimes we shared it with our best coke customers. You know…customer relations.

This seemed like a good time to break out some and try to calm Charlie down; he was still visibly upset over me bringing Kenny to the airport.

Charlie did five calendar years in Leavenworth and was super careful to make sure he never went back. He was an All-American in high school and went to college on a football scholarship. He played in college with the great Gale Sayers and would have gone on to play in the NFL, but an injury his senior year sidelined him and ended his career. So he became a school teacher—a school teacher who sold cocaine.

In 1970 when he got busted, he refused to cooperate, so when he ended up in front of Elmo Hunter, the federal judge, he decided to make an example out of Charlie. He got fifteen years under the old guidelines, which made him eligible for parole after one third of his sentence. I met him right after he got out in 1975 and we became great friends.

We smoked a joint of that good weed, and believe me, one joint was enough to do us all in for a while. When we were able to communicate, the joint was out and half of it was sitting in the ashtray.

Kenny came up with a proposition for us. He had been gone so long he lost his connection. If we would front him a pound of the new shipment of coke, he could put a six on it, turn it in two to three days, and it would help him get back on his feet. He, in turn, would set us up with some new clientele. Charlie told me to take Kenny home and let him think on it for the night. I dropped Kenny off and gave him a few grams to do. I told him I was sure Charlie would do it.

The next day I was back at Charlie's, starting to cut and weigh out our new shipment.

"Call Kenny and tell him we can't do it," Charlie said.

"What are you talking about? We're not helping him?"

"He's way too hot. I know he says he's not, but there's no possible way he's been down there with that dude and isn't being watched. I'll not take that chance."

"Okay, I'll call him."

"Kenny, Charlie says we can't do it, man," I said as he answered the phone.

"Bill, I love you...and I really like Charlie, but right now, I'd just as soon line you both up in my crosshairs." He hung up the phone.

I never talked to Kenny again. Our relationship had gone full circle, from being best friends to worst enemies.

That afternoon, Charlie and I rode in the back seat of a chauffeured limo heading out to western Kansas to pick up some money that was owed us.

"Oh, by the way, what did Kenny say when you told him?" Charlie asked.

I hesitated telling him, but finally said, "He said he'd just as soon line you and me up in his crosshairs."

"You think he means it?" Charlie asked, very seriously.

"I don't know. Why?"

"Because, if he does, I'll make a phone call now. I'm not going to live under a threat like that," he said.

It was there in the back of the limousine that I realized I had the power to make a phone call and have someone killed...or keep them alive.

"He doesn't mean it. I know him, and I know he doesn't mean it." The only reason I said that was because I cared so much for Kenny and I didn't want him killed. We had been through so much together. But I also knew he was crazy enough to do anything.

In my heart I was truly afraid he might literally line us up in his crosshairs. Kenny wasn't afraid to kill and did. I had seen Kenny sit for hours waiting for the chance to line someone up in his crosshairs. I never mentioned it again to Charlie.

Hardly a day went by that I didn't think of him sitting fifteen hundred yards away with a high-powered rifle looking at me through his crosshairs. Finally, I was able to sleep and quit thinking about it.

Kenny died in a horrific car accident on November 30, 1983, so I feel free to talk and write about him.

29

THE BIG OUTLAWS

There was a time in my heaviest drinking days when I was a welder on construction jobs. I couldn't hold my welding rod steady if I didn't drink. I got a half pint to last me from starting time to lunch, and another half pint for after lunch till quitting time. I was welding on the Sunflower ammunition plant out in Desoto, Kansas when I met Big John.

He was a major marijuana grower; but would work a few months out of the year as a front. He had taken a big fall with his brother-in-law several years earlier moving large amounts of heroin out of Mexico. He swore off narcotics and strictly dealt pot now. He came up with the best deal I could ever have gotten. John was friends with the people who owned the "Do Drop Inn" and had a room there.

We met in his "office," which was what he called the bar, and discussed our future plans of getting rich moving pot into Kansas City. I told Big John I had moved one hundred pounds a week and could do that for him, no problem. His only request was that I stop moving narcotics on any level, using it, or dealing it. The reason he wanted this was not selfish, but because he had seen it destroy his friends.

Several years later, John and his friend Big Lou physically carried me out of my house and took me to his farm, trying to get me off cocaine. He was a man I trusted in criminal activity and was a very good friend.

I will never forget when Big John trusted me enough to take me to the fields where he grew pot—he was one serious dude. He had irrigation systems set up in all his locations, which were scattered all over. He had several fields in about six different counties, so if the law found some, they didn't get it all. I knew the whole operation, from getting to meet some of the county officials he paid off; to the hit men he contracted to kill the candidate who might run against his man in power in the county.

Big John was one of my dearest and closest friends. He is a bright light at the end of the tunnel.

We moved a lot of pot in the time I was associated with John. He fronted me five hundred pounds at a time if I wanted it and could move it. I usually never took that much at once, but a couple of times we did move five hundred pounds. He was also one of my biggest suppliers of pills. He had a couple of druggist friends back then and they got him large amounts.

I saw people in that close-knit circle die. Big John's brother-in-law was found dead in a closet, where his body had been for six months. Somebody had paid the rent six months in advance. We looked for a long time for who it might have been, and wouldn't have thought twice about killing them.

I would have killed them for free, just to ease Big John's pain. Big John offered to kill people for me for free, so why wouldn't I do the same for him?

We buried some friends together. Big Lou was one of those. Lou was not called Big Lou for nothing. He was six foot, eight inches tall and weighed over three hundred pounds. His face looked like a road map because of all the many scars. He had been locked up all over the country and was even tougher than he looked. He would do anything for Big John or me, and was truly a guy you could count on no matter how bad things got.

When Lou died of cancer, he weighed less than a hundred pounds. John wouldn't let me go to the hospital to see him at the end. He didn't want me to see how bad Lou looked. What a hard thing for John to go through by himself. Lou was like a brother to him.

John and Lou tried their best to keep me away from narcotics, but I was determined to be one of the biggest dealers in the city. The crowd I ran with now was different. I have always divided serious law breakers into two different categories, outlaws and gangsters. Big John and Big Lou were outlaws. The sign on John's front door said:

THIS HOUSE PROTECTED BY SHOTGUN 4 DAYS A WEEK, YOU GUESS WHICH 4

There were also my friends in the city that I put in the category of gangsters. I liked them both, but considered myself more a gangster than an outlaw.

I GAVE MY WIFE TO A DRUG DEALER

A guy by the name of David was the one responsible for my reputation of moving one hundred pounds of weed a week. He was as good as gold for the money. I would just drop off any amount of weed to him and he would roll by my house in his Mercedes every day with sacks of cash. It started off with ten pounds a week, increasing to thirty, then fifty, and then one hundred. I wasn't making much per pound, but I didn't have to do anything except make one stop at David's house with the load, and wait till he brought the money.

David stopped taking my calls one day and I didn't talk to him for several months. I started rolling hard and fast in the cocaine sales, and one day I stopped by his house and knocked on his door.

He came to the door. "Bill, how you doin'?"

"Doin' good, man."

"I see that, come on in." He was eyeing all my jewelry.

I looked like a white Mr. T with four or five gold necklaces, a gold bracelet and gold rings.

I told him we were moving some of the best cocaine that ever hit the city and I would like to have his business back, and by the way, "Why did you stop taking my calls?"

"I heard you and your people were hot."

"Well, my friend, you heard wrong."

I told him he had definitely gotten hold of some bad information. We were probably some of the lowest profile dealers in the city and he didn't have anything to worry about. We actually got tipped off if the cops were on to one of our stash houses, and would move it.

We shook hands and were back in business. David became one of my top buyers, moving as much cocaine as any of my customers. He was also one of the biggest fences in town. We got any and all kinds of merchandise from him. One time, when big screen TV's first came out, he had ten brand-new boxed ones in his garage, which he traded a few ounces of coke for. At that time those TV's were worth about five grand each. He probably took one of my ounces he paid two thousand for and cut it four or five times before trading it for fifty thousand dollars' worth of television sets.

Another time, I brought a black trash bag home and threw it down in the middle of the floor. I said to Debbie, "Pick yourself out one of them, baby."

"What's in there?" She asked me.

There were two six-thousand-dollar mink coats and a twelve-thousand-dollar Russian sable in the bag that I had gotten from one of David's thieves. Twenty-four thousand dollars worth of coats traded for an ounce of cocaine I only had five hundred bucks in. He often had gallon-size Ziploc bags full of gold, rings, chains, etc. David was a gambler—drugs and fencing stolen goods were hobbies to him. He loved gambling and was good at.

He stopped by my house one day and said, "Hey man, can I borrow Debbie for about an hour?"

"What are you talkin' about?"

"I told some guys I was coming by, and I'd have a female in the car. I won't be gone long."

Debbie looked at me and shook her head, like, *Please...I don't want to.*

"Yeah, but she better be back real quick and in one piece," I said.

I can't believe I cared more about my business dealings with David than I did about the safety of my wife. Or maybe I just knew she would be okay, and that he knew if he didn't bring her back in one hour, untouched, I would blow his stinking brains out.

They were only gone about an hour, and everything was cool when they came back. Debbie told me later that he took her someplace she didn't recognize, left her in the car while he was gone, then got back in the Mercedes and drove her home.

I had no idea what that was all about—appearance I guess. Maybe he wanted them to think he had a white girlfriend. She also told me later that she was scared to death, and please never make her do anything like that again.

David and I pulled off some other scams—not drug related, but they paid well. We put together some insurance frauds and got away with them, car wrecks, etc. One time we came up with a scam we knew would put us on Easy Street. David had a guy under his thumb, and he did whatever he told him to. David had something on the guy. I never found out what it was, and didn't care.

The guy worked for a big name fast food fried chicken place. It was a nationwide chain and publicly traded. David's guy worked behind the counter and brought the food to your table when your order came up. David had him steal some of the batter that made their fried chicken famous; it was their own recipe. We planned to cut up a rat and fry it in *their* special batter; we knew the right temperature for the grease in the deep fryer, and how long to fry it.

David was going to send the fried rat to work with this guy, and I would go in and order some fried chicken. When my order came up he was to bring the rat out to me, and I would bite into it, then take it up and show the manager. It was going to be cut in a way that there would be no question it was a rat.

We had all the bases covered—a rat deep fried in their own special batter and I had the best lawyer in the city at the time. I lived in Riverside, and this was deep in the hood in Kansas City. I didn't know anyone working there, so there was no way to connect me to that particular fast food chain. It was absolutely the perfect scam, but the week we planned to do it, the guy who worked there got killed.

Another thing Dave and I worked on for over two years was an armored car heist at the Kansas City Chiefs stadium. We watched the transfer for a whole season and into part of another. We knew how much cash went through there on any given Sunday, and knew it would be a score of over one million dollars in unmarked bills.

The problem we faced in pulling this off was manpower. We needed six to eight trustworthy men, and just couldn't find that many we were comfortable with.

We planned a lot of things together that never happened, but we made a lot of money dealing weed and girl (cocaine). We probably planned all those big scores when we were high on cocaine. If you have ever done coke, you know what I am talking about. You can solve all the problems in the world.

HOPELESSLY HOOKED

I remember when I first started selling cocaine with Kenny. We were never going to do it; we were just going to sell it. We knew that if we started doing it, we would get paranoid and wouldn't make good business decisions. "That will not be us," I said to Kenny as we weighed out the coke.

When we sold cocaine to people, they wanted to try it to see if it was good, and it looked bad if we didn't do our own merchandise. I believe that if you go sit in a barber shop every day, you will eventually get a haircut. If you are going to be a bank robber, you need to hang out with bank robbers. Who you hang with is who you become. What is that saying, birds of a feather...?

The song, Cocaine, says, *She don't lie, she don't lie, she don't lie, cocaine.*

That's a lie! When I did cocaine, I thought I had every problem in my life figured out. If I had money problems, or marriage problems, or problems with my job, it didn't matter—I had the answer as long as the cocaine lasted. But, when it was all gone, the problem was still there.

I believe that is why I didn't want to stop. Somehow I knew that if I quit, my problems would come back, so I didn't quit till I had done it all. When the cocaine's gone, it is the worst feeling in the world.

If I had a small amount of heroin, I would do half today and save the other half for tomorrow. Cocaine is not like that; if I had a little bit of cocaine, or a dump truck load, I did it till every granular was gone. Sometimes I went for six or seven days at a time without sleep or food. We were never without cocaine but had to stop sometime, or we would kill ourselves. I learned how to do it after overdosing a time or two. I timed myself—after eighty or so hours, I stopped and slept for ten or twelve hours. After I slept, I ate something, and then went back to the same routine, partying and selling.

I would check into a five-hundred-dollar-a-night hotel and make my customers come there. Then there were times I stayed in budget motels, because I was so paranoid. Sometimes I checked into three or four different hotels or motels in the same day.

Sometimes I went home and slept after being on a five- or six-day run. I would always go home in the middle of the night while my wife and kids were sleeping. I would stop at 7-Eleven and buy two or three bottles of Nyquil and down them one after another. I did this trying to slow my heart, so that when I lay down beside my wife she wouldn't hear it beating. I drank two quarts of whiskey a day and never got drunk, because of the cocaine.

Cocaine is so powerful; it will take away your God-given desires. Sex has no appeal to you while you are doing coke. Scientists have experimented with chimps they have given cocaine to. They put a female chimp in heat, in with the male, but he ignores her while he has cocaine. When a male prefers drugs over sex, he should know there is something wrong with that drug.

When I competed as a power lifter, I weighed two hundred and seventy-five pounds. Now, because of the cocaine, I weighed one ninety or less and was going to self-destruct if I didn't get some help.

MY LAST CHANCE

Help comes in big packages. I don't remember this, but Debbie told me that Big John and Lou came to our house and literally carried me to their car. They took me to an old farmhouse John owned in Clinton, Missouri. I had my own room up in the attic and it was a very comfortable hideout.

I needed a hideout, because the case I was out on bond for wasn't going well and I thought I might jump bond. Big John took me to one of the most influential men in the state as far as criminal cases go.

He told John, "I've seen men with a monkey on their back, but Bill has an eight-hundred-pound gorilla on his."

There was one good thing about hiding at Big John's...I never ran out of weed, or prescription Valium or Percodan. John was one of the biggest outlaws in the country, but I felt totally safe there. He had the most powerful politicians in the county in his back pocket, and I didn't have to worry about anything.

One night I told Big John, "I'm going up to bed."

As I climbed the long wooden stairs leading to my bedroom, I looked at the wear and tear on them and thought, *They look like I am beginning to feel*. I was approaching forty but had a lot of miles on me, and was tired of running so hard.

I fiddled with the radio dial, trying to get it to bring the station in where I could hear it plainly. It kept drifting off the rock station I was trying to hear and over to some preacher saying, "God loves you, no matter what you've done."

"I don't want to hear that stuff," I said out loud.

I wanted to hear some music, not that preaching crap. I tried turning the knob ever so slightly to get it back to the rock station.

"Jesus will forgive you of all your past. Just ask Him to come into your heart."

This is not what I want to hear! I was really starting to get upset. I very carefully and slowly tried tuning it back to my rock station.

"Won't you tell Jesus you will live for Him?" the preacher on the radio said.

I was out of jail on a fifty-thousand dollar bond; our case was not going too well. It was April 15, 1983—seven months after we beat that lousy punk almost to death. He didn't die, but went to the state and gave them a twenty-page typewritten statement. He gave the names of everyone he'd been in any type of drug dealings with over the last eight to ten years. He implicated me and my partners as being some of the leading cocaine dealers in Kansas City. Because of this snitching little slime, I hadn't lived a normal life in months. I wasn't seeing my kids, parents, or anyone, for that matter.

I was sick of the life I had created for myself. And according to all that the attorneys were saying, I was going to prison...again. They had reduced the charge down to assault with intent to kill. That offense carried fifteen to life in Missouri. Then there was the first-degree burglary charge. That carried five to fifteen years, so I was facing a minimum of twenty years, and a max of life. I really felt like a taxpayer feels on tax day, like it is the last day you have. As a matter of a fact, this was April 15, and I felt like it was my last chance.

The words just sort of slipped off my lips, "God, if You're real and You can change Bill Corum, I will live my life for You."

I didn't really pray, I was just talking to God...if He was even there.

Finally, I fell asleep. When I woke up Friday morning, I didn't remember anything about the night before. But I did something that was very strange. I called Debbie.

"I think I'll come home. Do you wanna come get me?"

"Yes, I'll be there as quick as I can."

I stayed home for a whole week and mostly slept. One day, a thought came into my mind. *You haven't done any drugs for a week.*

Oh my, I thought, *that can't be!* I did drugs every day and night. I started to panic, thinking, *I'm going to die! I have got to do some drugs.*

Debbie was at work and had our only car. She had picked me up at Big John's and I'd left my car there. I waited at the door for her to get home from work. She came up the steps and I threw the door open and said, "I ain't done any drugs in a week."

"I know," she said, smiling from ear to ear.

"Gimme your keys. I have to get some drugs."

She wasn't going to argue with me, so she handed me her keys and I took off for a guy's house I knew had some good dope. I couldn't quit thinking about the fact that I hadn't done any drugs in a week. *I'm going to get so high!* I couldn't wait to get there. I knocked and walked in.

Ray said, "Where ya been hiding?"

"Never mind where I've been…give me some coke…roll me a joint."

I lit the reefer, but it was hard to light because it was so full of tar. I thought, *This is going to be good*. I took a real deep drag and held it. I let the smoke drift out of my mouth and nothing happened. It was like smoking a Camel cigarette. I did a couple lines of cocaine…it was like snorting a line of sugar.

"Where'd you get this trash?"

"Hey…don't call it trash! I got it from you, dude."

"You're a liar! This ain't mine," I said, sounding like I was going to smack him.

"Well…uh…yeah it *is* yours, Bill."

I jumped up. Ray leaned way back; I guess he thought I was coming over the table after him, but I went out his front door.

"Hey…you okay, dude?"

I didn't answer and got in my car and drove off. I turned on the radio and Debbie had it on some Christian station. The minute I heard it, I remembered the words I said one week ago. "God, if You're real and You can change Bill Corum, I will live my life for You."

I immediately had a thought come into my mind. *You haven't had a gun in a week and you're not afraid anymore.* I would never go out without a gun, and now I didn't even have one. I had left my guns at Big John's when Debbie picked me up and I hadn't even thought about them all week. Something very strange was going on and it was kind of freaking me out. I drove to our house—I will never forget this to the day I die. Debbie was at the sink doing dishes, and I walked up behind her.

"Debbie, one week ago today, I told God if He could change me, I would live my life for Him."

She started crying. He hadn't changed me that much.

"Shut up, what are you crying for?" She told me that she knew something had happened, because I woke up happy every day that week and she had never seen me wake up happy.

"And you haven't kicked my cat all week."

"I haven't?"

I wasn't even aware of the changes happening in my life—changes that would *continue* happening. Even as I write this book thirty years later, God is still making changes in me, and all for the good. Thank You, God.

That was definitely a miracle, because I kicked her cat every time it crossed my path. I was pretty excited about something new happening, but I was facing twenty years to life on the criminal case still pending. I can say with all honesty, I wasn't worried about it. I didn't know then, but the Bible says God can give you a peace that passes all understanding, and that is exactly what He had done.

I told Debbie that now we were both Christians we should read the Bible together, and she was excited about that. I asked her if she knew what John 3:16 said. She said she didn't, and I got mad at her. I learned it as a kid and thought everybody in the world knew what it said.

"You're a Christian, and you don't know what John 3:16 says?"

"No, I don't."

I was mad because she didn't know a verse. She started crying, and that made me even madder. I said I was going to just leave. She told me if I did, I couldn't blame it on her. It was crazy. So needless to say, we didn't read the Bible together that night.

While Debbie was at work one day, our phone rang. "Hello," I said.

"You can't walk out on us."

That was all I heard. I thought I recognized the voice, but wasn't sure. The people I had been involved with for the last few years did not let you just walk away. I controlled about seventy-five percent of all the business we did. They didn't know the people I sold to, and I didn't know who they sold to. They were not willing to lose my percent of the business because it was major money.

I sat down to try and think. I dozed off and dreamed I saw the barrel of a gun. I saw fire coming out of the end, and Debbie fall to the floor, dead.

I woke up in a sweat and in total fear. They were going to kill Debbie, not me! Their plan to kill my family would get my attention.

I thought back to the days of the River Quay and all the mob killings that took place. Execution style—you wind up in the trunk of your car. They might even put you on your mother's grave like one guy I knew. He was always saying, "I swear on my mother's grave."

That's where the police found his body.

Debbie's Bible was lying right there on the table beside my chair. I reached over and opened it. The only words I could see were:

"No weapon that is formed against thee shall prosper; and every tongue that shall rise against thee in judgment thou shalt condemn. This is the

heritage of the servants of the Lord, and their righteousness is of me." Isaiah 54:17

Then I flipped over a few pages and I saw these words:

"The Lord is my light and my salvation; whom shall I fear? The Lord is the strength of my life; of whom shall I be afraid?" Psalm 27:1

I wasn't asking anyone where to look, or sitting there digging through the pages till something came along that comforted me. It was totally God, and no one could convince me otherwise. I fell into a peaceful sleep. When I woke up, I had such a peace that everything was going to be okay.

A NEW CREATURE

Not long after I gave my life to Christ and started walking with Him, I went to see our attorney. When I entered his office, he looked like he had seen a ghost.

"What happened to you? You don't look the same."

"I'm not the same."

"Therefore if any man be in Christ, he is a new creature: old things are passed away; behold all things are become new." II Corinthians 5:17

Mike, my attorney, could actually see a difference in my physical appearance. I told him I really needed to talk to him about the change in me.

"We have a problem…Mike."

"What's that, Bill?"

"The reason I don't look the same is…I'm a Christian now. And God has made some radical changes in me. One is, I can't lie anymore."

My lawyer put his face in his hands and took a deep breath. "You're right, we *do* have a problem."

We had a plan of attack on this case, and had already entered a "not guilty" plea. We had stayed strong with our plans to go to trial, take the stand, and lie under oath or do whatever it took to win. I had told our attorneys that no matter what it cost, they had to win. There was an unending supply of money, and we didn't want to ever hear the words "plea bargain."

Now, I was telling Mike I couldn't lie. The case lasted for another thirteen months, and I never had to tell another lie. God did some miraculous things and showed Himself to me in many ways throughout the remainder of the case.

HEY, PAULA

I called an old friend of mine, Ray Hildebrand, who had been praying for me for ten years. His hit, *Hey Paula*, in 1963 had taken him to the top of the charts. He was now a Christian singer and song writer. He answered and I said, "Ray…its Bill Corum."

"Big Bill, is that really you?"

"Are you still praying for me, Ray?"

"Yes I am, every day."

"Well, you can quit," I said.

He replied, "Hey, man! I've got to see ya."

I thank God for that phone call and the trip to his office. I shared with him what I had been into in detail. Ray looked at me and leaned back in his chair. "Big Bill, if you want to grow, here's what you need to do. Your head is so full of trash…you need to force it out. If you try to pick it out one piece at a time, you'll never get it done.

"But if you fill your head full of good stuff and God stuff it will force the trash out. If you're gonna watch TV, watch Christian TV. If you're gonna read a book, read the Bible. If you're listening to the radio, listen to Christian radio. If you want to talk to someone, talk to a Christian."

I took Ray's advice and actually was preaching it as part of my message in churches I was asked to speak in. Let me just say… that was a bad idea. What worked for me may not be the answer for everyone (although it wouldn't hurt). I did, however, use it as a tool when I helped someone in their walk with the Lord. It works especially well with people who have come out of a lifestyle of drugs and alcohol.

GRASS YOU DON'T SMOKE

I didn't have a job, and hadn't worked for quite a while because of being a full-time drug dealer. I belonged to the plumbers union, but didn't want to go back into it, because I had sold cocaine to a lot of union members and didn't want to be around them. I took a job mowing grass for five dollars an hour. It was the summer of 1983 and was 106 degrees that summer. I was out at the Truman Library mowing grass; we also were in the process of planting six thousand ivy plants. I would be down on my knees baking in the sun, sweat rolling off of me, and crying tears of joy. I didn't understand it. I was still facing twenty years to life, but felt a peace I'd never experienced in my life and knew it would be okay.

I slowly got my strength back mowing yards and planting flowers. Hard work was what I needed. I got an offer to go to work for a guy as a laborer on a concrete crew for ten dollars an hour. Wow! That was double what I was making, so I jumped on it. If I thought mowing yards was hard work in the summer sun, was I ever in for a surprise. I was almost forty years old and just starting out as a laborer on a concrete crew.

I believed God was going to bless me, because I was doing exactly what the Word of God said I was supposed to be doing.

"Let him that stole steal no more: but rather let him labor, working with his hands the thing which is good, that he may have to give to him that needeth." Ephesians 4:28

This was a job for young men, but I liked the challenge and worked hard, and got stronger. I had previously been a competitive power lifter and lifted in the two-hundred-seventy-five-pound weight class. But when I got so messed up on cocaine my weight dropped all the way down to one ninety. By then I had already quit powerlifting. Now, as a Christian, I gained weight and felt like I could go back to lifting.

I had a gym in my back yard I built back in the days when the money was rolling in. At least I didn't have to pay to work out. I opened the gym back up, only the rules had changed—no steroids, just hard work and sweat. SWEATHOUSE GYM was the name we gave it. My son Larry even designed tee shirts for us. It had no air conditioning and when it was hot outside and full of bodies, it was a sweathouse. I got stronger and set some new personal records, which was pretty cool since I was now drug free.

I went to the meets and guys I used to sell steroids and cocaine to would come up to score drugs, and I would tell them about Jesus. It was a joy having my two sons lifting with me and they even entered some power meets. We had great times together, and they got a glimpse of the dad they had grown up without.

Ever since my conversion, Debbie and I were faithful tithers. God proved to us He would provide. I went from making five dollars an hour mowing grass to ten being a laborer. He then opened a door for me to make fifteen dollars an hour as the master plumber for Macy's construction. I took the job and got my oldest boy on. It was a great time for him and me to get to know each other and be together. I still didn't think I was ready to go back into the union, but I knew God would show me when the time was right.

A GIFT FROM GOD

I got a call from our attorneys and they said we needed to talk. I drove down by myself, because Charlie and Mark were still dealing and using. When they arrived, we went into a conference room where our attorney told us that if he could keep us from going to prison, it would be a victory. He told us the direction the case was headed; the only way to keep us out of prison was to ask for a plea bargain. I had been the one so opposed to plea bargaining, so Mark and Charlie both looked to me for a hint of what we should do. I, of course, saw this as God's way of delivering me from having to lie.

Our attorneys explained to us that the deal was not guaranteed. The judge had the final say, and could deny the plea. The prosecutor was in favor of the attorneys' proposition and was willing to cut a deal. He knew that something was wrong in our case because of all the problems going on in the preliminary hearings. The case was a fiasco from the beginning, and our lawyers were sure the judge would agree to the plea.

The majority of the money and drugs found at the scene of the crime had not been turned in. I knew exactly what was there. I put it in sacks and took inventory as I did it. Since I was stealing it, I wanted to know what I was taking. Of course, we weren't going to say anything about what was actually there, or what the police claimed they found. But we knew that the crooked cops, who stole most of the evidence and a large percentage of the money, knew that we knew. They started disappearing. When our attorney called for a statement from one of the officers, someone would say, 'That officer is no longer here'. He would say that the officer quit the police department and was now living in New Mexico or some other state.

That happened with two or three of the officers our attorney wanted to question. Not only did most of the drugs and money disappear, but also my friend's car I drove that day. The police towed it and I had the keys in my pocket when we were released. I asked to get it back and was told it was being investigated because of the out-of-state tags. It ended up taking six months and costing my friend over ten thousand dollars to get his car back. He hired an attorney and in his investigation found that the Chief of Police had changed the locks and was driving it.

Even though the state had a strong case against us, our attorney felt sure that because of the discrepancies in the officers' testimonies, and other things that had happened during the past seven months, the prosecutor was not as confident as he should have been. Which made our attorney feel that they would accept a plea bargain. I considered it a gift from God.

THE VOICE OF GOD

The night before I was to go to court for what might be the last time, I kept waking up in the night and thinking, *Psalms 50*. I would go back to sleep and wake up with it stronger on my mind than before, *Psalms 50*. It was driving me nuts. I needed to get some sleep. I would check the clock and close my eyes... *Psalms 50*.

Finally, I thought, *I wonder if this is God speaking?* I'd never heard His voice and didn't know what to expect. I got out of bed quietly so I wouldn't wake Debbie. I walked through the house into the kitchen, all the while thinking, *I wonder if this is God speaking?* I opened the Bible to Psalms 50 and couldn't believe my eyes.

You have to read it slow and meditate on it like I did that night:

"The Mighty God, even the Lord, hath spoken, and called the earth from the rising of the sun unto the going down thereof." Psalm 50:1

I guess that answered my question. He said the Mighty God even the Lord has spoken. It couldn't get much clearer than that. He really had my attention. The next day, I was scheduled to stand before a judge who had my life in his hands. I read on to verse 6:

"And the heavens shall declare His righteousness: for God is Judge Himself." Psalm 50:6

So the judge was not really the one I needed to be concerned about, because God is my Judge. But I was still a little worried because I was really in trouble. I read a little further to verse 15:

"And call upon Me in the day of trouble: I will deliver thee, and thou shalt glorify Me." Psalm 50:15

I said, "Oh Father, I'm in trouble, will You deliver me? I've been an evil and wicked man, but I repent." As I read on, I saw these words in verses 16-19:

"But unto the wicked God saith, what hast thou to do to declare My statutes, or that thou shouldest take My covenant in thy mouth? Seeing thou hatest instruction, and castest My words behind thee. When thou sawest a thief, then thou consentedst with him, and hast been partaker with adulterers. Thou givest thy mouth to evil, and thy tongue frameth deceit." Psalm 50:16-19

Every word I read was exactly who I'd been. When I saw thieves, I joined up with them. I lived a life as an adulterer and ran with others who were too. I had a filthy mouth and planned evil with it. God knew I wasn't that man anymore. I was praising Him continually and when I got to verse 23, I couldn't believe my eyes.

"Whoso offereth praise glorifieth Me: and to him that ordereth his conversation aright will I shew the salvation of God." Psalm 50:23

He said if I offered praise it would glorify Him. I had been praising Him since the day I came home. I had ordered my conduct aright and He said He would show me salvation. The next day I went to court and got a pardon. God is so awesome and His Word is truth and light.

The day we went for the plea bargain, I let Debbie go with me. She had never gone with me before. I knew that if the judge denied the plea bargain and sentenced us this could be the last time I would see her for a while. She waited across the street in the lawyer's office and we went into the courthouse. She prayed and asked God to tell her something. He told her to read Isaiah 55:7.

"Let the wicked forsake his way, and the unrighteous man his thoughts: and let him return unto the Lord, and He will have mercy upon him; and to our God, for he will abundantly pardon." Isaiah 55:7

I walked into the lawyer's office a few minutes after she prayed and Debbie asked, "What happened?"

"I got five years' probation and a five thousand dollar fine."

To us, that was…an abundant pardon, just like verse seven said. I went across the street, paid my five thousand dollar fine, and they said I would hear from a probation officer within a week.

That was in May of 1984. One week went by, a month, and then another month. I still never heard from the Board of Probation and Parole.

In August my nephew got married in Wisconsin. I knew I wasn't supposed to leave town without permission, but didn't have any one to ask permission from. So, I packed up Debbie and Richelle and we went to the wedding in Racine, Wisconsin and afterwards vacationed in that area for a week. It was the first time I had ever taken Debbie and Richelle anywhere.

When we came back, I went back to work. I wasn't reading my Bible yet but ended up working on a job with Chuck Hanna. Yep, Chuck—the Bible thumper—who taught Debbie the Bible after she became a Christian. Except now, I didn't consider him a Bible thumper, I saw him as a man of God. We worked together for a couple of years and he taught me how to study the Bible—how to fast, and pray, and how to get to know Jesus personally. Chuck and I have remained friends all these years and I still consider him one of my best friends.

What a privilege it is when I go somewhere to give my testimony and Chuck travels with me. I always introduce him as the guy who taught me how to study the Bible, fast, and pray. Not many men get the honor of walking in fellowship for over thirty years with the man who helped them grow in Christ.

One year had passed since I reported to the courts and paid my fine and still no word from the Board of Probation and Parole. One day in June of 1985 a guy showed up at my front door.

As I opened it, he handed me papers. "You've been served."

I was being sued by the guy we beat almost to death. I had seen God do so much already and felt such peace that I figured there was nothing He couldn't take care of. I just ignored the paperwork. One day I told my dad about it, and showed him the paperwork.

He said, "You need to get a lawyer, you can't let this go."

I spent hours every day in the Bible, and knew what Psalms 1:1 said, *"Blessed is the man that walketh not in the counsel of the ungodly, nor standeth in the way of sinners."*

So I asked Ray Hildebrand if he knew of any Christian lawyers, and he sent me to see Jim Smart. Jim said he would take the case, and as I left his office I told him that one year earlier, I had paid my fine but never heard from the Board of Probation and Parole.

He advised me to write them a letter. This is the letter I wrote to the State of Missouri Board of Probation and Parole:

June, 1985

To whom it may concern,

My name is William L. Corum. I was arrested September 5, 1982, and was charged with first degree assault with intent to kill and first degree burglary. The case lasted twenty months and in May of 1984, I entered a plea bargain and the charges were reduced. I was fined $5,000 and given five years of supervised probation.

It has been thirteen months since I paid my fine and reported as directed, but I have never been told where to report for my probation. I would like to be supervised, please contact me.

Sincerely,

William L. Corum

A few days after I wrote that letter, the authorities showed up on my front porch. They told me when and where to report. My first trip to the probation office was a little unnerving because I had no idea what to expect, since I had initiated the process.

My probation officer was a nice lady named Kay King. She told me that according to everything she could see, my paper work had been lost. If I had never contacted them, they probably would never have known. I thought, *Was this a mistake?*

You know the truth is, if I *hadn't* written that letter, I would still be looking over my shoulder. So I am very glad I did.

She questioned me about my past drug use—the types, amounts, frequency, etc.—and determined that I needed to go to drug rehab classes. This was not good news to me, because I had not used any drugs in over two years and was actually speaking at schools and churches against drugs and alcohol. I didn't want to act disappointed though, so I told her I would do whatever she requested. She gave me a guy's name and phone number to call who would evaluate me and set up the classes.

I said, "Can I go see him today? I don't want to take another day off work."

"He is really busy…there will be no way to get in today." She then told me my five years of supervised probation would start that day.

"Ma'am, I haven't had any supervision for the last thirteen months, and I haven't even had a traffic ticket."

"I'm sorry Bill…it starts today."

"That's fine, ma'am. I have changed and will do what you ask."

"I would like to believe you have changed, but every client tells me he's changed."

I thanked her and left. On the way home I prayed and asked the Lord if He would work it out for me to get in that day to see the man who was to evaluate me. When I got home, I called him.

"Sure, come over now."

I thanked the Lord for opening the door that day and I drove to his office. He was like a psychiatrist. He had big couches in his office and I was hoping he wouldn't ask me to lie down. My mind went back to the prison psychiatrist I hated. Under my breath, I asked God for grace and strength to get through this.

He told me to take a seat. "So, Bill…what have you been doing for the last ten or twenty years?"

"Are you kidding me?"

"No, I really want to hear."

"It would take me hours."

"Let's just start, and see how far we get."

After three hours, he told me he would like to hear more, but had another appointment coming up. I got up, thanked him for his time, and shook his hand. I wanted so badly to ask him if I had passed, or if he was going to recommend I take drug rehab classes, but I knew I shouldn't ask him.

Then he said it…"Bill, I have two different drug rehab classes I conduct."

My heart sank, I was so disappointed.

"I would like to have you come speak at both of them."

I couldn't believe my ears! What a mighty God I was serving! This guy wants me, a former drug user and pusher, to speak to his classes. WOW!

A few months later, I received a message to call my probation officer, Kay. I wondered what it was about. I had followed all the rules to the letter, I thought. When I called her, she asked me if I would be interested in speaking to a group of college students in a criminal justice class. She told me a friend of hers was a college professor and wanted someone from the *other side* of the law to come speak to the class.

When I arrived, the professor told me they had heard judges, lawyers, police officers, and prosecutors. They were interested in hearing a criminal's point of view. I told the professor I would love to speak that day, but there were some conditions.

"What are the conditions?" he asked.

"On April 15, 1983, I said, 'God if You can change Bill Corum, I will live my life for You.' I have had a radical change in my life. I cannot, and will not, tell that story and leave God and His Son out."

The professor told me whatever I wanted to say was okay, and we went to the class. I had spoken for only a few minutes when I pulled my Bible from my briefcase. I opened it up and began quoting Scripture in that secular college. After I finished, the professor asked me if would speak at the class again the next year.

FROM POT TO PRAISE

Not too long before I was a Christian, I told a friend of mine I might quit using cocaine someday. I might quit drinking. I might quit cheating on my wife, and even go to church someday, but I would never quit smoking weed. Pot was most assuredly my drug of choice.

I am a hyper person by nature and pot slowed me down. I used to go to a lot of professional fights, and if I smoked some good weed first, those three-minute rounds seemed like ten. If there was ever a person who couldn't stop smoking marijuana, it was me. God delivered me and I am thankful. I can talk to anyone addicted to pot and consider myself an expert, because I smoked ten to fifteen joints a day.

Christmas 1982 and Thanksgiving 1983

In 1982, Debbie had been a Christian for a year and looked so happy. I carried two pistols on me in this picture and would shoot you for looking at me wrong. She had no business being with me. The picture on the right was taken seven months after I asked Jesus to change me. The Bible says the eyes are the windows of the soul. My soul was extremely dark in 1982.

After I asked the Lord to change me and was back living at home with Debbie, she asked me to go with her to a Bible study she attended. The people hosting the study, and those who attended it, welcomed me with open arms. They were excited to meet me and finally get to lay eyes on the person they had prayed for. I told them that night, that if I had known they were praying for me before I was saved, I might have blown their house up.

Debbie and I became very close friends with the couple hosting the Bible study. We were at their house one night a few months later when Kay gave me a book that changed my life—*There's Dynamite in Praise*, by Don Gossett. I highly recommend it. In this book the author explains the power of praise and how praise is a key that unlocks doors nothing else will unlock.

Praise is the most mentioned commandment in the Bible for a good reason. Psalms 22:3 says the Lord "inhabits" our praise. Inhabits means dwells, stays, lives, etc., so when we praise Him, He comes. If He comes, He wants to stay. How do you get in His presence and stay there? We can achieve that by continually praising Him.

I have looked for joy in a multitude of ways in my life. I bought eleven brand new cars in thirteen years. I used drugs, drank alcohol, bought jewelry, chased women, and they only brought me temporary joy. I have now found joy unspeakable.

Psalms 16:11 says *In His presence is Fullness of Joy*. I experienced what I thought was joy in a lot of different ways, but had never experienced Fullness of Joy until I was in the presence of the Lord. I have learned that the key to staying in His presence and, therefore, having Fullness of Joy, is to praise Him.

I remember my mother telling me a few years after I had been serving the Lord, "Bill, do you know why you are as close to the Lord as you are?"

"Why's that, Mom?"

"You have learned the secret of praising Him."

I had only been a Christian for two or three years when she told me that. I meditated on what she said for a while, and came to a conclusion. This is my own opinion, not something I can back up with Scripture.

I believe there are Christians who have walked in the light for twenty or thirty years but have never found the key or the secret of praise. Then there are those who have found that secret in the first few months of their walk with Christ. Are both of them going to make it into Heaven? I believe they will without a doubt.

I believe that the person who is praising the Lord has the advantage of being in the presence of the Lord and experiencing the joy of the Lord. The Bible says *The joy of the Lord is my strength*. So when I am going through a rough time and feeling very weak, He is my strength.

I have been praising Him now for over thirty years, and have found strength when I am weak. I have enjoyed Him walking beside me continually, because He is living in my praise. And it has been comforting to know that I have a Best Friend who is all loving, all powerful, and all wise. Praise the Lord!!

BACK IN THE STREETS

Not long after I became a Christian, Debbie and I started going into the streets to witness. We went into the darkest part of the city where the prostitutes and adult bookstores were. Sometimes we stayed out there for hours just walking, praying and witnessing to whoever would listen. It probably wasn't wise taking our nine-year-old daughter with us, but God protected us in our ignorance.

I felt like I needed to do something, to make up for all the wrong I had done in the streets. I was a brand-new Christian and didn't know that I didn't need to earn God's love. His love is unconditional and when we say "yes" to Jesus, we don't have to do penance.

We had some divine appointments on those streets. One of those was with a young man named Sam. He lived in a very dangerous, old apartment building. He did whatever he could to make enough money to pay the rent. He was eighteen and had spent years of his life in mental institutions and juvenile homes. His father abused him as a child and he was terribly damaged because of that abuse. His life was in constant turmoil and he lived every day in much fear.

I sent Sam to several rehab centers and Christian programs, trying to get him some help. He always headed right back to the street life and the drugs and alcohol. One time, I told him there was a program that could change his life if I could get him in it.

Teen Challenge was started by David Wilkerson back in the 50's and is one of the best treatment programs around. It took me a while to get Sam in because of the long waiting list. Finally, after weeks of phone calls and letters, he was approved and was going to Little Rock Arkansas. I was excited for him. I just knew this was going to be the program to turn him around. I bought him some clothes, gave him money, and put him on the Greyhound.

The very next day my phone rang. It was Sam. "Hi Bill, how ya doin'?"

"Sam, how are you using the phone?" I knew that they weren't allowed to use the phone for the first few days they were there.

"Oh . . . I left. I didn't like it there, Bill . . . I'm in a motel right by your house."

"Stay right there. I'm coming over to kill you." I obviously wasn't going to kill him, but I felt like it.

This kind of thing went on for many years. Sam went through countless programs—some he graduated from, and some he quit. Sam wanted God on his terms not God's. Men say to me sometimes, 'I tried God and He didn't work.' And I always reply, "He didn't work the way you tried Him."

I prayed for grace to get through all my trials with Sam, and learned how Jesus must feel waiting on us. Sam is serving the Lord today. His heart is for the down and outers because that is where he came from and he wants to give back. He travels all over the country preaching and teaching to those who are going through the kind of things he went through. We have remained friends for almost thirty years now. I love him and consider him my brother in Christ.

RESCUE MISSION

During the time we did street ministry, we also volunteered at the Kansas City Rescue Mission two or three nights a week. We helped serve the meals to the homeless and wash dishes. On occasion, I got to share my testimony with those who came into the chapel.

I will never forget the night a man came through the line, handed me his dirty dishes, and asked me, "Why do you wash my dirty dishes?"

"Because Jesus loves you, and so do I." I replied.

He asked me if he could talk to me later. When we got together, he told me he was a doctor. He had lost his family and began drinking. He became an alcoholic and, over time, lost his practice and everything he had. He became homeless and had lived in the streets for years.

I met with him for several weeks and he finally made a decision to try Jesus and get his life back on track. He then returned home and reconciled with family. He was a changed man.

The mission used to be at 5th and Walnut Street down in the River Market area. The river is just a few blocks north. On the banks of the river was an area called hobo jungle. The homeless guys built houses out of plywood scraps, cardboard, or whatever other discarded items they found. I would leave the mission and walk through the jungle to share Christ with those guys. Sometimes I sat and drank coffee with them. I always prayed and asked God to protect me, because they sometimes used an old paint can over a campfire to brew the coffee.

One year, at Thanksgiving, we served a big meal at the mission for all the homeless. Usually, the guys living in hobo jungle wouldn't come up to the mission. They had their own food and didn't want our help. But I decided to go and invite them to come for turkey dinner anyway. I felt like the Lord told me to take my daughter with me. She was ten years old at the time and, although it wasn't a very safe place, I knew that if God told me to take her there was nothing to worry about.

When we served the turkey and all the trimmings, several men from hobo jungle showed up. One guy in particular, I knew God brought there for a purpose. He told me the only reason he showed up was because some guy came into the jungle with his little girl and invited them to come. He didn't even know it was me, and I never told him.

UNION PLUMBER

In 1985, God told me it was time to go back into the plumber's union. The last time I worked steady in the union was in 1975. When I quit, the boss told me to call if I ever wanted a job; I called him ten years later and he hired me.

The first job he sent me on, I ran into a guy I used to sell large amounts of coke to. God had prepared me and I was ready to be around people who knew me from the past.

I had an awesome time telling him how God changed me, and that I was not the same Bill Corum he had known. I will never forget it because we stood and talked, and construction workers were walking right past us the whole time. I went home and told Debbie it was like God put an invisible shield around us and the other workers couldn't see us. I was so bold telling this guy the whole story of my conversion, how I felt, and about the tremendous peace I had.

I must have talked to him for thirty minutes, and no one told us to get back to work. I knew God set up that divine appointment.

My boss on that job was a young man named Pete Olson. We became pretty good friends and I shared the Lord with him several times. I tried my best to be an example to him but never saw him surrender to Jesus. That was in 1985 and I didn't see Pete too often after I left that job.

When I ran into him in 2010 coming out of a restaurant, his face was shining brightly and he was all dressed up.

"Where have you been all dressed up, Pete?"

"I've been to church. I gave my heart to the Lord a few years ago."

What a thrill it was for me to hear that. I wondered if some of the seeds I had sown might have influenced his decision to follow Christ. Pete and I have seen each other since then and he is a man of God.

Many men saw a changed Bill Corum over the next few years. If I asked the Lord every morning in my time with Him to bring someone to share Christ with, He never failed to do that. All we have to do is ask...*you have not because you ask not*.

THE PRISON PROPHECY

In 1985 we had a conference at our church, and there were a lot of people from out of town. I was waiting for my wife to come out of the restroom, and one of the visitors walked past me and then came back. "Excuse me, sir."

"Are you talking to me?" I asked him.

"Yes. I just saw something on the back of your head; it looked like bars...prison bars. They were on the back of your head, like that's something in your past. Does that mean anything to you?"

"Yes, it does. I've been in prison."

"They were gold, and I think it means God is going to give you a golden opportunity to go into prisons. He will open every door He wants you to go through, and close any door where He doesn't want you."

"What's your name?" I asked this stranger.

"Kevin Prosch."

About that time, Debbie walked up and I said to him, "Tell her what you just told me."

He didn't tell her, but looked her right in the eyes and very quietly said, "God wants you to know...you are not a barren woman."

He turned and walked away as Debbie started crying. I wanted to go find him and punch him for making her cry. She told me that the devil had tormented her, telling her she was barren and that she would never bear any fruit for the Lord. She had never told anyone that, so it had to be God.

I wouldn't see Kevin again for years, but was convinced that what he said was true. I wasn't even sure I wanted to go into a prison, let alone *prisons*. I made a vow when I got out in the 60's, never to go back, and I didn't. I stupidly came very close to spending the rest of my life there, but God delivered me this time. I would be happy to never see another jail or prison again.

About two years later, God opened the door for me to start going into prisons with Bill Glass. I have continued doing that now for over twenty-six years. I have been in prisons and jails all over America, and even other parts of the world. Only once in the last twenty-six years was I denied access to a jail. I have always remembered what God told me through Kevin. After they said I couldn't come in because of my record, I walked away with total peace, knowing He didn't want me in that one.

When I ministered in a prison for the first time, I didn't want to leave those guys and go home. God so broke my heart for the inmates that I knew this was my life's calling. The Lord confirmed His calling to me with this verse:

> "The Spirit of the Lord God is upon me; because the Lord hath anointed me to preach good tidings unto the meek; he hath sent me to bind up the brokenhearted, to proclaim liberty to the captives, and the opening of the prison to them that are bound."
> Isaiah 61:1

COMING CLEAN

Since God healed our marriage, Debbie and I believed there weren't any marriages beyond hope. Our marriage had been a mess. I seldom came home, and when I did, I didn't treat her very well. Every time I came home, it didn't matter if I had been gone a day or for weeks, she asked me if I had been with another woman. I always lied and told her no. The truth was, there were other women almost every time I left her. I even brought diseases home to her, and would lie about how I might have caught them.

After I came to Jesus, she asked me one last time to tell her the truth. I lied and told her I had never been with anyone else. She went into the bedroom and talked to the Lord about it.

"I know he's been with other women."

The Lord spoke to her and said, "You know it, and I know it, but if any man be in Christ he is a new creation. Can you trust Me on this?"

Debbie made up her mind that day to never ask me again and to honor the fact that I said I hadn't cheated on her. She trusted what God told her.

After her conversation with the Lord, two or three times people asked her if I had been unfaithful to her. She told them no. I cringed every time I thought the subject might come up. Finally, I told the Lord that if she ever told someone I hadn't cheated again, I would tell her the truth no matter what the consequences.

I prayed like everything that she would never say it. But one day, while talking with someone, she did. After the person left our house, she was getting ready to go to bed and I asked her if we could talk.

She and I sat down and I asked her if we could pray before we talked. I confessed all to her, crying through most of my confession. I told her how unfaithful I had been to her and asked for her forgiveness. I also told her there was something else bothering me and I needed to get it off my chest.

I told her that keeping this from her had been tormenting me in more ways than one. Whenever I spoke somewhere, I would start worrying before I even got there that I might run into one of the women from my past. I couldn't go on in my walk as a Christian another day unless I came clean.

She cried and told me she already knew. The Lord showed her a long time ago and after watching my life for over two years, there was no doubt I had changed.

Often, when I work with men in prison who have given their lives to Christ, they ask me if I will call their wife and tell her they have changed.

"How many years did you cheat on her and beat on her?"

"Fifteen."

"Do you think she is going to think you've changed, just by me telling her?"

I tell them that the people in their life need to *see* the change, not hear about it. Anyone can say they have changed, but the people they are around every day really know the truth. A person can go to church every Sunday and their pastor doesn't know if they've changed. He only sees them for a couple hours on Sunday.

If you are reading this, and you have changed your life, you're walking with the Lord, and are trying to convince someone of the change...stop. Don't say another word about the changed person you've become. Let them see the change, not hear about it. It is like telling someone you love them, but your actions don't show it. St. Francis of Assisi is supposed to have said, "Preach the Gospel always; if necessary use words." In other words, let your walk speak louder than your big mouth.

FALSE PROPHET?

I was back in the union and landed a good job inside for the winter. We were on the big Hallmark cards building down in Crown Center in Kansas City. It was cold outside and I would be working in the heat all winter in a tee shirt.

The church I attended was having a week of meetings and we were going every night. We were also on a seven-day fast. It was the first time I had ever fasted, and I was blown away by the grace I had. Our pastor invited a guy in from out of town, and before every meeting he prophesied over people. I copped an attitude about how he did it, and thought he was a con man. At the end of the meeting one night, our pastor got up and instructed us to seek the Lord and ask Him to show us if we had hidden sin in our heart.

The next morning while praying, I asked Him, "God, do I have any hidden sin in my heart?"

"You have the sin of doubt and unbelief."

"What is that supposed to mean, Lord?"

He told me to read I Thessalonians 5:20, so I opened up my Bible.

"Despise not prophesyings." Just those three words, they were real clear. There was no way I could get out of it. It was the guy at church last night...I had been despising him for sure.

Lord, if You're talking about the guy from church...uh...if he's Your servant, please forgive me. Please clean up my heart.

I went to work that morning and sat in the car with a friend of mine who was also a Christian. I was fasting and praying, and felt close to God. It was time to go into the job trailer and start our day. I didn't want to be around all the dirty jokes the other plumbers told, or the filthy pictures on the walls. I told my friend what I wished I could do.

"I would like to just walk in there and whisper, "Jesus," and they would all fall over."

We got out of the truck and went to work.

That night before the service, Mike called John Paul up again.

"The man in the white sweater, and the lady next to you…I believe she's your wife. Will you both stand up?"

I started sweating and looked around to see if there was another white sweater. There wasn't. So we stood up.

"In the past, you have used your fists to get people's attention. You've kicked doors down to get to them. God is going to give you the ability to speak one word as soft as a feather and people will fall over."

I lost it…I cried like a baby. No one in that church knew I had been an enforcer. No one knew I was on paper for kicking a door down. My friend who heard me say earlier that morning, 'I wish I could just whisper, "Jesus," and they would fall over', didn't go to our church.

I went away that night and was completely humbled and broken, knowing that God uses who He chooses and I had better keep my mouth shut. I wish I could tell you I have never had any more problems with my mouth, but I can't. In Proverbs 21:23 it says, *"Whoso keepeth his mouth and his tongue keepeth his soul from trouble."*

PEACE THAT REMAINS

I heard that the guy I used to run the Country Club Plaza with back in the 70's was getting baptized and I went to watch. There was another friend of his who was there to watch also.

He asked someone, "Who's that big guy over there?"

"That is Bill Corum, he was Kenny's cocaine partner."

Kenny dealt to people I didn't know, and I dealt to people he didn't know. This guy had been one of Kenny's customers. He came over and started talking to me, and said he had a desire to know and follow Jesus. I got excited about the possibility of helping him to do that. I gave him my phone number. He didn't call for several weeks. After we became good friends, he told me he didn't call because he knew that if he started hanging out with me he would have to change his lifestyle.

We became very close and saw each other several times a week. I told him how I was transformed by renewing my mind, and taking Ray Hildebrand's advice.

One day, Tom said, "Why don't you stop being so religious, and watch a football game some Sunday with me?"

"Okay I will."

"You will?" he said, with a glimmer of hope in his eyes.

"I will, if they'll show the beer commercials with a guy hugging a toilet throwing up, or beating up his wife, or wrecking his car. Because that's the true, honest, just report of alcohol. Not the one that says you'll be the life of the party, and leave with the sexiest looking girl. There would be no alcohol sales if they told the truth about what it does to you, so they have to tell lies that portray it as something good."

I felt peace for the first time in my life and did not want to lose it. I found the secret to it in Philippians.

> "Be careful for nothing; but in everything by prayer and supplication with thanksgiving let your requests be made known unto God."

> "And the peace of God, which passeth all understanding, shall keep your hearts and minds through Christ Jesus. .

> "Finally, brethren, whatsoever things are true, whatsoever things are honest, whatsoever things are just, whatsoever things are pure, whatsoever things are lovely, whatsoever things are of good report; if there be any virtue, and if there be any praise, think on these things.

> "Those things, which ye have both learned, and received, and heard, and seen in me, do: and the God of peace shall be with you." Philippians 4:6-9

I went to visit a pastor friend of mine one day and his wife said he had gone to the doctor to get something for his anxiety. I asked her what was wrong. She told me that when he read the paper or watched the news, he got stressed.

I said, "I could've saved him a doctor bill; he needs to quit watching TV, and reading the newspaper." This was the same thing I had shared with Tom a few weeks earlier. I wonder how many people are on medication, like my pastor friend, as a result of watching and reading all the bad reports on TV and in the newspaper.

UNION PEACEMAKER

One day, I got a call from the union business agent and he said, "Hey, Bill, we're having some trouble down on the new GM plant and need you to go there."

"Jim, I don't carry a baseball bat anymore, I carry a Bible."

"I don't care what you carry. Your presence on the job will help."

I told him I needed to pray about it and would call him back. But before I called him back with my answer, I prayed and fasted. I had carried out a lot of contract work for the unions and knew what they expected. I had a reputation for getting the job done, but was through with that life and wouldn't use my old skills anymore. God would show me how to do it His way.

Three days later, I called Jim and told him that I would go.

"Good, we will set you up as an area foreman, and you will be working for Dravo Company on the underground piping... they're an out-of-town contractor."

I was anxious to see what God had in store for me. I knew He was up to something, but I would just have to trust Him and see what it was.

I had been working inside at Crown Center where I wore a tee shirt every day. But I would need to wear my thermal underwear to go down by the river where the new General Motors plant was being built. It was November and starting to get cold. Even though I knew the working conditions were going to be brutal, I was excited.

It was the biggest job that had ever been done in the Midwest. Over 1.2 billion dollars; the building would be seventy-eight acres under one roof. It was almost twice the size of the largest building in Kansas City.

I will never forget that very first day on the job. I went into the trailer to warm up, when two plumbers I didn't know walked in and started talking. They were going so fast, they sounded like a machine gun.

"We know who you are, you're Superman...we've heard all about you...wow, we couldn't wait for you to get here!! We know you're going to get things straightened out around here. Everybody on the crew has been talking about what would happen when you got here. We're glad you're here, Superman. They say you don't put up with any nonsense."

I am certain my response to their flattering welcome blew their minds. "The Bible says, blessed are the peacemakers, for they shall be called the children of God."

"WHAT?" one of them said.

"The Bible says, blessed are the peacemakers, for they shall be called the children of God. I came here to make peace...but not the way you were expecting."

They turned around and walked out of the trailer, shaking their heads. They were totally confused because they expected the guy they'd heard about to use physical force to get things squared away. What took place over the next two years surprised everyone.

My tract, *Heart of Stone*, was originally titled *Death Sentence* when I wrote it in 1985. Proverbs 14:27 says to avoid the snares of death we must fear the Lord. I had been facing life in prison, but the real sentence I faced was death, because I didn't fear the Lord. I carried those tracts in my shirt pocket so that the only word you could see was DEATH.

As area foreman, and later general foreman, I rode all over that seventy-eight acres on a four wheeler with that word DEATH peeking over the top of my pocket. At peak, there were over five thousand men on that job, and hardly ever a day went by without some guy I didn't know flagging me down and asking, "What is that?" pointing to my pocket.

I would hand them one and say, "Here, read it; it's the story of my life."

A couple of days later, he would flag me down again—this time, to ask me questions about how Jesus changed my life.

After we got all of the underground piping in, I was appointed by the union as the general foreman on the above-ground piping job. It was a 17.5-million-dollar job. I now worked for Limbach National Piping Company out of Pontiac, Michigan. Many interesting things took place over the next year that I worked for them.

FREE AT LAST

One of those interesting things was that God gave me a revelation about something. We had Motorola two-way radios on the job and they cost about fifteen hundred dollars each. The company I worked for had about thirty, but a couple were broken, so we borrowed a couple from another company. When it came time to return them, my boss told me, "When you take those radios back, take our broken ones and keep the good ones."

One of the men who worked for me overheard him, and came over and said, "Are you going to do it, Bill?"

"No."

As I said no to him, I got a revelation about something. I whirled around and stuck my finger in his chest. He jumped back.

"You know what else, Steve?"

"What?"

"I not only don't *want* to lie anymore. I don't have to." I went on to tell him, "I can still cheat on Debbie, but I don't have to anymore. I don't have to steal, I am totally free."

I had been going to church for over three years. I read my Bible, prayed daily, and was experiencing peace like never before. But not until that moment, did I realize I was truly free. I knew the verse in John 8:36 says; *Whom the Son sets free is free indeed*. This was different. I really knew it, not just in my head, but in my heart. I knew there had to be more in the Bible that explained why I felt so free.

I started asking God to show me through His Word. Not long after that, the Lord revealed it to me:

> *"Know ye not, that to whom ye yield yourselves servants to obey, his servants ye are to whom ye obey; whether of sin unto death, or of obedience unto righteousness?"* Romans 6:16

I had been a slave to the devil and was obedient to him, so I would lie, steal, and cheat on my wives and girlfriends. I did anything he told me to do. Now I was submitted to God, and didn't have to do those things anymore. It was truly a revelation and it changed my whole way of thinking.

You may think you're not a slave to the devil, or to God; you're just doing your own thing. That would be fine, except the words Jesus spoke say you can't do your own thing.

> *"He that is not with Me is against Me; and he that gathereth not with Me scattereth abroad."* Matthew 12:30

In other words, there is no such thing as doing your own thing... you are either serving God or the devil.

If you don't know the freedom I am talking about, you can know it right now. Ask Jesus to forgive you of your sins and tell Him you want to know true freedom. You don't have to pray any fancy prayers. He wants to be your best friend, and you can just talk to Him like you would one of your friends. If you ask Him into your heart, get a Bible and start reading in the Book of John. The Bible is the only Book ever written where the author will stand beside you and explain it to you. Ask Him to come close every time you read His Word and help you understand it.

A FINAL CONFRONTATION

It didn't take me long to find out the real reason the union wanted me down on that job. There was a lot of controversy over whose work was whose, and one of the unions had a guy on the jobsite who weighed over three hundred pounds, and was their enforcer. This guy had the foulest mouth—he would cuss his own men out and they wouldn't say anything back.

Jerry and I had already been in several confrontations since I arrived on the job. The fact that he couldn't get me to lose my temper was making him hotter. It wasn't easy for me to take the abusive language from him, but the word says, *"And the servant of the Lord must not strive; but be gentle unto all men, apt to teach, patient."* II Timothy 2:24

Before I became a Christian I had a reputation as a guy who didn't take anything from anyone. I would always, *always* get even, no matter how long it took. Now I was on a job with five thousand men, and was letting everyone see me get pushed around. I even remember times there, when my son questioned why I took some of the things I did. I was studying God's Word and trying to live by it. It was telling me that the man God would look at was the man who trembled at His Word (Isaiah 66:2). I had walked with Him long enough to know His Word was truth and I wanted the truth. I wanted to do everything His Word commanded me to do. James 1:22 says, *If you just hear it and don't do it, you deceive yourself.* I don't know about you, but I don't like being deceived. And I especially don't want to deceive myself. So I live by every Word.

One day he and I really got into a heated argument, and I had to pray in the Spirit to keep from blasting him. I let him cuss me out like I was a cur dog, and say all kinds of things against me, but thought of the Scripture that says, *A soft answer turns away wrath.* I said something very calm and quietly to him. He just turned, threw up his arms, and walked away. Many of the foremen and other men who were working on the job stood fairly close when he and I stood nose to nose.

Word spread quickly throughout the jobsite that we were probably going to fight that day. A few minutes after our run-in, Steve, one of the foremen I had working for me, came up and said, "Bill, I'm going to quit if you don't put that guy in his place."

"When your enemy is thirsty, give him a drink of water."

"What is *that* supposed to mean?"

I told Steve that when somebody is your enemy and you're nice to them, it confuses them and they don't know how to handle it.

"That don't make any sense and I'm going to quit if you don't do something."

"Steve, you're one of my best foremen and I need you. If you quit, that won't help anything. Please trust me. I know what I'm doing with this guy."

Less than an hour had passed since the three-hundred-pound mauler and I faced off, and he called me on the radio. "Corum, where are you?"

"I'm in the penthouse of section eight."

"Stay there. I'll be right over."

Everyone had been waiting for this since the day I came on the job. All of the foremen carrying radios heard him call me out, men from all over the job headed for section eight.

"You still up there, Corum?"

"Yes sir, I am."

"I'm at the bottom of the stairs."

As I started down the long flight of steel steps leading to ground level of section eight, my old dark side tried to take over. I resorted back to my old way of thinking. My hands were empty and Jerry was standing right at the bottom of the stairs. Not a good place for him to be, because when I got close enough, I would put both hands on the railings and swing my two hundred and forty-five pounds up and catch him right in his fat face with both feet. Before he hit the ground, I would pound him senseless.

Then, I thought, *Jesus, You said love your enemies...now would You help me love him?*

When I got to the bottom of the stairs, Jerry reached his hand out to shake. "Forgive me, Bill, I'm sorry. I just found out I'm sick and I was out of line."

"You don't know what that means to me for you to ask for forgiveness. I know you're not a man who does that. I forgive you. What's wrong? You said you're sick."

"I just found out today I have cancer of the tongue."

Many times in the Bible it says Jesus had compassion on them. I was moved with compassion as I said to him, "Jerry, the Bible says, we should lay hands on the sick and pray for them. Can I pray for you?"

"Yes, you can, Bill."

So with half the men on the job peering out from behind trailers, columns, and piles of pipe, expecting to see this fight between the bouncer and Superman, I prayed for Big Jerry. A few months later, Jerry had a heart attack and none of his own men went to see him.

I went to the hospital to see him and took him a Bible, and prayed for him. As I was leaving, he asked me to come back towards the bed, and he reached up and gave me a hug. That was monumental for the big guy.

AFRICA? NO WAY

The church we attended was supporting a mission project in Africa and they decided to send a few men from our church to check out the work being done. One of the men going asked me if I would like to go with them.

"I'd really like to go, but I can't," I said.

"What do you mean, you can't?"

"I'm on paper and can't even go to Kansas without permission."

I knew for a fact, I wouldn't be able to leave the country. On top of that, the trip was super expensive and I wasn't a drug dealer anymore, I was a plumber. My wife and I couldn't afford for me to be gone seventeen days to Africa and Israel.

"What if God made it possible? Then would you go?"

"If God makes it possible, I'll go for sure."

I said it with confidence because I knew it couldn't happen. I had never met my new probation officer Dan Hernandez. I just mailed my reports to him each month. I knew this guy wouldn't let me go.

I went down to his office and asked his receptionist if I could see him. She told me that my old probation officer had eighty clients, but Mr. Hernandez had over eight hundred. There would be no way I could get in.

"Would you mind just asking him, please?"

She dialed his office and told him I wanted to see him, then said, "Oh, okay, sir."

She looked at me, completely flabbergasted. "Mr. Hernandez says for you to come on back."

I had been sitting there praying for favor. God is good. I went back to his office and introduced myself as I looked at the mountainous stacks of papers on his desk.

"I know you're very busy, sir. I appreciate you taking time to see me."

I told him about the trip to Africa and asked him if he would give me permission to take this trip with the men from my church. He peered around the stacks of paper. "Bill, you can't even go to Kansas without permission...so no, you can't leave the country."

"I didn't think so, sir. I just wanted to ask."

I shook his hand, thanked him again for his time, and headed for the door.

"Bill...if you will write a letter to the judge who sentenced you, and he gives you permission to apply for a passport, I will let you go."

"Oh, thank you, Mr. Hernandez."

I went right to work on it. I wrote the letter, and Judge Carl Gumm gave me permission to apply for a passport. I put my passport application, the fees, and the letter from the judge in the mail. I sent it off and called all the guys I was supposed to go with and told them I was going. One guy told me not to get too excited. He said the trip was only three weeks away, and it took a long time to get a passport. Then he *really* discouraged me. "It's Christmas time, the mail is moving slow, and I doubt you'll get it in time."

I went to the mailbox on my front porch exactly five days later, and there was my passport. Five is the number of Grace. I stood on the porch and cried. I told God, "You are truly a God of miracles. You must really want me in Africa for something."

We were in the air for many hours on the trip to Africa and I got to know all ten men a little better. At one point while sitting with Charles, he asked me about my life. I told him about the high-speed police chase in the Corvette in Cape Girardeau. He looked at me very intently and asked, "Did that chase go over into McClure, Illinois?"

I was in a state of unbelief. "Yeah, how did you know that?"

"My dad was the Chief of Police and that was the talk of the town for years."

I couldn't believe it. Here I sat on a plane going to Africa...with a guy whose dad chased me twenty-five years earlier.

The day after we arrived in Johannesburg, South Africa, I found out one of the reasons God wanted me there. He was getting ready to circumcise my heart.

This was part of the men I traveled to Africa with in 1987.
The miracle was that I was on paper, and my PO let me leave
the country. I always talked with my hands, must have
picked that up from my Italian friends. Capiche?

I was walking along a path with several of the men I came to Africa with, when I almost stepped on a grasshopper. I reached down and threw it aside. It flew into a small puddle of water. I asked the men I was with to wait. They stopped and I walked over and lifted the grasshopper out of the water and put it in the grass.

When I caught back up with them, they asked me, "Why did you do that?"

"I didn't want that grasshopper to drown." I began to cry.

They asked me why I was crying.

"Four years ago, I would kill someone for money. Now I don't want a bug to die."

> "A new heart also will I give you, and a new Spirit will I put within you: and I will take away the stony heart out of your flesh, and I will give you an heart of flesh." Ezekiel 36:26

This was one of the biggest miracles of all—seeing God take my heart of stone and give me a heart of flesh. He brought me to Africa to do it.

But there must be more....

In the evenings we ate our meals with all the people living on the farm. Afterward, we went into the community center living room and talked, prayed, and sang praises to the Lord. Every man on the trip with me was either a pastor, prophet, or in some type of leadership. All except one—yours truly.

On the last night we were there, each one of the men in our group had a prophetic word for the people living there. Everyone, except me. I told them I wasn't a prophet, a preacher, or any type of leader, I was just a plumber. I hadn't had any dreams or heard God tell me anything about any of them. Actually, I felt intimidated by those men who had all those profound things to say.

I told them the only thing I knew was that the love of Christ was what saved me. I also knew that even though I had been a hopeless drug addict and a selfish, unpredictable man, Jesus Christ loved me. He loved me enough to die for me and give me life. I told them, I Corinthians 13:8 says *Love never fails*, and if they loved the natives they were trying to reach, they would be victorious.

The people living there on the farm told us about the dissidents living in the mountains. They had been killing whites in Africa since the war ended in 1980. They were heavily armed defectors who broke away from their army, and were a serious threat to our friends in Zimbabwe.

The dissidents had come on the property not long before we arrived and had kept everyone at gunpoint all night. They left before daylight, and our friends were spared. We prayed for them and kept them in prayer after we returned back to the States.

Part of our itinerary on the return trip was stopping in Israel for three days. One of the men in our group had done missionary work there for years, and he knew every sight to go see. He took us to places you would never get to go with a tour guide. Only God could have set up what I experienced when we traveled to Masada.

Masada is an ancient fortification in the southern district of Israel, on top of an isolated rock plateau on the eastern edge of the Judean desert, overlooking the Dead Sea. We drove past the Dead Sea on the way there. I was disappointed because it was a very cloudy day—bad for pictures. Charles pointed to the Judean hills telling us those were the caves David hid in while running from Saul. I snapped pictures in spite of the clouds.

When we got back home and got the pictures developed, I couldn't believe what I saw on one. It was a picture of the Dead Sea I'd snapped while Charles told us about the caves on the other side of the road. Light beams shone down through the clouds brightly; they made a streak of light across the water.

"Debbie, look at this picture of the Dead Sea."

"Oh wow, that's really cool."

"It's more than cool, honey…there just has to be a Scripture for this."

This is the picture I took that day, look at the beams of light coming from HIS chambers.

The more I looked at the picture, the more I knew it was God. I really felt in my heart there was a Scripture connected to the scene I captured. I couldn't get it off my mind. I kept praying and asking God where it was, and He led me to Psalms 104:3. One version of the Bible says, *He lays the beams of His upper chambers on the waters*. There is no doubt in my mind that David was sitting in one of those caves hiding from Saul, and saw what I saw in the picture I took.

God so touched my heart in Africa. I felt He was calling me back to help build two weirs (dams), and that I was to take Debbie and Richelle with me. This would even be more of a miracle, because I wasn't going to ask my probation officer if I could take a short trip, I would ask him to let me move there for months. I also knew the dangers involved in taking my wife and daughter to a place where dissidents were killing people daily. I asked Debbie if she would pray about going. I knew she heard from God and He would tell her if it was safe for me to take them.

After a fairly short time, she said the Lord had spoken to her and told her to submit to me. That freaked me out, because I hadn't even been praying. I was relying on Debbie. Now I had to get serious and really hear for myself, and there could be no mistakes about it. I was sure that if He told us to go, He would protect us. God sovereignly put me on a fast. He made it clear to me that we were to go.

God was going to really have to step up to the plate on this one. Our airline tickets were going to be twenty-one hundred dollars each. I was still paying child support and we had a house payment, utilities, and other expenses. Overall, it would cost over ten thousand dollars for us to take this trip. I was a new enough Christian that I wasn't sure even God could pull this one off.

Then all of a sudden, one man offered to pay my child support for as long as we were gone. "I will pay it for one month or one year, as long as you're gone."

We would come home from church, and find one-hundred-dollar bills stuck in our Bibles. Money came in the mail, with no return address. People always say God's ways are mysterious...not to

Him. He supernaturally put that trip together and we were able to go with money to spare.

At the time, I was running the paint kitchen at the new GM plant, working overtime, and making the most money I'd ever made legally. Some of the men on the job found out I was going to Africa, and asked me how much I was going to make over there. When I told them I was going as a missionary and wouldn't get paid, they couldn't comprehend it. They wondered why someone would quit a good job and go work for free. I knew my rewards would be in Heaven. One of the hardest things I did when I left the GM plant, was leave my best plumber...my oldest son Billy.

I hired him to work with me at the GM plant, and he came on board when we started building the paint kitchen. He was an apprentice, but I was able to get him journeyman wages. That was just one more blessing from the Lord, because he was married and could use that extra money because they were starting a family.

Billy is really good with math so I put him in charge of figuring all the bends on the stainless steel pipe. I heard through the grapevine there were some old timers who thought he was too young and inexperienced. There were forty lines coming out of the paint kitchen going to the booths. In order for them to look right, every bend had to be perfect. None of the experienced paint line guys thought he could do the job.

There were miles of pipe to be bent and it had to look good to be approved by General Motors. It was a huge undertaking and he impressed everyone there with his ability to figure and make the bends. When the job was finished, the old timers all had a meal together and the main course was crow.

It was good getting to work with my son, and letting him see his dad as a Christian instead of a man totally out of control.

THE POWER OF A FAST

God spoke to me about a fast before I went to Africa the second time. He told me the day to start and the day to stop. It was frightening and I was sure I heard wrong. He told me this was to be a water-only fast for twenty-one days. I was doing everything I could to prove I didn't hear right.

One Sunday, the Lord told me there were two other men I was supposed to fast with, and I should talk to them at church. Church was over and I hadn't seen anybody who I thought would want to go three weeks without food.

Ron Freeman and I were scheduled the next night to speak at McCune Home for Boys. He was supposed to drive, but I wanted to verify it. As I walked up to him and his wife, he said, "Hey, Bill, I'll come by your house tomorrow night to pick you up."

"Why don't you come early and eat dinner with us?"

"I'll come early...but won't eat with you."

"Why? You don't like Debbie's cooking?" I laughed.

"No, it's not that. I'm starting a fast tomorrow. Why don't you fast with me?"

"You know how long yet, Ron?"

"Yes, twenty-one days."

There was no getting out of it, so I told him I might. There was still a possibility; if I couldn't find that other person...I wouldn't have to fast.

I saw Kevin Mangold walking towards the door. I thought the Lord said, *"That's him."* I was clear on the other end of the building and thought, *If he's still in the parking lot when I get out there, I'll ask him.* I walked slowly, knowing he would be long gone when I got out there. When I walked out the door, Kevin was right there talking to someone. I waited till he finished and walked up to him.

"Hey, Kevin, have you been thinking about fasting?"

"Yes. As a matter of fact, I'm starting a twenty-one day fast tomorrow."

"Are you doing it with Ron Freeman?" I quizzed him.

"No, didn't know he was doing one," Kevin said, shaking his head.

I was blown away, but was starting to feel the grace for it. I had no idea what was to come. We spent that next three weeks encouraging one another and praying for each other. God revealed His Word to me in new ways during that fast and my spirit man got stronger and stronger, but I figured my physical man was getting weaker.

I was training for an upcoming powerlifting meet. During the whole fast, I skipped training and didn't go to the gym once. I decided, on the last day of the fast, to go to the gym and assess the damage. I had lost forty-three pounds and hadn't been in the gym in twenty-one days. I was about to have my mind completely blown and so was everyone else who was in the gym that day.

I started out slow, knowing I was going to be weak after not eating for so long. Everything I felt was really light, so I kept going up. I ended up setting personal records that day in the squat. I did ten reps with the most weight I'd ever had on my back. Everyone in the gym knew it wasn't possible for me, because of how much weight I had lost and after missing that many workouts. When I came up from the bottom on that last rep, I wanted to scream out, "GOD, I BELIEVE IN YOUR POWER!"

It was awesome. God is powerful and the ultimate power lifter. He can lift the heaviest burdens.

NON-UNION CONSTRUCTION

The farm we were to live on for the next few months was about forty miles over rough roads from the nearest city, Bulawayo, Africa. It was in the bush area called Esigodini. We had no electricity, gas, or propane. My wife and daughter learned to cook on a wood cook stove, and found it *was* possible to live without a curling iron. We even got to use an outdoor loo (outhouse). Water was rationed out to us. We had plenty of drinking water, but were limited to a two-gallon bucket of water each day for bathing.

I was there to help build the weirs. They were like dams, and we were going to build two in a dry river bed. Zimbabwe had been in a seven-year drought and desperately needed rain. If we built these two dams, five hundred meters apart with the same top elevation, when it *did* rain, it would make a reservoir. When the river ran over the top of the first weir and then filled up and ran over the second, the five hundred million gallon reservoir trapped between them could be pumped to the gardens.

Just as before, God worked out all the details and we were able to go in the summer of 1987. My parole officer gave me permission to be out of the country for ninety days and we built two weirs in that time. That meant thousands of bags of concrete, all mixed by hand, with some of the hardest working men I have ever worked with.

Picture of my crew who had never worked construction and did an awesome job. They taught me to speak their language.

My helpers were twelve Matabeles from the village of Mbezingwe. They ran through the bush six or seven miles every day to work for four dollars a day. We worked long, ten-hour days, then they ran back home at night. They made twenty dollars a week. Their twenty dollars only bought them a fifty-kilo bag of maize (corn) which they made mealy meal out of. It was the staple food of the Matabeles. When I ate with them, we ate with our hands.

We saw God do some miracles while we were there. Once, we threw a party for all the village children. We sent the invitation by bush telegraph…it was faster than instant messaging. We bought a goat and asked one of the natives to cook it—he made it taste like prime rib. We also had mealy meal, which they all loved. We had some cool drink (soda pop), which was a rare treat for them, and most of the native children had never tasted it.

We got word that there could be as many as two hundred and fifty children coming to our party—we planned enough food for that number. Once the party was under way, they kept coming and we ended up with five hundred. When it came time to eat, we didn't have nearly enough food. The Bible says that Jesus Christ is the same yesterday, today, and forever. We knew He fed the multitudes with very little, so we asked Him to do a biblical miracle. I was there and saw with my own eyes—the food did not run out until every child had eaten.

The Matabeles were an off-shoot of the Zulu tribe, but their language was different than the Zulu's. I learned to communicate with them in their language, called Ndebele. It sounded like "en da belly." Those men were a joy to be around and I worked right by their side.

Someone told me one day that I had a way of motivating men without intimidating them. I did that by working with them. When we unloaded one-hundred-pound sacks of cement off the truck, and I would grab a bag under each arm and run with it, they would try to do the same and fall down, and we would just laugh together. One day, one of the natives said to me through an interpreter, "It must rain a lot in America."

"Why do you say that?" I asked.

"You are so big."

The whole group broke out in laughter because, at a little over six foot two and two hundred and fifty pounds, I dwarfed the biggest of the Matabele workers helping me.

They were in a seven-year drought and it takes rain to make things grow. Cattle were starving to death and lacked water. When a cow walked towards you, the only thing you could see was its head. Its sides were that sunken in.

There were dissidents living in the Matupo hills and our lives were threatened the whole time we were there. We had confidence that we were going home safely though, because the Lord confirmed it to us.

Before we left home, Debbie had nightmares about being killed by wild beasts and dissidents. The Lord gave her a promise out of His Word.

> *"The Lord shall preserve thy going out and thy coming in from this time forth, and even for evermore."* Psalms 121:8

We went to church the week before we were to leave to hear a special speaker. At the end of his message, he asked for the couple and their daughter, who were going to Africa, to stand for prayer. We stood up and he prayed over us, and said, "God, would You protect this couple and their daughter as they go to serve You in Africa? And God says to you, The Lord shall preserve thy going out and thy coming in from this time forth, and even for evermore.'"

We were pretty pumped, the word God gave my wife, He just confirmed to us. We were ready to go now.

A couple of days before we left, we went to my sister's for dinner. My dad prayed for the meal, and as he finished the prayer, he said, "God, would You protect Bill, Debbie, and Richelle as they go and will You preserve their going out and coming back in?"

The same words God had given Debbie and the same ones He gave the visiting pastor. My dad knew nothing of the dream Debbie had, or the words spoken over us at church. It was a real confidence builder for us to know we were coming home and that God confirmed it three times.

We were privileged to have been on the continent of Africa with some of the most amazing people we have ever known. Even though it was only three months, I learned lessons there that are forever etched in my mind. Those sixteen people were like family to us; we made eternal heart connections with them.

But the threats from the dissidents were not idle threats.

November 25, 1987, I got a phone call from a guy in Washington. "Bill, this is Joseph, are you sitting down?"

Literally, the first thought that came to my mind when he asked me that was Psalms 112: 1, 6-7. The man who delights himself in God's Word will not fear bad news and will not be shaken.

"No, I'm okay, what is it?" I asked.

"They have killed everyone on both farms."

"All of them?"

"They left Laura Russell alive with a note for the authorities and Matthew Marais escaped, everyone else is dead, sixteen in all, Bill."

The dissidents came in the night and brutally murdered our sixteen friends—the friends we lived and prayed with, and ate our meals with. These were friends God allowed us to know and love. They were chopped to pieces with one of their own axes. All were gone now, even a six-week-old baby who had been born the week before my family left.

What an awesome promise, in the world we live in today, that our heart can stay steadfast and will have no fear of bad news; we can trust in the Lord. Blessed is the man who fears the Lord, not a fear like being afraid of Him, but a reverent fear. He is Holy and we should revere Him. I had been asking God daily to give me the spirit of the fear of the Lord. So when Joseph told me they all had been murdered, I silently said the first verse of Psalm 112, *Praise the Lord*….

You might be thinking I didn't care about them. That's not the case at all. I would have been devastated by that news had I not been grounded and rooted in His love and His Word.

"Thanks for calling, Joseph. Talk to you soon." I hung up the phone.

Our friends who were murdered had prayed for years for rain so that the natives in the bordering villages would have food to eat. When they first started the farms, they prayed in shifts 24/7. But then they started praying according to Psalms 55:17, which says we should cry out morning, noon and night.

The day they were murdered it started misting. A few days later, they had the funeral service for them. At high noon, the sky turned as black as night. It started raining and didn't stop for more than a week. The weirs overflowed and created their intended five-hundred-million-gallon reservoir of water for the natives to use for watering gardens. God is sovereign.

I remember that phone call like it was an hour ago, although it has been over twenty-five years.

39

PRISON VOLUNTEER

The year was 1988 and I had been a Christian for five years. I was being asked to speak at youth meetings and did some high schools, taking an anti-drug message with me wherever I went.

Someone asked me to go on a prison weekend with a ministry out of Texas. Bill Glass was the man behind the ministry. Bill Glass had been an All Pro football player for the Cleveland Browns and when he retired from the NFL, he started preaching on platforms with Billy Graham. People believed he would be the next Billy Graham. In 1972, someone asked him to get some athletes and go into a prison.

Sharing the gospel with an inmate on a Bill Glass weekend.
Probably not the best shirt I could have picked to wear that day.

I am honored to say that I have been going into prisons as a volunteer with Bill for over twenty-five years. He has truly been a
mentor to me in many ways and I am proud to call Bill Glass my
friend. My wife and I were privileged to attend the 40th anniversary of his ministry in 2012; we celebrated over one million
incarcerated men and women who have made decisions to follow Christ.

In 1985, I began feeling a call to full-time ministry and started
praying about it, but prayed for several more years before I got
an answer. Every time I really sought the Lord in prayer about
going full time, He would lead me to the same passage, and I got
sick of it. He always took me back to Isaiah 66.

> *"The heaven is My throne, and the earth is My footstool: where
> is the house that ye build unto Me? and where is the place of
> My rest? For all those things hath mine hand made, and all
> those things have been, saith the Lord: but to this man will I
> look, even to him that is poor and of a contrite spirit, and trem-
> bleth at My word."* Isaiah 66:1, 2

This is my interpretation of that passage: The heavens are where
I live…My house. I use something as small as the earth to rest
My feet on. What can you build, Bill, to impress Me? Will it be
a big prison ministry? Do you want a big television ministry?
How about a radio ministry? You can only do one thing that
will impress Me. That is to have a broken and humble heart, and
tremble at My Word.

The reason I hated it, was not because I didn't have a humble
heart, or because I didn't tremble at His Word. The reason I hated
it was because I knew I could do those things just as well being
a plumber, as I could being a preacher. So I would say, "Okay,
Lord, I'll wait on You."

One thing I did for sure was tremble at His Word. When I first
got saved, He revealed to me clearly that the Bible was true from
cover to cover. I have heard of certain denominations holding
big conferences and voting on which parts of the Bible were to be
taken literally, and which parts not. It says in Revelation 22:19,
we should not take away or add to the words from the Book. I
always have been of the belief that if one verse wasn't true, then

maybe John 3:16 wasn't true. I believe the Bible in its entirety, because Jesus Christ saved me, but the Bible changed me.

> *"All scripture is given by inspiration of God, and is profitable for doctrine, for reproof, for correction, for instruction in righteousness."* II Timothy 3:16

It doesn't say *some* Scripture, it says *all*. So, you can't just pick out what you don't like and use it to suit yourself. If you allow it to, it will make you a new person. I was amazed at what giving myself wholly to God, and letting His Word be a light unto my path and a lamp unto my feet, had done for me. I did things I never thought possible.

I spoke at Full Gospel Businessmen's meetings and was still going into prisons with Bill Glass. That, in itself, was a miracle, because I was still on paper and was going into prisons, death row, and lockdown as a convicted felon. No way was that supposed to happen.

In 1989 I was asked to be on the 700 Club. When the show was aired nationwide, thousands of people called in and prayed to receive Christ over the phone. That opened more doors for me, but I still wanted to be in full-time ministry. God had not yet released me. I kept trusting Him and waited.

GOD'S NOT ASHAMED OF YOU

A friend of mine called me one day and said he knew I did prison ministry and could I help him. He asked me if I would help a guy who was being released from prison into a Kansas City half-way house. I told him I would like to pray about it.

I called him back a few days later. "Give me his name and how I can reach him."

I met Mark downtown on a street corner; he told me he would be wearing white jeans and had real long hair. When I got there, his description of himself couldn't have been more accurate. He had on white jeans and his hair was just below his broad shoulders. Like most inmates before they are released, he had been hitting the weights hard. He was friendly, and very grateful to have someone who understood prison pick him up.

He voluntarily told me that he had been locked up for cooking meth. I didn't care what he had done, I just wanted to be his friend and see him find peace. I never ask inmates what their crimes are, because it can be an embarrassing question. I dropped him at the Federal Bureau of Prisons half-way house, and told him I would see him later.

When I got home that day, my wife asked, "Well, how did it go with the new guy?"

"The Lord told me to give myself to him."

"What in the world does that mean?"

"I don't know, honey…He has never told me that before."

I helped Mark find a job and spent quite a bit of time with him, lifting weights and just hanging out. One day I dropped him off at the half-way house and told him it was time for him to make a decision about Jesus. He called me a couple of hours later; he decided to make Jesus Lord of his life. I drove back to the half-way house and we prayed together.

I found out over the next few months exactly what the Lord meant about me giving myself to Mark. He got a job and was working at 18th and State Ave. in Kansas City, Kansas. Every night I picked him up at 18th and State Ave. I'd then take him to 3126 Forest and he would sign in and sign out. We would head to my house in Raytown to eat dinner. Afterward we'd go to our church in Grandview till nine at night. Then back to the halfway house at 3126 Forest Ave. Whew!

On Tuesdays we went to church in Grandview, on Fridays to a church in Olathe. Sunday morning and Sunday night we went to church in Grandview. After most services ended, I would say, "Let's go fellowship," and we would go to a buffet and eat. One day Mark said to me, "I think I'm starting to get the hang of what fellowship means…it means eating."

When we weren't in church, we just hung out. I loved every minute of those times; sure it was a lot of driving and a lot of work, but when God gives the grace, it is pleasurable. It was an honor for me to do it and a blessing.

On Friday nights, we had baptismal services at our church in Olathe. Mark felt like he was to be baptized, and I would have the pleasure of baptizing him.

He called me a couple of days before I was to do the baptism. "Hey, Bill, would it be okay if I wore a sweatshirt?"

"I guess it would, but why?"

"I don't know...you know...I got all these tattoos."

"If you would be more comfortable, wear a sweatshirt."

I tell people that Mark only has one tattoo...it starts on his left wrist and goes to his right. He is like so many guys who go to prison with four tattoos and come home with four hundred. I told Debbie what he said about the sweatshirt, and while she was praying, the Lord spoke to her.

I called him. "Mark, God told Debbie to tell you something."

"Really? What did He tell her?"

"He told her, He could've called you into His family before you had any tattoos...but He waited until you were covered with them and He's not ashamed of you."

When he came out to get in the baptismal that night he wore a wife beater shirt. It was a proud moment for me to get to baptize Mark and he was proud God wasn't ashamed of him.

WALKING, NOT TALKING

As much as I wanted to be in full-time ministry, I was still working on construction jobs as a plumber. I ran a big job down near Sedalia, Missouri. This turkey-processing plant had a massive amount of pipe in the ground. There was over twenty-five thousand feet of pipe, inside a building that was six hundred feet square.

I had a couple dozen men on the job and a lot of backhoes, rubber tire loaders, and dump trucks. The architects would not allow any of the dirt to go back into the ditches. Every ditch had to be filled and compacted to specifications with Missouri river sand. The main line coming in was seventeen feet deep. We put in the mains, left stub outs on them, and covered them. When we were ready to put in a branch, we would dig down to the stub out and tie on.

One day, one of my guys came running over, all out of breath, and looking very nervous. "Bill, we just broke that main line, trying to dig to one of the stub outs."

"Well, you'll have to dig it up and fix it."

"You mean you're not mad?" he asked me, looking confused.

"You didn't break it on purpose, did you?"

"No, of course we didn't," he said, almost smiling.

"Then why would I be mad?"

I drove to work the very next day, complaining to the Lord. *"I've been on this job for months and no one even knows I'm a Christian."*

A few days later, I told a friend of mine that there was a contractor on the job who was hiring, and that he should try and get on. He was in the trailer filling out the application when the boss asked him, "That Bill Corum a friend of yours?"

"Yes he is. He told me to come see you."

"Is he real religious or something?"

"I don't think so…I think he just loves Jesus. Why?"

He told my buddy about the way I reacted when my plumbers broke the seventeen-foot-deep line. He told him most guys would have thrown things and cussed and raised a ruckus. I just acted like it was no big deal and didn't get mad.

That very morning I'd told the Lord that I didn't even get to share Christ with anyone. I didn't realize that all along, I had been sharing Christ without saying anything. Preach the Gospel always, use words when necessary.

CHAPTER

40

DEATH LEADS TO BIRTH

November 5, 1991 was a Sunday. My niece called me and said they thought my dad had suffered a heart attack. I drove to the house to be with Mom, my sister and brother-in-law. As I approached their neighborhood, the Lord told me my dad was already gone.

I prayed, *"Father, let the death of my dad be the birth of something in me."*

The Lord had already prepared me. I wasn't shocked, and was happy knowing Dad was with Jesus. God sovereignly arranged for me to see him earlier that morning. I always took Debbie and Richelle to church on Sunday mornings. That morning, I told her I was sure the Lord told me to skip church and take her and Richelle up to a game preserve a couple hours away and look at geese.

Debbie looked at me, very shocked. "Are you sure?"

"Yep, I need to call Dad and borrow his binoculars."

We went by Mom and Dad's and got the binoculars. I had not seen him for several days and when I left, we hugged, and I kissed him and told him I loved him. If we hadn't gone to see the geese, I wouldn't have seen him that day.

The day after he died I was at Mom's house. She asked if I would like to look through some of Dad's things. I found a cassette music tape that belonged to him. The title of the cassette was, FIRST DAY IN HEAVEN. Since this was the day after my dad died, I considered it a little kiss from God. He let me know Dad was with Him.

In January of 1992, God answered the prayer I prayed the day dad died. I started the prison ministry; **Prison Power Ministries, Inc**. He confirmed it to me through His Word. I was waiting on Debbie at church one day, and said, "If that's what I'm supposed to call it, Lord, confirm it to me."

I felt He said, "Romans 1:16."

I opened my Bible to read, *"For I am not ashamed of the gospel of Christ: for it is the power of God unto salvation to everyone that believeth; to the Jew first, and also to the Greek."* Romans 1:16

God began opening doors all over the place for us. One of the first doors the Lord opened was at Municipal Correctional Institution, Kansas City, Missouri's city jail. I heard they didn't have a chaplain so I went up to apply for the job.

I will never forget the day I met with Mr. Burt and Bill Howard. Mr. Burt was the superintendent and Bill Howard was a captain who had been there for many years. Mr. Burt told me they had known for a long time there was a chaplain coming—they just didn't know what he would look like.

I became the full-time volunteer chaplain. I received no pay from the city, but God supplied all of our needs. Debbie and I decided when we started Prison Power Ministries we didn't want to ask anyone for money. Professionals told me we would never make it unless we followed the fundraising models. God took care of us the entire time we ran the ministry; we were never late on a bill, and never missed a payment.

My role as chaplain at MCI took several hours a day, five days a week. They gave me freedom to move around the entire complex. I had an office for counseling and was able to build relationships with many men there over the years. I have so many memories of inmates I met at MCI. I am still in relationships with some of them today.

One of the saddest things I saw in my time there was fathers and sons locked up there at the same time. On one occasion there was a grandfather, father, and son all locked up at the same time.

They were there on three separate cases. When I saw generations locked up together, it always reminded me of the Scripture that says the sins of the fathers follow them for generations.

This was a municipal jail and many of the inmates were there for drinking. I remember one told me that in the last twenty years he had been locked up there at least once a year, and sometimes two or three times a year. I find that sad, but that is the result of alcohol so many times.

A short time after I formed the ministry, I began doing more than just the city jail. I started going into prisons and jails statewide.

I attended a church where eight active Kansas City Chiefs football players also went. I got to know them and they started going into the prisons with me. By networking with some of them, I met Kansas City Royals baseball players and professional basketball players and other pro athletes. I started using those professional athletes for prison outreaches. They didn't go in just to speak, but to play softball or basketball against the inmates.

Ken Ufford was a friend from my powerlifting days, and was the world's strongest policeman. He would go in and challenge any inmate to a bench press or deadlift. I used to put up posters in the prison a couple of weeks before the event to try and get as much interest as possible. Ken asked me one day if I could change the wording on the posters. I asked him why. He pointed to one as we walked into a prison. There, hanging on the wall in maximum security, was a poster with the time and place, describing Kenny as being the world's strongest policeman.

But the boldest words were BEAT THE COP.

"Bill, could we change that to CHALLENGE THE COP?"

I laughed and said, "That's a good point, buddy."

Kenny was a DARE officer and I always waited till there was a good-sized crowd on the yard before I popped the question. "How many you guys like cops?"

No hands would go up.

"How many of you don't want your kids on drugs?"

Not one inmate wanted their kids on drugs. I told them Kenny was a DARE officer, and was in the schools trying to educate their kids against drugs. Before the event was over, those inmates were shaking Kenny's hand and patting him on the back. Many of them wanted his autograph.

No one ever came close to him in the deadlift. He toyed with them, letting them lift as much as they could, and then put on a show for them. He could deadlift over eight hundred pounds and truly was the world's strongest cop.

Another thing we did was take pro athletes in to play basketball or softball against the inmates. We put up posters that read, CHALLENGE THE PROS. I listed the names of all the pro athletes who were coming to play. It was such a thrill for the inmates to meet and rub shoulders with players who had a Super Bowl ring, or had been an All Pro.

We held a basketball game once in maximum security at Kansas; the score ended 123 to 124. What a game! Wow, some of those inmates had been playing together for fifteen or more years and they were good. They played against professional athletes who were not easily beaten and it was a thrill for both the inmates and the pros.

For about ten or twelve years, I took The Good News Garage Band into the prisons and did outdoor concerts on the prison yards. They were amazing and the inmates and officers loved them. One time, we did a concert on a big prison yard and I was getting ready to go up and speak, when an inmate walked up to me and said, "Could I talk with you for a minute?"

I told him I was about to speak, but I had a few minutes.

He said, "I am thirty-two years old; I've been in the system since I was twelve. For twenty years I've either been locked up or on parole or probation. I'd like to be a Christian, but I'm afraid it will be too boring."

I couldn't believe the words that came out of my mouth next. "You're right...it *is* boring."

Then I told him, "If you're talking about taking your Bible off the shelf and taking it to church on Sunday, then going home and putting it back on the shelf till next Sunday, it's boring. But if you're talking about living for Jesus 24/7, there's nothing boring about it. I'm not a man who can live a boring life. Let me tell you a little about my life before I was a Christian.

"My partner, Kenny, had a Turbo Carrera Porsche that would go 185 mph. We used to get in it and go 150 mph on I-70 through downtown Kansas City. If you think going three times the speed limit with an Uzi laying in the backseat is boring, you should go with me.

"I used to go into a shooting gallery—and I'm not talking about a place to target practice, I'm talking about a place you go to shoot dope. I would walk in and lay my .357 Magnum on one side of me and my .9mm on the other. I'd open a box with six or eight ounces of cocaine and ten thousand dollars or more in it, just hoping someone would try and take my cocaine or my money so I could shoot them. If you think that's boring, you should go to a shooting gallery with me.

"I'd get on a motorcycle in Shawnee, Kansas and ride to Ray-town, Missouri, in ten or twelve minutes. I'd go 140 mph across I-670, lying down on the bike with my .9mm and my .357 Magnum, carrying cocaine and thousands of dollars. If you think that's boring, come ride a motorcycle with me. Remember…I said I can't live a boring life.

"Now, as a Christian, let me tell you what I do. I go to death row and sit on a concrete floor. I hold a man's hands through the bars of a six-by-nine foot cell he's been locked in for seventeen years, and pray with him to receive Christ. If you think that's boring, come go with me to death row.

"I go to San Quentin prison where there are six thousand inmates. More than half of them never get a letter or a visit. When you're in prison for fifteen or twenty years and never have a letter or a visit, you get pretty angry. They let one thousand men at a time out on the big yard. I go down to the iron pile and lift weights with some of the angriest men in the world. If you think that's boring, come go to San Quentin with me.

"I go to the AIDs wards where men can barely whisper, they are so weak. They whisper, "Please pray for me." Sometimes I get to lead them to Christ before they die. If you think that's boring, come go with me to the AIDs wards."

I shook the young inmate's hand and walked up the steps of the platform to speak. The Lord had me tell the whole crowd of over two hundred about a young man who wanted to be a Christian, but was afraid it would be too boring. I told them the story I had just told the man at the bottom of the steps. When I gave the altar call, that young man was one of the first ones to come forward. Praise the Lord.

KEYS TO CITY HALL

In 1989 when I was on the 700 club, the producers asked me if I would consider making a movie of my life story. I declined. Only six years had passed since I was living that lifestyle and I wasn't willing to re-live it through a video.

A man approached us in 1993 about making a movie of my life. I thought maybe God wanted us to do it, but wasn't sure. We decided to do it, but did it with apprehension, and for good reason. It ended up being one of the hardest things we ever attempted. We had to go back and relive those dark days and even reenact some of my unfaithfulness to Debbie. It had only been ten years at that time and was very hard on both of us, but especially my wife.

All of my kids played a part in the movie except my oldest daughter, who said she had lived through those actual days and couldn't be in the movie because it would be too painful. I blessed her for her decision and understood.

Heart of Stone covered twenty-one years of my life from the time I was eighteen years old and escaped from the military prison, until I was thirty-nine and was implicated as being one of the leading cocaine dealers in Kansas City. It was not a high-budget movie and never hit the box office, but we put it in some prisons around the country. I received letters from inmates who gave their hearts to Jesus watching it in the chapel. That was our goal, to reach inmates in the prisons and jails.

Some amazing things happened during the making of it.

We needed some really big muscular guys for some of the prison scenes. I stopped to get gas one day and there was a really big guy filling up his car. I told Debbie there was a guy we could use.

She said, "What…you're just going to go ask him if he wants to be in a movie?"

Being shy has never been one of my weaknesses. That's exactly what I'm going to do."

I walked up and told the guy we were making a movie and asked him if he would like to be in it. He said he might, and I asked him his name. He said John Corum. I told him my name was Corum too and he didn't believe me. So I took my driver's license out and showed it to him. Turns out, we were second cousins and had never met. He agreed to be in it, and did an awesome job. We got to know each other a little.

The Raytown police were so much help to us and furnished all the police officers and guns we needed for various scenes. This was amazing to me, because this is the same town the police wanted to run me out of thirty years earlier.

The most thrilling part of the whole movie for me was when we shot the courtroom scene. The director said we needed a courtroom to shoot the scene of my final appearance in court. I went to City Hall and asked if it was possible to use the court room. To my surprise they said yes. I called the director to tell him and he said we would shoot that scene the next Sunday, but we wouldn't get to that particular scene until around midnight.

I called city hall and asked if we should get the police to let us in on Sunday night when we were ready. The person in charge said, "Just come by before we close on Friday and we'll give you a key."

I couldn't believe my ears! *Me…a key to city hall in Raytown!*

This was right up there with the parting of the Red Sea. It wasn't like they didn't know anything about me. There had been several stories in the paper for the last month we were shooting. The press built it up as though it was a pretty big deal in Raytown.

Even some of the one hundred forty-three actors who were in it got saved, either during the filming or afterward. Only one person out of one hundred forty-three played their *own* part in the movie, and that was my friend Tony Moreno, aka Mr. T., who played a big cocaine dealer I sold to. Tony is one of the lights at the end of the tunnel.

CHAPTER

DEATH ROW MINISTRY

One of my very favorite places to minister in prisons is death row. I think the main reason I like going to death row is because I get blessed and touched by God more than the inmates do. You wouldn't think that would be the case, but it happens more often than the other way around.

On one occasion, I got to visit death row in the old United States Disciplinary Barracks at Fort Leavenworth, Kansas.

Walking into that place, I couldn't help but notice the medieval look of the prison—the weathered and worn, native stone walls—built by forgotten prisoners when *hard labor* meant exactly that. This old prison had witnessed thousands of prayers, curses, and pleas over the past one hundred and some years. As the military chaplain and I headed to the row, I said, "This is like we're stepping back in time."

The chaplain replied, "Yep, we almost are. You'll see."

I couldn't believe we were getting to go to death row at this prison. Very few civilians ever get to see this part of the USDB. Most people don't even know it is there. When a member of our armed forces commits a crime that carries capital punishment, they are sent to Fort Leavenworth USDB death row.

Death row was in the basement of the main prison. We had to go through the boiler room to get there. It was summer time and ninety degrees outside. I couldn't believe how hot it was down there—no air stirring, and no air conditioning. As soon as we reached the bottom floor, I noticed the size of the stones the foundation was made of. I pictured convicts in leg irons moving those monstrous stones with teams of mules or oxen in 1875 when construction began.

When we reached the end of the cells, the chaplain sat at a desk and let me go on my way. I walked to the end of the row and stopped in front of a guy's cell. I sweat more than most people, and felt like I'd taken a shower with my clothes on. I was sweating so badly, water ran off the bill of my cap. Normally, I would have complained about how hot it was, but not to this guy.

I stood there talking to him, looking at his living conditions. The over one-hundred-year-old stone walls of his cell were painted, but the paint was peeling off. His cell measured about five by nine feet, and I am sure it was hotter in there than where I stood. I asked him if he was a Christian and when he smiled, I knew he was. I told him I would be praying for him, because I could see, his living conditions were rough.

"Thank you…but I make it through my days, praying for those who are suffering more than I am in here."

I didn't even know how to respond to the guy. I felt like I was such a complainer, thinking about how hot it was, when this guy, who had spent the last decade or so in a tiny cell, was praying for those who had it worse than him. I came away from there blessed and feeling very humbled to have met him.

MISSISSIPPI DEATH ROW

I kept my hand up high and even waved a little as they asked for volunteers to go to death row. We were in Parchman, Mississippi on a Bill Glass prison weekend. It was back in the days when we spent three days in the same prison. This meant all day Friday, all day Saturday, and half day Sunday.

Death Row Mississippi. The guy hadn't touched his breakfast, but just pushed it back out under his cell door. I asked him, "You not hungry? Or not feeling well?" He told me, "Neither. I just get tired of the same food after 15 years." He'd been in that 7' x 9' cell for 15 years. He went on to share with me how much peace he had since asking Jesus into his heart.

There were forty-three men on death row and I would have time to talk to all of them, but of course, there were always some who didn't want to talk. I probably visited with thirty men that weekend, but one in particular stood out in my mind. I have used his story as an example for many years. Most of the inmates on this death row had deep southern accents.

I stopped in front of a cell and quietly asked, "Do you mind if I watch?"

He shook his head no and continued doing martial arts exercises. I'd never watched someone do martial arts in person, only on television. I didn't know what style it was until he told me later.

After a few minutes, he stopped and bowed to me.

"Is that Karate?"

"No, it's Kung Fu," he said, with a strong accent that wasn't from the South.

"Where're you from?"

"Brooklyn, New York."

"Well, I knew you weren't from these parts, so what in the world are you doing in Mississippi?"

"That's a long story."

"I got three days, you wanna tell me?"

He told me he had done a few years in Florida prisons—caught a case there buying drugs to take to New York. He did time with a guy who knew of an easy score on some diamonds in Florida. The guy even had a connection in California to sell them. They got together when they got out, stole the diamonds and were on their way to California. He said when they passed through Mississippi they got thirsty. They stopped at a little tavern and had a couple of beers…and then a few more. Some redneck started trouble with him, so he went to the car, got his pistol, and shot the guy and one of his friends. The story seemed fresh to him as he told it, which made me think it happened within the last year.

"How long ago was that?"

"A little over ten years ago."

"So you've been living in this seven by nine foot cell for ten years?"

"Yes, I have."

"I bet you wish you'd drunk Coke that day, huh?"

He was already a Christian and had stopped appealing his case after his conversion. I just encouraged him and prayed for him.

I use his story when I speak to groups about the choices people make and how a bad choice can change your life forever. I have never heard of anyone killing someone after drinking too many Cokes.

WOMAN BANK ROBBER

Debbie and I went to Denny's to have lunch with a lady some-one told us we needed to meet. Countless times in our years of prison and street ministry we've been to Denny's for these meetings. They say Denny's isn't somewhere you plan to go, you just end up there.

I would say, in our experience that is not true. We have planned a lot of meetings there. This meeting turned into a long-term relationship with a real live woman bank robber. Her name was June Frye and she ended up being one of our good friends. She and Debbie became really close and Debbie was influential in helping her grow closer to Christ.

June's life was colorful to say the least. She rode the rails, she owned and operated a night club in Oklahoma, and at one point in time was the girlfriend of a mob-connected guy. She was also a drug dealer and a bank robber. We spent hours swapping stories of our individual drug dealing escapades.

She became born again when a cop, who arrested her, led her to Christ. June was all ears when Debbie taught her spiritual things. She was like a sponge, soaking up all the nuggets of wisdom my wife shared with her.

One thing she longed for was to see all of her children accept Jesus Christ as their own savior. She had been estranged from them and wanted badly to be reconciled. When she was dying of cancer, we were able to spend some time with her and were there to see her children gathered around her bed at the end of her life. That is something only God can do.

Debbie and I attended June's funeral at the church she attended, and large numbers came to pay their respects. It was one of the best funerals we have ever been to. Her pastor spoke so well of her that day and we look forward to seeing her in heaven. When you see a person who was where June was at one time in her life, and see how the Lord redeemed it, you know all things are pos-sible with God.

I have a special keepsake from June. She loved doing needle point and cross stitch and made me a nice bookmarker for my Bible. She has been gone over twenty years and I still use that bookmark. I especially like anything a convict or former convict makes me. I keep them like treasures.

CHAPTER

RECONCILIATION

I talk to men and women in prison all the time who feel as though they have lost their children and there is no hope for reconciliation. I encourage them in the fact that the Bible says there is nothing too difficult for God. No matter what the situation, God can turn it around if they trust Him and pray. It might not happen in a day, or a week, it may take years. When they share with me that they have spent years messing up their families, I tell them it may take years to fix things. Then I share with them my story, and how I felt like the worst dad in the world.

I spent the first ten years of my new life in Christ doing street ministry and volunteering at Kansas City Rescue Mission. I became very involved with Promise Keepers, a men's movement emphasizing the importance of being a promise keeper to your family. I was also a volunteer with Bill Glass' prison ministry. During those years I heard messages on being a good father and blessing your children.

I was a brand new person in Christ according to what the Bible says,

> *"Therefore if any man be in Christ, he is a new creature: old things are passed away; behold, all things are become new."*
> II Corinthians 5:17

It had been ten years since I used alcohol, drugs, or tobacco. I hadn't cheated on my wife or told lies. I didn't swear anymore—there had been all kinds of changes. But while I was out ministering to all those strangers who needed God's touch in their lives, I ignored my own children.

I was talking to my ex-wife on the phone one day, and told her how I felt. I felt like I had been a terrible father and that there was nothing I could do to fix it.

"My kids are all grown, Marsha. It's too late for me to be a dad to them."

"Bill, I'm almost fifty years old, and I still need my dad."

That was the changing point in my life. I had almost quit the ministry because I didn't feel I was worthy to represent God to those inmates and people on the streets, while ignoring my own family.

I asked God to help me know how to reconcile with my children. He led me to a verse, the last verse in the Old Testament. I don't think it's an accident, that it is the very last verse before something new.

> "And he shall turn the heart of the fathers to the children, and the heart of the children to their fathers, lest I come and smite the earth with a curse." Malachi 4:6

It says in Isaiah 63:7 that we are to remind God of His promises. I started praying and reminding God of His promise in Malachi 4:6. I asked Him to restore my heart to my children. I noticed the verse starts with the father. He doesn't really need to be reminded of what it says, but likes to know we are reading and trusting in His promises.

The Lord gave me a plan. I don't know about you, but I always need a plan from Him. His Word says in Proverbs 19:20, we have many plans, but it is His counsel that will stand.

I called my oldest daughter. "Could we get together for lunch, just you and I?"

When we got together I asked her if she could forgive me for being a lousy father and give me another chance, starting that day. As I called each one of my children, they individually agreed to have lunch with me. Every one of them said yes. They wanted to give me another chance.

I wish I could tell you everything is perfect today, like it would have been had I been a good father all along. I regret to tell you, our relationships are not the same as they could have been. I know that they never will be, but am happy to report, we are a great work in progress.

Left to right Larry, Laura, Billy, Richelle

We have the best relationship we have ever had. I have spent more time with my sons and daughters in the last few years, than I would have if I had not asked them to forgive me. Only God knows the pain each one has gone through individually. As I wrote this book, I cried and my heart was broken thinking of all the things I put them, and my wives, through.

If you have a family you want to reconcile with, it is never too late. There is nothing impossible for God. He will pick up all the pieces and put them back together again. Just ask Him for wisdom (James 1:5). I don't think any man knows how to be a good father until he has learned how to be a good son to HIM.

God changed me, and if He can change me, there is no person He can't change. I could tell you all day how much I have changed, but you don't know if I am telling the truth. I invite you to ask my wife and kids. They know the kind of man I was, and who I am today. They have watched and lived with me for thirty years now.

GOD SENT A HELPER

In 1994 I hired Ricky Beach to work with me full time at Prison Power Ministries. He was one of the best things that ever happened to our ministry. God started opening doors for us out of state and Ricky and I traveled and ministered together. Although he was more than twenty years younger, *he* mentored *me*. I was open to his rebukes and corrections. He heard from God and we learned together.

Rick and I were in a jail one day and I told the inmates a story. "There were three black guys and three white guys in the room...."

While driving home that day from the jail, Rick looked over, and asked, "Why did you say what you did when you told that story?"

"Why did I say what?"

"Why did you say, there were three black guys, and three white guys?"

"Because that is how many there were."

"In your story, skin color didn't matter. It was a prejudiced statement. You could just say there were six guys."

I got so upset with him. I was ready to fire him. In my quiet time with the Lord the next morning, I asked Him, "Lord, why is what Rick said yesterday bothering me so much?"

I felt like the Lord answered me, but I didn't like the answer. "It's because the truth hurts."

I was so convicted about still having prejudice in me, because I thought I had dealt with all that a long time ago. I repented and asked the Lord to forgive me. I then went and thanked Ricky.

Another time Rick and I were driving to Colorado to minister in some prisons. I was driving about 85 miles an hour in a speed zone clearly marked 70.

"Slow down, Bill."

"Why do I need to slow down?"

Ricky told me that the devil wanted to kill us bad enough without us helping him. He reminded me of the Scripture in John 10:10—the devil comes to steal, kill, and destroy. He told me we are under God's umbrella of protection, as long as we are doing what is right. When we break the law and do things we know we shouldn't, we step out from under that umbrella. When I know the speed limit and am purposely driving fifteen miles an hour over it, I step out from under the umbrella.

I sometimes got upset when I was rebuked or corrected by this young guy who hadn't been in prison, or ever done any of the things I had done. But the Lord always told me Ricky was right and I needed to listen to him. I have no doubt God put him in my life, and for that, I am very grateful.

Ricky wanted to start a street feeding project, so we found a spot on Independence Ave. in Kansas City and started feeding on Thursday nights. We cooked hot dogs in the summer and served chili in the winter. It didn't matter if it was raining or snowing, we never missed being out there on Thursday nights.

A year or so into it, I said to Ricky, "I think we need to end the feeding project."

He raised his eyebrows and said, "Why in the world would we do that?"

"In the year we've been serving food, I don't think anyone has been saved."

"My Bible doesn't say they will, it just says feed the poor."

"Then it looks like we will keep feedin' 'em, Ricky."

He has been doing that continually now for almost twenty years.

I found out Ricky was capable of running the ministry without me, when in 1995 Debbie and I were asked to go to Germany. They wanted me to come speak in some churches, prisons, and do some radio and television interviews. We had about forty meetings on our agenda, spread out over a period of twenty-seven days.

When we arrived in Frankfurt, we found that all of our bags had gone to Florida. That was a little alarming to us, because I was scheduled to speak not long after we arrived. I have the highest praises for the airlines we traveled on. They delivered all nine bags (there were three of us) in less than twenty-four hours, to the house where we stayed, which was about seventy-five miles from the airport.

GOING TO GERMANY

After my first television interview in Germany, our contact's phone started ringing.

Doing a television interview in Wurzburg Germany

They wanted me to go here and there. Before we were done, our schedule changed from forty meetings to sixty-five. We did all that in twenty-seven days. It was hectic to say the least. I am wired differently than my wife and love fast-moving things. She normally cannot go at that kind of pace. It was amazing to watch God's grace helping her keep up with me day after day. Finally, after twenty non-stop days in a row, while we were getting ready to go again, she said, "I can't go with you today."

She was afraid of what people would think of her if she didn't go. I told her to rest and we wouldn't worry about what they thought. She rested that day and went with me every day after that.

We ministered in prisons, jails, schools, churches, coffee houses, and television and radio stations. I spoke in a prison in former East Germany where no American had ever been. They allowed me to share my story and preach to the entire staff and new officers in training. It was most likely the first time some of them heard the Gospel, and the Spirit of the Lord really moved.

I was told when we arrived in Germany I should not give altar calls, because German men were very reserved and would not respond. There was never a time when I did not feel I was supposed to give men the chance to give their hearts to Jesus. The men who advised me not to give altar calls were amazed. I told them it wasn't me, but the Holy Spirit drawing them.

One unbelievable thing that happened was in a large prison in Wurzburg. I joked around about needing an interpreter, because they couldn't understand my language, otherwise. The inmates were laughing, my interpreter was laughing, and I asked if there was anyone who *did* understand my English. A guy way in the back held up his hand.

I asked without the interpreter, "Where're you from?"

This unmistakable, deep southern accent rolled out. "Mobile, Alabama."

I was a little embarrassed for being a wise guy, and shocked that someone from the United States was in prison in Germany. I preached and gave an altar call; there were several men who responded, and the guy from Alabama was one of them. We talked after the service, and he told me his whole story.

He had been in jail in Alabama on a murder charge and had escaped. He ended up in Germany on the run and caught a manslaughter case for killing a guy in a fight.

He wrote to me after I returned to the states. He was found not guilty on his case in Germany and went back to Alabama. He turned himself in, because he wanted to serve God. That is true repentance.

I thought I had seen just about everything in my life, but when we did street ministry in Frankfurt it went up a notch. We walked through the red light district of that city; it was similar to what I had seen in Amsterdam when I was there. We walked the entire length of it and then back. Hookers advertised themselves out in the open everywhere. The difference was how we saw drugs being sold and used out in the open.

Junkies shot dope right on the street. The police drove up and down the streets and were looking at us more suspiciously than the people using. We were there several hours and never saw anyone get arrested. Two or three junkies would squat down right in the middle of the sidewalk. They used a Coke can turned upside down to cook their dope. Every fifty or one hundred feet we would have to walk around them.

I saw one guy leaning in a door way and watched as his buddy hit him in the neck with the hypodermic needle. Blood ran down his neck and all over his white dress shirt. The drug addicts and hookers were so thick in places it was hard to walk. This was a place they could go and not be bothered by anyone— even the police. I never figured out why the police even drove through there; they did nothing. It was a very sad and depressing place. The people we went there with have a ministry on those streets.

I only had the same interpreter about five or six times out of all those meetings. It was hard, because I could never get into a flow with them. Same with our drivers—if I had four meetings in one day, I might have two or three different drivers. That is the way the whole trip went.

Some of the places I spoke at gave me an honorarium. A few times, a driver taking me to the next meeting told me a tragic story of something that had happened to him and I ended up giving him all the money I had on me. I called my eighty-nine-year-old mother one day from Germany to see how she was feeling. I told her I had been giving away all the money I got. She told me I should keep some of it, because we had needs too. But, I kept on giving it away the rest of the time we were there.

The last Sunday before we left Germany, I spoke at a very large church in Frankfurt. They took up an offering and it was a big one. We got back to the house where we were staying and I told Debbie I felt like I should give some money to the people who hosted us for twenty-seven days. I gave them a good amount and kept thirteen hundred dollars.

When we got back home after being gone for almost a month, the first day back in the office, Ricky told me we had financial problems. We had bills due and no money to pay them.

I asked him, "How much do you need?"

Ricky looked at me and said, "Bill, we need thirteen hundred dollars."

I reached in my pocket, and pulled out exactly what we needed. God knows your needs, before you do.

JEHOVAH JIREH, MY PROVIDER

God was always faithful to supply our needs. Philippians 4:16 tells us that He will supply all of our needs according to His riches in Glory. It doesn't say our wants, but our needs—food, clothing and shelter. God always did that and so much more. He also gave us a lot of our wants while He supplied our needs.

When we originally started Prison Power Ministries, Debbie and I agreed we would not ask for money. The experts told me that if I was going to make it and have a successful ministry, I had to do what everyone else did. They advised me to build a strong support base. In order to do that, I would have to campaign for funds. I needed to get a mailing list and start sending out information.

We told everyone that if God had really called us, then He would provide. If not, I would go back to plumbing and we would live happily ever after. I can honestly tell you, not one time in the years of our prison ministry did we miss a payment or be late on a bill. God supernaturally provided for us, but even when He did that I would still doubt on occasion.

One time while flying to San Quentin Prison in California, I was sat next to a guy who was going with me. While he slept, I sat there worrying about bills that weren't even due yet, and how I was going to pay them. I looked out of the window and saw the most awesome sight I had ever seen. I thought, *It can't be the Grand Canyon, because that would not be on our route.* I knew on the map where Kansas City was in relation to San Francisco, and I thought we would just fly straight towards it.

I stopped a flight attendant serving snacks and pointed, "What is that we are flying beside?"

"That's the Grand Canyon."

There was not a cloud in the sky and the sun was just starting to set. We cruised at five hundred miles per hour and it took thirty minutes to fly the length of it. The colors were so magnificent, I started crying. From my vantage point beside the window, I saw parts of it that were eighteen miles wide. There are mountains down inside. In places it is over a mile deep. As I looked at the colors reflecting from the setting sun glisten off the rocks, I thought I was looking through a kaleidoscope. God gave me a thirty-minute show of the beauty of His creation. I cried and felt so small. I had been worrying about where our provision was going to come from. He showed me that He owns it all, and He was my Provider.

When we got to San Quentin, they told us there were twenty-five hundred men on lockdown and some of us could go there. I got my hand up quickly to volunteer. When I minister on lockdown I have to talk to men through the slop chute. It is a little flap on their cell door where a food tray just fits through. It is about waist high so we went from cell to cell bent over looking through a small slot in the door talking to the inmates.

I went up to one guy's cell and started talking to him and he said he was Jewish and didn't want to hear anything about Jesus. I told him I served the God of Abraham, Isaac, and Jacob, and that my God loved him and me very much.

I then told him the whole story about God loving me so much that He gave me an awesome show on the way there. I went into great detail and tried to describe what it looked like. When I got ready to leave him that day, I asked him if I could pray for him. He allowed me to, and I prayed that God would show him how much He loved him by giving him a dream that night. The next day, I was way down the tier talking to another inmate, when he called my name. I went up to his cell, and he said God had given him a dream the night before. I don't know what happened with my Jewish friend, but I can tell you for sure God got his attention.

PLEASE FORGIVE ME

One thing I do when I speak in women's prisons, or to women in county jails, is ask their forgiveness. A large majority of the women in prison and jail have been involved in prostitution. I tell my story of taking my money back from prostitutes. I tell them I know it wasn't any of them, but it might have been their mothers or aunts.

I start off telling them how, after I was a Christian, I was working on a construction job at a college, with guys who always made dirty remarks to the girls. I got so mad one day I was going to knock a couple of them off the roof.

The Lord spoke to me and said, "You were a lot worse than they are."

It made me feel bad to think He watched me do all the things I did to women. Today I tell women they are precious in God's eyes and that He wants to be their Husband. I tell them if they have boyfriends or husbands who are looking at pornography, they don't deserve that. I tell them that if they have boyfriends or husbands who beat them, they don't deserve that. If they have boyfriends or husbands who are cheating on them, they deserve better.

I usually quote I Peter 3:7, that says husbands should honor their wives so their prayers won't be hindered. I ask them if they have a man who honors them. Does he call you his old lady? That is not honoring you. Does he open the door for you when you get in the car? I tell them that when they get out of lockup, they need to find a man who will treat them the way God planned. God gave woman to man to be his helpmate, not his doormat.

This message to women incarcerated has never failed to touch them. I pray and ask the Lord to come close to them and hold them. I then ask them to forgive me for treating women the way I did. Sometimes I hear shouting from the back of the room. "We forgive you, Bill, we forgive you."

I get healed a little more every time I do that, and I think they do too. Sometimes forgiveness is more healing for you than the person you're forgiving. Do you know forgiveness breaks the devil's back? He can't stand it when we forgive someone. Jesus defeated the devil hanging on that cross, when He said,

> "Father, forgive them; for they know not what they do." Luke 23:34

A PRISON DIRECTOR

One day I got a call from The Salvation Army; they were looking for a new Director of Correctional Services. I had been speaking for a few years at Salvation Army events and prison ministry fund-raising banquets. I really felt like this directors job could be beneficial for me, but how could I just shut down Prison Power Ministries? What would happen to Ricky? I really prayed and sought the Lord for an answer. I fasted…I prayed. I had to hear.

I went for the interview, and they liked me; they wanted me to take the job. I couldn't give them an answer till I talked to Ricky. I went nervously to talk to him. I felt like I was abandoning him and that he would be left without a job. I told him all about the offer and the interview and that I really felt good about it. I just didn't feel good leaving him out in the cold.

Ricky looked at me—all twenty-some years of him—and said, "Sounds like God to me."

"But Rick…what about you? What will you do for work?"

He looked at me, cocked his head and said, "Bill, God's taken care of me all these years. You think He's gonna quit now?"

That was the wisdom of an old man who had been walking with God for years, not something I expected to hear from a young man.

Then my wife had the best idea. Why not let Ricky take over Prison Power Ministries? That is exactly what we did. I went to work for the oldest and largest prison ministry in the world—founded in 1878. When I accepted the job, they apologetically told me they could only start me at twenty-seven thousand dollars a year.

I said, "Praise the Lord."

Debbie and I paid taxes on less than half that amount for the last few years in full-time ministry. To us, twenty-seven thousand dollars was huge a raise.

Most people don't know that The Salvation Army has a prison ministry. Most people think they just ring bells outside of stores at Christmas time. That's the picture most people have in their minds when they hear the words, "The Salvation Army." I didn't know much about them when I first went to work, but fell in love with the people and what they do. William Booth is one of my heroes and when I get to Heaven I want to see Jesus first, and then William Booth. The others—King David, Paul, Moses—they all can wait. In one of his sermons William Booth said these words:

"While women weep, as they do now, I'll fight;
While little children go hungry, I'll fight;
While men go to prison, in and out, in and out, I'll fight;
While there is a drunkard left,
While there is a poor lost girl on the streets,
Where there remains one dark soul without the light of God –
I'll fight!
I'll fight to the very end!"

Doesn't that sound like something you would expect from some young, on-fire Christian? William Booth said those words in his last sermon when he was eighty-three years old, and was almost blind. When he was about to die, he said, "I'll fight to the very end." I don't know about you, but that sounds like someone I want on my team.

My time with The Salvation Army was an eye opener. I became a member of the ACA, which is the American Correctional Association. I got to go to conferences all around the country and see all of the newest and most modern equipment being used in prisons. We set up a booth, along with about six hundred other vendors, and let the conference participants know what we did in the prisons. I was a part of a very large prison ministry that was in one hundred and twenty different countries.

My territory was called Kansas and Western Missouri. That meant I was over every jail and prison in the entire State of Kansas and Western Missouri. I had over one hundred and fifty volunteers and we tried to have some presence in those jails and prisons on at least a weekly basis.

We did a project every year at Christmas called Angel Tree. We took volunteers into the prisons and jails and met with any inmate who wanted to send his or her children a gift for Christmas. We brought samples of gifts for all ages, girls and boys. The inmates picked a gift for each one of their children and we bought those gifts from vendors. With volunteer help, we wrapped and mailed one to each child. In our division we wrapped and mailed over five thousand gifts at Christmas. Sometimes the gifts came back, because the mother or father wouldn't let the kids have anything from the prisoner. It was a very sad thing to get a gift back—but of course, we didn't tell the inmates unless they asked.

When I was director, my office was in Leavenworth, Kansas. There were eight prisons and jails within twenty minutes of my office; we did a lot of ministry there. I had over one hundred volunteers throughout the whole division. We held Bible studies daily in different prisons, and on Sunday, with the help of our volunteers, we held morning, afternoon, and evening services. My time with The Salvation Army was priceless and will be an everlasting memory.

FROM JUNKIES TO JESUS

Prison ministry is not the most rewarding ministry a person can get involved in. If you are looking for high numbers of success stories, you won't find them in prison ministry. I can't count the times I had my heart broken over someone who I worked with—one I really thought was going to make it—and they fell.

I have literally sent some men to a half dozen or more rehab programs and they come back home, and appear to be doing well... then relapse. There was one young couple in particular Debbie and I were really drawn to. We had high hopes for them, that they wouldn't be just another statistic.

Ray and Lisa Stribling were different from some of the others we had worked with. We saw so much potential. We prayed hard that they would not fall back into the life of drugs and madness the Lord brought them out of.

Ray had given his heart to the Lord at Municipal Correctional Institution, which was the jail where I later was chaplain. Ray was a serious drug dealer and had no intentions of quitting his profession—but God interrupted his miserable life, and gave him hope. His wife Lisa also gave her heart to the Lord and they started coming to our home fellowship group.

This was me visiting Ray in prison in 1992.

Each of them had been on the needle for many years. Their arms were covered in tracks and it was not going to be an easy road for them to travel. Before they accepted Christ, Ray faced prison time on drug charges and Lisa faced charges for writing bad checks. They pleaded guilty and were sentenced to prison. We prayed God would keep them strong and protect them while they were away for a while. They had four children at home and it just didn't seem possible these sweet new Christians were going to go off to prison and leave their kids. Lisa was sentenced first and got shipped off to the women's prison in Chillicothe, Missouri. Debbie and I went to visit her in prison and it nearly broke our hearts seeing our new friend locked up.

There was something different about her and Ray. We believed they were going to make it and make a difference for the kingdom of God.

Ray took care of their four children until his sentencing, and then he went to do his time. Their family was faithful to take care of the children while they were both gone. Lisa came home first and took up where Ray left off taking care of the kids alone. We took Lisa to the prison with us to see her husband.

Today they are the leaders of the inner-city ministry Debbie and I are involved in called Hope City. I have lovingly dubbed them our pastors. The church is in the heart of the hood and we are bringing HOPE to those that have no hope. We serve lunch every day at noon and a hot meal on Monday and Friday nights. The prayer room is open to the public from 8:00am till 10:00pm, five days a week. There are evening services held, and we have a food pantry on Wednesday. Men and women can come in off the streets and take a hot shower and feel loved.

It is such an incredible blessing to minister with this couple God brought into our lives over twenty years ago. I have taken them both into prisons with me; we have traveled hundreds of miles together doing HIS will and trying to let our light shine. Praise the Lord!!!

Ray and Lisa 2013
as the leaders of
Hope City

GOING BACK TO JAIL

After a few years with The Salvation Army, God began tugging my heart in a new direction. I had a volunteer named Ronnie who went in with us on a regular basis. He had been in prison himself for quite a few years and could really relate to the inmates. He was in a wheelchair, but could do about anything anyone else could do. He was super strong, because he wheeled about twenty or more miles a day, just to stay in shape.

He told me one day that he wanted to build a private jail, and would like for me to be involved. I told him I didn't have any interest in building a jail, but would pray for him on a regular basis. A year or so went by and he told me some of the disappointments he was experiencing. Things were not going well with his partners on the jail project. Finally, he asked me to pray that his partners would back out of the deal, because he wasn't feeling good about them. God answered the prayers and they decided not to be involved with Ronnie. Shortly after that the Lord told me to get involved.

I told Ronnie and he got real excited. "I knew you were going to be involved!"

I didn't want him to get too excited, because at that point I thought I was just going to be an advisor. I didn't have near the faith Ronnie had, but of course I never told him that. I thought since he and I were both felons and neither of us had any money; there was no way we could build a jail.

One day I told him, "We have a real problem."

"What's our problem?"

"You own a car and a wheelchair...I own a car and a house. Neither of us has a savings account."

I knew it took deep pockets to build a jail and that wasn't us, we had holes in ours.

"Bill, do you think God would put this in my heart and not provide a way for us to do it?"

Wow! He had faith. "You're right, Ronnie, let's start meeting together and praying."

We started meeting every Monday night and got on our knees and cried out to God for wisdom and direction. Another friend of ours, Phil, started meeting and praying with us every week. God brought several more Christian men into the picture. Without going into every detail, and to make a very long story short, the Lord provided the money we needed to build.

We bought one hundred and fifty-two acres in an unincorporated county, so there were no rules against us building the jail. If we were the general contractors we could save hundreds of thousands of dollars. With my years of experience running construction jobs, I volunteered to run the job. We bought a construction trailer and set it up on the jobsite. I quit The Salvation Army and put on a hard hat.

Someone didn't want us building our jail in that county and started campaigning against us. The State of Missouri got involved and they also tried to stop us. We hired a lobbyist to go to the Capital and work for us. I will never forget the phone call I received from the lobbyist at nine p.m. one night. 'Gentlemen... start your bulldozers.'

We started the site work on July 5, 1999. We felt the Lord gave us *Integrity Correctional Centers* as the name for the jail. When we started construction, Missouri had no jail standards. We didn't want to own and operate a jail without being accountable to someone. Because of my experience with The Salvation Army and the standards I saw in the prisons I was in every day, I wanted us to build this jail according to ACA standards. It is the highest standard available for adult correctional facilities. If we could get an accreditation from them, it was the gold seal of approval and we would be accountable to them.

We had every intention of this being one of the top accredited jails in the country, one that the State of Missouri would be proud to say was in their state. Although we had opposition, we were determined to get the jail built and be operational. We just weren't aware of how the devil would use whatever means possible to put us out of business.

In November of that year, my mother died and went to be with Jesus and my dad, who she had missed so much for the past eight years. At ninety-three years old, she was ready to go Home.

Construction went well and we were on a fast track. We built five buildings, totaling twenty-five thousand square feet. We put in over a mile of eight inch water main and over a mile of three phase electricity. We brought in a thirty-thousand-gallon propane tank. I didn't realize how big it was till I saw a ten-thousand-gallon tanker filling it. The tanker looked like a Tonka Toy sitting beside it. We built a one-hundred-and-fifty-thousand-dollar sewage treatment plant that could accommodate five hundred beds. We put up thirteen hundred feet of FIRST DEFENCE, costing one hundred dollars a foot. It was a fence with a guarantee no one could climb.

We opened our doors in January, 2000—seven months after starting dirt work. At the time we built the jail, the cost of building jails was from twenty-five thousand dollars a bed to sixty-five thousand dollars a bed. We built our jail for thirteen thousand dollars a bed—Two hundred beds, for 2.6 million dollars. The miracles that took place while building the jail could fill a book.

In the few years I ran the jail we saw many men and women touched by God. When we had about sixty-five people on staff, we told the Christian staff members, we wanted them to preach the Gospel every day, but we didn't want them to say anything. We told them that men and women in jail have heard about Jesus till they are sick of hearing about Him. They don't need to hear about Jesus, they need to see Him. If you do something out of line to an inmate, go back and tell them you are sorry; they are not used to hearing that.

Another thing we did was try to put *correction* back in corrections. We told inmates when they came in our jail, "Where you've been before, you may have run the jail, but you're not going to run this one. We run this jail and if you don't obey the rules, you'll be reprimanded." Most of the men and women who are incarcerated have not had any one care enough about them to correct them. We found that they actually appreciated having someone care enough about them to correct them.

The administrator we hired came to us with twenty years of experience from the Jackson County Jail. Our security administrator came with twenty-six years of experience from Kansas City, Missouri's city jail. One of our captains had over twenty years of experience from the same jail.

We underwent some intense spiritual warfare over the next few years. One day, a friend of mine came by the jail and took me to lunch. Afterward, we rode around and he prophesied over me for an hour. He told me that morning over breakfast he asked his wife, "I wonder if the men who've gotten involved with Bill Corum have any idea what they've gotten themselves into?"

This is what he told me: When you give your heart to Jesus, you get a target on your back. When you decide to start a business and run it with Christian principles—not cheating on your taxes or doing anything under the table—that target doubles in size.

When you have the audacity to name your business one of God's characteristics, INTEGRITY, you have just doubled the size of the target again.

He then told me I was entering into a business different from all others. The two places on earth where demons run wild are in mental institutions and prisons. He then added, "Bill, you are getting ready to jump into hell's fire and pull people out."

He told me we need some real intercessors praying for us. Looking back, I'm certain we didn't have that piece in place.

Our founder/chaplain, Ronnie, kept a stack of letters from inmates. One inmate wrote after he left.

I have been locked up in jails in New York, Florida and California. I have never been treated like I got treated at ICC, thank you for treating me like a human being.

My wife received a letter from a girl sentenced to prison, and she wrote, *Would you please call the Independence Police Department and thank them for putting me in your jail?*

Those letters were what I was after, to know that we were letting those inmates see Jesus and not just hear about Him.

The spiritual warfare manifested through the weather one day. I had just left the jail and was probably twenty miles or more up the highway, when our administrator, Dave, called. He and Ronnie, our security administrator, Bill, and administrative assistant, Marilyn, were standing in the parking lot.

Dave said, "Hollywood doesn't have the technology to do special effects like we're seeing here. There are three long clouds a hundred feet or so overhead. They are about a quarter mile long and almost touching each other. The bottom one is rolling in one direction, the middle one the opposite direction and the top one the opposite of that. They are different shades of black and the ugliest thing we've ever seen.

At the very moment he told me that, I felt the Holy Spirit say, "That is a picture of the spiritual warfare that is going on over that jail."

THE 700 CLUB AGAIN

I t was 2001 and had been twelve years since the 700 Club aired my story on nationwide television. I ran into the kitchen to answer the phone.

"Debbie, I just got a phone call from the 700 Club."

"What did they want?"

"Pat Robertson wants to do some archive stories. They wanted to know what I was doing today."

"What did you tell them you were doing?" "I told them I was back in jail, but that I was one of the owners and not locked up."

"You never told me what an archive story is." She said.

What they told me was, some of the stories they aired over the years received higher than normal response, and they wanted to see what those people were doing today. My story was one of those they decided to follow up on. We felt honored to have the story of the jail go nationwide, and give all the glory to God.

They brought the 700 Club film crew into our jail and shot for a whole day. The filming process, with candid shots and interviewing different people lasted five or six hours. When it aired on television, it was about five minutes long, but very powerful. We had a blast doing it and heard the response from viewers was good. A large number called in for prayer. That's what it's all about.

Time after time, year after year, the enemy tried to close our jail down. We wanted so badly to see it work, but struggled financially.

One day, the main stockholder came to me and said they had figured out why we couldn't get a federal contract. He told me the reason was because I was a convicted felon and the Feds wouldn't do business with us because of that. Two of the stockholders came one day and said they had a chance to hire a retired Federal Bureau of Prisons Director, and he probably could get them the contract with INS. I had been trying, unsuccessfully, for over three years to get in with them. In order for the Bureau guy to get the contract, they needed to take my name off of every document and I could, in no way, be connected with the jail. I agreed that if that was what it took, I was willing to step down. It was one of the hardest things I have ever done in my life, but I wanted the jail to survive.

However, there was a master plan for the jail to fail. The enemy hated it that we treated inmates humanely. Our plan was for inmates to leave our jail knowing there were people in the world who genuinely cared for them. We were concerned, not only for them in the present, but we cared what happened to them eternally. We desperately needed prayer warriors, and were told by a prophetic couple who came over to our house one night, that we needed intercessors. We just never did get them in place. We had people who prayed for us, but never had true intercession going up day and night.

On January 15, 2003, Charlie Turnbow came out of retirement and went to work for us. He told the owners he would work for ninety days, and if he didn't have them a federal contract in those ninety days, they weren't going to get one. Charlie had been with the Bureau of Prisons for thirty years— twenty-three as a warden and the last seven as one of only six directors in the United States. He had power, and if anyone could do it, he could. The first day he was in my office, he picked up the phone and called John Ashcroft in Washington, DC.

He planned my retirement party for January 31, 2003. Two weeks after he arrived, I was gone. He wanted my name off of everything. I was president of ICC and ICC management, as well as being on the board, and being one of the stockholders. Once everything had been restructured, my name was taken off all records. Charlie went to work, and at the end of ninety days, he called the board members together.

"I can't get you a federal contract, but I want you to know one thing…it's not Bill Corum's fault."

So my leaving wasn't necessary, but God had another plan. I have to admit, I was pretty messed up over the whole deal—physically, mentally, emotionally, and spiritually. I didn't backslide, and I wasn't mad at God, I was just sort of numb. After I helped design, physically built, and ran the place, Ronnie's dream had become my dream too.

I remember my son Larry calling one day. "Dad, I can't imagine the Pope without the Catholic Church, and I can't imagine the Catholic Church without the Pope. I can't imagine ICC without you, and I can't imagine you without ICC."

It took several months, but God slowly began to heal me. My wife and I had a pastor pray for us one day. He said, "God is going to do a "SUDDENLY" in your life."

He told us God was going to do something that would change our lives and it would be suddenly, and also our finances would change suddenly. We didn't know what to make of it and so kept on with business as usual. I was having trouble finding a job. I couldn't get back into the plumbers union, even though I tried.

It seemed God was closing every door I tried to go through. I paid our bills by selling old car parts on eBay. I worked for a friend in his classic car store, cleaning cars. Even though I was not making much money, I felt rich in God's grace.

SUDDENLY

I went by to see a friend of mine at his office; I hadn't seen him in years. As I was leaving, he said, "You know something, Bill? I would like to be in business with you someday."

I drove away confused as to what he meant. He was in the car business, and I had been in some sort of prison ministry for many years. I wasn't sure how the two could come together. We had a few lunches and dinners together, and I introduced Don to my friend, John. John was interested in hearing about Don's plans to start his own business. We got together and John brought his nephew, Jason, along.

That made four of us talking about the business. We bought a piece of property in Overland Park, Kansas and formed two corporations. We hired staff and were in business all within five months of my first meeting with Don. I would call that a SUDDENLY.

Our business became very successful and every year we grew and prospered. All three of my partners were Christians and encouraged me to continue doing prison ministry while being a business owner. For me, it was an honor to be in business with three men who loved God. We sought biblical wisdom in all our business decisions. When we started out, Bob Tamasi, a good friend of mine, told us there was one word that would make us successful: "Serve."

We have seen the power of that word come true after nine years in business—if you serve people, you will be successful.

Another thing I know made us successful is that we listened for the voice of the Lord. While we planned the business, Don told us God had given him something to share with us.

He said, "The Lord gave me 7 P's."

1. Prayer (pray about everything you do).

2. Plan (you have to have a plan for what you are going to do).

3. Place (you have to have the right location to launch your project).

4. People (you have to have the right people working for and with you).

5. Provision (plenty of money).

6. Priorities (you have to keep your priorities in order).

7. Peace of God (if you are doing the others right, the peace of God will be there, and if it's not, something's wrong).

We all believed without a doubt, it was from the Lord. I believe the 7 P's the Lord gave Don could be a business model for anyone. If you are a committed Christian, and are starting a business, I would recommend you use that formula; serve, and run your business with Godly principles, and see what God will do.

Bob Williamson, a friend of mine, said we should add two more P's—Perseverance and Patience. That makes nine P's and just about covers everything. I would suggest leaving prayer at the beginning and the peace of God at the end. In November of 2012 we celebrated our ninth year in business and these principles work.

Over the last few years, I wrote a couple of letters to my partners requesting that they release me back into full-time ministry. I felt the Spirit of God woo me and gently call me back. He wanted me giving myself fully to prison and street ministry. My partners had let me do ministry any time I wanted to, but I felt there was something more I was to do. They graciously figured out a way for me to go full time to what I know God called me to.

I retired December 31, 2012, the day before a new year started, so that I could start 2013 with Jesus Christ as my CEO. By the time this book is in print, there will be a new ministry up and running.

It had been twenty-one years since I first formed Prison Power Ministries. When Ricky Beach took over the ministry in the 90's, he changed the name. Right before I retired, I checked with the State of Missouri, and guess what? The name was available. So I am now working for **Prison Power Ministries, Inc.** again.

The Bible tells us in Hebrews 13:3 to remember those in prison. Jesus said, when we visit those in prison we are visiting Him. When we do it to the least, we are doing it to Him.

I always used to tell Debbie, "I want to die of a heart attack on a prison yard telling men and women how God changed my life."

"Please don't say that, Bill."

"Ok, Honey. How's this...I want to die of a heart attack on a prison yard telling men and women how God changed my life, when I'm ninety-five."

"That's okay," she says with a big smile.

Will I ever retire? Oh yeah! Whenever they get about 70,000 miles on them, I will put four new ones on...probably Michelins.

RICHEST MAN ALIVE

Even though I don't have enough money to be considered rich, I feel rich. I don't just feel a little rich, I feel like the richest man on earth. I have been given things that no amount of money could buy. God gave me my mind back. In 1983 I couldn't carry on a conversation with you, because in the middle of a sentence, I would forget what I was saying. I did so many drugs and drank so much alcohol my mind was getting fried. God renewed my mind and made it better than it was before I ever used drugs or alcohol.

The Bible says, *"And be not conformed to this world: but be ye transformed by the renewing of your mind, that ye may prove what is that good, and acceptable, and perfect, will of God."* Romans 12:2. How much would you pay to get your mind back?

God gave me back my wife. I used to kiss her goodbye and tell her I would be back that night. I might not come home for weeks. God healed our marriage and gave her grace to put up with me. She was able to forgive me of all the wrong I had done to her. How much would you pay to get your wife back?

God gave me back my sons and daughters. I wasn't a good father. On weekends I was supposed to see my kids, but I wouldn't be around. Through years of prayer, and sitting down one on one with my kids and repenting to them, our relationship is being restored. How much would you pay to get your kids back?

Before Christ I did no less than five hundred dollars' worth of cocaine a day, drinking two quarts of whiskey a day, and taking all kinds of other drugs. I would have taken a birth control pill if I thought I could get high on it. I would take any kind of pill that was out there if it was illegal and it would get me off.

To date I have not done an illegal drug since 1983. I have not taken a drink of alcohol. I was delivered from drugs and alcohol without ever going to any kind of drug or alcohol rehab. Jesus is the only explanation I have for my change. *"If the Son therefore shall make you free, ye shall be free indeed."* John 8:36. How much would you pay to get off drugs and alcohol?

The greatest thing I have enjoyed over the last thirty years is peace. Never in my whole life have I had peace like I have now. When I faced going to prison for the rest of my life, I was completely at peace. In the natural that is not possible. It seems like I would have had anxiety, but I had none. I just knew everything was going to be alright. I was trying to do the Word, not just hear it (James 1:22).

Philippians 4 instructs us to think on certain things and God's peace will be with us.

"Finally, brethren, whatsoever things are true, whatsoever things are honest, whatsoever things are just, whatsoever things are pure, whatsoever things are lovely, whatsoever things are of good report, if there is any virtue and if there be any praise, think on these things. Those things which ye have both learned and received and heard and seen in Me, do: and the peace of God shall be with you." Philippians 4:8-9.

How much would you pay for peace?

Family picture taken at my wife's 60th surprise birthday party in 2013. How blessed I am to have 4 children, 2 sons-in-law and 2 daughters-in-law. Also I have 10 grandchildren, and 3 great grandchildren. Psalms 127:5 says "Blessed is the man whose quiver is full." Looks like I am real blessed. The only one of the family missing in this picture is my granddaughter's husband.

I feel rich because I am laying up treasures in Heaven that rust can't corrupt and thieves can't break in and steal. Those treasures are the only ones that will last.

My friend, Bob Williamson, whose testimony is that God brought him from rags to riches, has written *Words for Today* for the past fifteen years.

This is an excerpt out of one of those words:

> "Eternity is forever and this life is but a vapor. It seems that the entire world wants to chase the things that mean the least. The money, the material things, the power, the titles, the accomplishments, and streets, bridges, and buildings named in our honor. In the end though, we will face God alone and we will take nothing with us, (including those Rolex watches and diamond rings), even our families and friends will all be left behind."

THE ULTIMATE PARDON

DEDICATED TO DAD AND MOM

There is no one I know of on my mother or dad's side of the family who ever went to prison or got into trouble like I did. I don't know of anyone in my family who was a drug addict. I don't think there were any real criminals in my family tree. I believe if you traced my family tree back several generations, they were all just hard-working people with good morals.

How is it possible for someone who came from a family like mine to rebel and do everything that goes against all they were taught? I can't blame it on going to the sixth grade at the high school, because I was rebelling with Jesse at eight years of age. It wasn't because of the crowd I ran with, because a big portion of my life I committed crimes alone. I have to take responsibility for my own actions; no one held a gun to my head. I made choices. I know if there was ever a black sheep in a family, it was me—and I was the blackest of them all. I am so thankful I am now as white as snow; I have been washed by the blood of the Lamb.

There is one commandment in the Bible that comes with a promise. It says, if we honor our father and mother, we will have long life. I would not be honoring my parents if I didn't tell you this about them.

After doing prison ministry for over twenty-five years, I have personally never known anyone whose parents loved them like mine loved me. I am not saying there is no one…I have just personally not met them.

Most inmates I have talked to over the years have come from broken homes. My parents were married sixty-three years.

My dad and mom celebrating their 60th wedding anniversary.

Drugs and alcohol have plagued most inmates' homes since their birth. My folks never touched a drop of alcohol in their lives. My mother and father didn't smoke or use any kind of drugs. I never heard a cuss word come out of either one of their mouths. The only time in my life I remember my dad saying anything that could be considered cussing, was when I was with that fifteen-year-old girl in the motel, and he asked me what I had done to her.

I worked by my dad's side building houses and never heard him swear or tell a dirty joke. I did see him walk away when other people told them. My mother died when she was ninety-three years old, and she had never been in a movie theatre or to a dance. They were the most loving, unselfish people I have ever known in my whole life. I remember Mom would put my sister and me to bed at night, and if Dad asked for a bowl of ice cream, she would not get him one unless she got Sharon and I up and gave us some too.

They visited me everywhere I got locked up. When I got locked up in Clarksdale, Mississippi, they drove five hundred and fifty miles to see me. When I was waiting to go to trial in Oxford, they drove six hundred miles to see me. Dad told me years later that sometimes they drove down...visited me...then drove home, bathed, changed clothes and drove right back. It was a twelve hundred mile round trip and they made it many times.

I remember one time they came to see me and asked if I wanted a chocolate malt. I wanted one for sure, but there were ten or twelve other inmates in the big cell I was in. Dad asked the jailer if he could bring everyone malts. The jailer gave him the okay. In a few minutes they returned with malts for everyone, including the jailer.

When my friends and I hopped the freight train and got locked up in Tucumcari, New Mexico, my dad made the thirteen-hundred-mile round trip to get us out of jail and take us home. When I was sent to Ashland, Kentucky for a sixty-day observation, they made a fourteen-hundred-mile round trip to see me. I was there with guys who had been locked up for years and their families only lived an hour or two away, and they never got a visit. No wonder I hated and cussed that psychiatrist at Ashland, when he told me it was Mom and Dad's fault that I turned into a criminal.

They visited me in San Diego when I was in boot camp, which was sixteen hundred miles one way. When I was in the brig in Millington, Tennessee, they drove over five hundred miles to see me. Englewood, Colorado is another place they drove six hundred miles to see me. I figured it up once—my dad drove over twenty-five thousand miles one year visiting me. The average mileage on a car back then was ten thousand miles a year.

If I came in at eleven o'clock at night with a couple of buddies, my mom got out of bed and asked if we were hungry. All any of them had to do was nod his head, and she whipped up a five course meal. She loved to cook for me, and loved to watch me eat. I think she tried to kill every friend I brought around with food. There was no one who could cook like my mother. She didn't use recipes and everyone in our family has tried to copy her cooking since she's been gone, but no one's mastered it.

Are you starting to get the picture of how much my parents loved me? No matter what I did, they loved me. My sister and I came first and they were second. They did everything possible to help me, and still, I was a rebel. If there was ever a human on this earth who should have excelled and never been in trouble, it was me. I had their blessing from the time I was born until they died. If they did all that for me when I was rebellious...how much more would they have done if I had not been rebellious? I don't believe they would have done *any* more, because their love was not conditional.

Mom used to have dreams about me; she wore her knees out praying for me. She told me so many answers to the prayers she prayed for me, I could fill another book. When Debbie started praying for me, mom encouraged her and they prayed together. My saintly mother prayed for almost forty years for me to surrender to Jesus. She prayed many times, "Not my will, but Thy will be done."

My dad gave me Godly advice all my life. He tried everything he knew of to point me in the right direction. Although I didn't listen to him at the time, thankfully, he saw me walk out of the darkness and into the light before he died in 1991. We got to spend eight years together on the same page. Mom got to enjoy seeing me love God, and love my Dad, those last eight years of his life.

My sister and I with our mother after dad had passed away. This was on her 90th birthday. She was still a prayer warrior.

Mom died in 1999, but she spent the last sixteen years of her life praising the Lord for His answer to her prayers for my salvation. We had many good times together. Mom and her best friend in life, Dad, are together again in Heaven. I look forward to the day I join them.

CHAPTER

48

THE BLESSING

One of the messages I have heard so many times on prison weekends is the message Bill Glass gives on the father's blessing. He often tells the story about a guy getting a divorce. The judge asked the man, "How often do you tell your wife you love her?"

The man replied, "I told her the day I married her, and that applies until I tell her different."

No, it doesn't. You have to speak your feelings. A blessing has to be spoken and must communicate three things: Love…Value… Belonging.

Inmates often say, 'My dad never told me he loved me, but I know he did'.

If your father never said it, then he didn't bless you. Men don't like to hug and say, 'I love you'. Inmates hug their wives and girlfriends in the visiting room, but push their little boys and girls away. They say, 'I can't hug him, he's a boy, and I am a convict'. If you don't hug him, he will grow up and be a convict.

You can't put conditions on the blessing, either. Fathers always tend to keep the blessing just out of reach.

The kid says, "Dad, I got A's on my report card."

"If you would have gotten A+'s, you would have made the honor roll."

Somewhere across town, a high school senior runs out of the locker room all excited. "Dad, I scored four touchdowns!"

"I saw you, but five would've been the state record."

They always keep the blessing just out of reach. You watch an NFL football game on television and see the guy score a touchdown, and then he does his little dance. When he gets to the sideline for a breather, he takes off his helmet, looks into the camera, and says, "Hi, Mom."

It is always that same nauseating, 'Hi, Mom'. Why don't they ever say 'Hi, Dad'? I will tell you why. It's because dad was never there, and if he was there, he was on the phone, behind a book, or doing something he wanted to do.

My good friend, Bill Glass, has a saying. 'When you are where you are, be there'. Don't be on your cell phone when you are on a date with your daughter, or out to lunch with your son, or playing golf with a friend. Bill told me that one time he took his teenage granddaughters somewhere, and his cell phone started ringing.

One of the girls said, "Grandpa, your phone's ringing."

"I know it," Bill said.

"Aren't you going to answer it?"

"No."

"How come you're not?"

"Because, whoever is on the phone is not as important to me as you are."

This actually happened to me recently. My oldest daughter, son-in-law, and fourteen-year-old grandson came over for dinner. During dinner I wanted to look something up on the Internet. My phone was in another room, so I asked my daughter for hers. She said, "I didn't bring it."

I said to my grandson, "Give me your phone, J.D."

My daughter then said, "None of us brought a phone."

I asked her if that was by design and she said yes. They wanted to spend the evening with us, uninterrupted. I cannot tell you how much that blessed me. She had never heard Bill Glass' saying, 'When you are where you are, be there'.

At the baptism of Jesus Christ, God said, *"This is My beloved Son in whom I am well pleased."* Matthew 3:17

That is a powerful unmixed message. We shouldn't tell our kids *I love you, because….* If we tell them *I love you because* you are pretty, or sweet, we are putting conditions on our love. Tell them *I love you, you are mine, and I think you are terrific.*

Many years ago there were sixty thousand inmates in Florida prisons. Someone asked how many of those inmates at the time were Jewish. There were only thirteen. The reason is because it is a Jewish custom for fathers to bless their sons when they reach a certain age.

Every single man on the earth needs his father's blessing. God blessed His Son at His baptism as an example of how important it is for us to bless our sons and daughters. Pick up your little girl and hold her on your lap. Kiss her and hug her, because if you don't, when she is a teenager, she will find a man who will. Girls need their daddy's blessing too.

I was asked to share my testimony in a large church in Frankfurt, Germany. I was told in advance to only take about thirty minutes. During the music part of the service, God told me to speak on the father's blessing. I told God, "They only gave me thirty minutes and that isn't enough time to do the message any justice and pray for men afterward."

During the announcements, the Lord *again* told me to give the father's blessing message. I told Him I knew the United States had the problem of men not blessing their sons and daughters, but I didn't know anything about the German culture. *Again* during the offering, God instructed me to do the father's blessing. I told Him I would…but was concerned about the allotted time.

When they brought me up and introduced me, the pastor spoke German, of course, and the interpreter translated for me. The pastor started to walk off and turned back to my interpreter and spoke.

The interpreter smiled at me. "He said take all the time you need this morning."

I knew I had no choice but preach what God told me to. Over one hundred men came forward for prayer to receive the father's blessing. I prayed for each one of them—it took two or three hours. I was so glad God persisted with me, because so many men were touched that day.

I have received many blessings from God myself since I began teaching and preaching on the father's blessing. I believe my heavenly Father wants to bless me all the time. One of the many blessings I have enjoyed in the last few years was the blessing of writing for the Gospel Tract Society.

YOU WANT ME TO DO WHAT?

My friend, Tom Buttram, at Gospel Tract Society asked me to write a monthly article for the *Harvester* magazine. His father started printing tracts in 1926 when God spoke three words to him—'print My Word'. *Harvester* magazine became part of that ministry. I felt as humbled and honored as when I went to work for The Salvation Army. Both ministries have been in operation for decades, and both are deeply rooted in Christ. The opportunity to be associated with them wasn't something I took lightly.

I not only quit high school, but when I *was* there I *wasn't* there. So I felt like I didn't have much to offer an eighty-some-year-old ministry—no writing skills, no theology training—but the one thing I had was… knee-ology.

Tom has a heart for the incarcerated. Gospel Tract Society has been sending Bibles and tracts to prisoners for decades. He was thrilled to partner with someone who went into prisons full time. He felt it would be good to have an article every month built around those particular men and women. I was no journalist, but sure could put on paper some of my personal experiences as a former inmate and criminal, and now as a prison preacher.

I wrote an article every month for over two years and then took a break. It was such a blessing reading some of the letters Tom got as a result of those articles. I believe God used me during that season of my life to reach some people who otherwise might not have been reached. I give Him all the glory.

I want to share an excerpt from one of my *Harvester* stories with you. The article is found in the April 2008 edition. Remember my experiences in the Marine Corps? I was an embarrassment to the Corps, but God even turned that around almost fifty years later:

SEMPER FI

At my first court martial, I stood before a Marine Corps Colonel who said, "If you don't straighten up, you will be in the penitentiary before you are twenty-one."

I laughed in his face and was in Federal prison when I was nineteen.

Two Marine Corps officers came to a Federal prison and gave me my discharge. I was glad to get out. When I got out of prison, I continued my life of crime and was as rebellious as ever, just determined never to get caught again. Over the next twenty-plus years I never felt ashamed of being a rebel in the Marines. I was kind of glad I had not bowed down and let them make me obey.

In 1983 when I gave my life to Christ at almost forty years of age, I began to wish I had done things differently. I felt so ashamed for the way I conducted myself and wished I could do it over, but there was no way to undo the past. When I saw a Marine in uniform, I wished I could go up and tell him of my time in the Corps, but was too ashamed.

I loved the saying *Semper Fi*, which is something only Marines say to each other. It is Latin for Always Faithful. Since I had not been faithful, I didn't feel I had the right to say it. I carried this shame around and wanted so badly for it to go away, but couldn't do anything to fix it.

In 2007, after serving God for over twenty-four years, I spoke in some Texas youth prisons that were like boot camps. Most of the staff was made up of retired Marines. I found myself surrounded by them, most of who were decorated. As I spoke to one of the groups, there were about four or five Marines in the room. I talked to the kids about choices and consequences and some of the mistakes I made in my life. I told them I had one regret that I could never undo. I felt very nervous telling the whole story, but confessed to the kids and those decorated Marines everything about my time in the Corps.

After I finished, one of the Marines approached me and said, "*Semper Fi*, once a Marine, always a Marine."

He took off his belt, unscrewed the Globe and Anchor from the buckle, and gave it to me. I broke down and cried. At that moment, I felt totally forgiven by the Marines. I found out later that the man who gave me his Globe and Anchor was a decorated Marine. His belt buckle was the one he wore when he was on duty at the White house.

Now when I see a Marine, I walk up and say, *"Semper Fi."*

That moment of destiny in 2007 changed my life. While telling the story to a group of men recently I broke down and cried again. I will never be the same. God healed me of something that happened forty-five years ago.

After telling the story the other day to a former Marine, he took off his red hat that read ONCE A MARINE ALWAYS A MARINE on the front and SEMPER FI on the back. He gave it to me.

God just keeps on blessing me (red just happens to be my favorite color). Is it at all possible that God may be a Marine, since He is the one who is ALWAYS FAITHFUL?

THE ULTIMATE PARDON

started applying for a pardon from the State of Missouri in 1995. I asked my former probation officer about the proper steps in applying for it. He said I needed to put together a package and send it to the Board of Probation and Parole at the State Capital. I needed as many letters and documents as I could get to prove I was a changed person, and was now doing something constructive with my life.

I obtained letters from wardens of prisons I did ministry in, police chiefs, mayors, a state senator, and many business people who were friends of mine. Certainly the best letter and the one that carried the most weight was a letter from Judge Carl Gumm, the judge who sentenced me. He said in his letter, 'If a man ever deserved to be pardoned, it is Bill Corum'.

I also sent flyers from schools where I did anti-drug meetings and high school assemblies, flyers from churches I spoke at, and posters we put up in prisons when we brought in pro athletes. I put it all together and sent it to Jefferson City, Missouri.

About a year after I sent it, I called a friend, who was a state senator. He checked and said it had been sent to the Governor's office. I waited another year and called the Governor's office. They told me these things take time. After three years I gave up hope that it would ever happen.

Five more years passed. In 2003 I received a call from a probation officer telling me she had been assigned to reopen my executive clemency case and would I come see her. Wow! I didn't think I would ever hear from anyone. I went to see her. She told me that all the paper work I sent to the Capital eight years earlier had been lost, and instructed me to get some letters of reference from some other people.

The problem was—Judge Gumm had died, and his letter was the most influential of all. My friend, the state senator, was not in politics any longer. Some of the wardens had retired. Police chiefs were no longer in office. I finally asked her if I could write a letter myself, asking the governor for mercy, and not ask my friends to take time out of their busy schedules to write another letter. She said okay.

After two more years passed, I called her and was told again that these things take time. I already figured that out on my own, because over ten years had passed since I first applied.

Another year went by—I gathered some letters from several people, including, Charlie Turnbow, former director of the Federal Bureau of Prisons, a Kansas City, Missouri police officer, and some highly respected business men in the state. I put together a nice package and sent it to the proper authorities. I had been pursuing a pardon from the State of Missouri for a long time. They never said no, they just never responded.

Finally…a response came in January of 2009, after fourteen years and four Governors.

> The Governor has considered your application for Executive Clemency. I regret to inform you that the Governor has denied your application for Executive Clemency on December 19, 2008.

I was extremely disappointed, as you might imagine. I worked so hard to live a life of integrity and honesty since my conversion to Christ twenty-six years earlier.

> *"But he that shall endure unto the end, the same shall be saved."* Matthew 24:13

It has been over thirty years now, and I still refuse to give up. I am going to continue being one of the best American citizens I can be, and pursue a pardon from my state. If I get it, I will praise Him. If I don't, I will praise Him.

After I received that letter in 2009, I complained to the Lord about it just not being fair after all these years. He reminded me of Romans 5:10; it says that while we were the enemies of God, Jesus died for us. He also told me no matter what man said about me, to Him, I was righteous. I thought of what the Bible said in II Corinthians 5:21, that Jesus who knew no sin was made sin on my behalf, so I could become the righteousness of God in Him. WOW!! God looks at me and sees me as righteous.

My hope in all this comes from the fact that over 2000 years ago, Jesus died on an old rugged cross, and all of my and your sins were nailed to that cross with Him. He was buried, and on the third day rose from the dead, so you and I could receive *THE ULTIMATE PARDON.*

So, although man may not be willing to forgive us of our past sins, the Lord Jesus has. He is alive and I am totally forgiven of my past. Are you forgiven of your past sins and mistakes? You can be right now.

> *"That if thou shalt confess with thy mouth the Lord Jesus, and shalt believe in thine heart that God hath raised Him from the dead, thou shalt be saved."* Romans 10:9

Won't you ask Him to come into your heart and take control of your life, so you, too, can experience THE ULTIMATE PARDON.

In HIS grip,

Bill Corum

THE ULTIMATE PARDON

BRIGHT LIGHTS AT THE END OF THE TUNNEL

I promised you some bright lights at the end of the tunnel. Well, these are the stories that make those lights shine so brightly. Some of them are stories of the people I wrote about in this book, and how an encounter with God changed their lives. For some it happened at the end of their lives; it is an example of the merciful God we serve. Not all the characters in this book had happy endings to their lives. Some of them were so tragic and sad there is no getting over them. However, I am going to tell you about some happy endings that will make you smile, and hopefully will be bright enough to get you out of a dark place in your life.

I want to start with a story that is one of the brightest lights to me, personally. It is about an act of forgiveness and the redemption that can only come through God.

Over twenty years ago I was praying for my four children and God told me, "If I would honor a father's prayers for his children, how much more would I honor a father and a stepfather praying together for the same children?"

My ex-wife's husband and I were working on the same construction job, so that day I told him what I felt like God told me. He said he had been praying, and asking God for someone to pray with. Since we worked on the same job, we decided to start riding together. We began using the time we drove to and from work each day to pray for our children.

We decided one day, we needed to take it up a notch, and include our wives in the prayer meetings. So my wife, Debbie, and I began meeting with my ex-wife, Marsha, and her husband, John, to pray. We have been doing that now for over twenty years. I would like to say we have never missed a week, but that is not the case. It has been on and off again because of busy schedules, but we are determined to be faithful to the end.

To me, this is one of the bigger miracles God has done in my whole story. It may not be unusual for divorced couples to still be friends, but not many women who had husbands like I was, would ever want anything to do with, or even lay eyes on them again. Marsha and Debbie chose the higher road of forgiveness.

Midnight Dolan

When I originally started Prison Power Ministries, I was the volunteer chaplain at the city jail in Kansas City, Missouri. One day, while walking through the jail, I noticed a young man about eighteen years old. I hadn't seen him before, so I asked him his name. He said his name was Bobby Dolan. I wondered if it could be my old high school friend's son. I asked him about his father and told him I knew his dad. I will never forget what he said.

"You don't know my dad."

I guess he figured no jail preacher would know his infamous, criminal father. I asked him if he knew the story about his dad going down through Missouri and Oklahoma then jumping in a boxcar in Texas. He said he did. I proceeded to tell him I was the guy driving the car on that trip. He opened up to me and told me he would tell his dad I wanted to talk to him. His dad lived in Las Vegas. I asked Bobby to send him my little tract, *Heart of Stone*.

He did, and soon we were writing each other. Midnight's mother got sick, so when he came to see her, we got together for the first time in thirty-two years. He told me he had legally changed his name to Midnight B Dolan and preferred being called that. I started sending him tracts, and Chaplain Ray's life changing books such as: *Jewels for the Journey*, *Where Flies Don't Land*, *The Catch Me Killer*, and *One Bad Dude*.

Midnight surrendered to Jesus and today we go into prisons together and share the love of Christ. Go ahead…try and tell me there is no God and that He doesn't have power. Two guys, who stole together over fifty years ago, are now freely walking in and out of prisons. Both of us are convicted felons and don't have all of our rights restored because of the choices we made. We should not be allowed to go in and walk around freely in prisons, but are now going behind the walls, telling inmates that Jesus is the way, the truth, and the life.

When someone debates with me about my faith, I stop them, saying, "A man with an experience is not at the mercy of a man with an argument." Midnight Dolan and I have both experienced God changing our lives. I know what kind of men we were, and I know what we are today.

Essie Ray

Remember Eddy, aka Essie Ray? I stayed friends with him up until he died on June 4, 2010. He suffered with many health issues. He had been a diabetic all of his life and was supposed to take shots every day; like most men, he didn't always do like he was supposed to. As a result, he had numerous heart attacks. I tried to go see him whenever he was in the hospital. One time, I visited him every day for thirty days.

One day his ma called me…the hospital was recommending hospice, because he wasn't going to last much longer.

She said, "Superman, I ain't ready for him to die."

"Then we're gonna pray."

Debbie and I prayed and several days later, while visiting him, I asked him if he would like to ask Jesus into his heart. That day was one of the happiest days of my life, because he said yes. I loved Eddy and that day assured me I would see him again.

God's plans and the hospital's plans are not always the same. His mom took him home a few days later. We went to his house and barbecued hamburgers and had cake with him on his birthday. Al and Patty, some of our good friends, went with us. Patty played her guitar and sang to him. We gave him a goofy bobble head dog for a gift and he fell in love with it. He lived almost another year and his momma put that bobble head dog on his grave.

The last time he went to the hospital they were going to cut off his legs, because of the diabetes. He went home to be with Jesus before they could do it. I can't wait to see his smiling face when I get to Heaven. I loved that guy as much as any friend I've ever had.

Big John

Big John called me after I hadn't seen him in years and asked me to come down. He had moved and I had to look for the house out in the country. I wasn't sure I was at the right one until I walked up to knock on the door and saw the sign:

"THIS HOUSE PROTECTED BY SHOTGUN 4 DAYS A WEEK, YOU GUESS WHICH 4"

I knew I was at the right place. I went in and he weighed about a hundred and fifty pounds, down from his normal Big John two hundred and eighty. He had cancer of the tongue and wore a morphine pump. He could barely speak and didn't want to talk about Jesus.

He wanted to ask me two things. Would I take care of his two sons, Little John and Thomas? And would I preach his funeral? I told him I didn't want to preach his funeral, unless I knew where he was going to spend eternity. I told him I was sorry, but I couldn't promise to take care of his sons; I didn't even know if they wanted me to.

I left that night very sad, because John didn't want Jesus and I couldn't promise to take care of the boys. About two or three weeks later a hospital in his home town called and said he wanted to see me. When I called them back they said he was gone.

I felt horrible and said, "When did he die?"

They told me he hadn't died, but was gone from the hospital. I didn't know what to do. I didn't know anyone who knew John and had no idea how to get in touch with his sons. I took a gamble and called his house. A woman answered, and I asked, "Who's this?"

"Bernice."

"What're you doing there?"

She and Big John had been divorced for years. She told me she was there to take care of him till he died and that he wanted me to come.

I went down that night, and when I arrived, she met me in the yard. She wanted to warn me about how he looked. I told her I had seen him a few weeks earlier, but she said he had changed a lot in those weeks.

I went in to find John sitting at the table. He probably weighed less than one hundred pounds, and couldn't talk at all.

"You didn't ask me to come down to visit did you?" I asked him.

He shook his head no.

"You want to get right with Jesus tonight, don't you, John?"

He nodded his head very emphatically yes.

I prayed with him, and Big John gave his heart to Jesus that night; he went to be with the Lord the next day. I had the privilege of preaching his funeral and got to give an invitation. God only knows who asked the Lord into their hearts that day. I know I will see him in Heaven when I get there. He and Essie Ray are probably up there together fishing.

Bill H

Bill H was my friend who paid me to burn his house down—the one where Kenny was blown through the back door. Bill was bringing in the purest cocaine I ever saw from Bogota. In 1979, just a few weeks after I left Bill in Florida, the FBI showed up at my door looking for information on the whereabouts of him. I had no information for them and never heard any more about Bill until I got arrested in 1982.

I went to see a lawyer that Bill and I both used. I mentioned Bill's name and he said he knew where he was. Bill was in Spain, and as long as he stayed there, he would be safe. Florida charged him with capital murder, which carried the death penalty. Spain would not extradite anyone if they faced death.

Fast forward to 1999 and I was chaplain for the Raytown Police Department. Yep, you heard me right, that's the same Raytown I ran wild in thirty years earlier.

The Police Chief told me one day that Bill was in prison in Florida. He knew about it because Bill had a case in Raytown that was never closed, and they kept track of where he was. I looked him up on the internet and thought I would take a chance and write him. I had not had contact with him for twenty years. He wrote back and told me that he accepted Christ as his Lord and Savior since he had been locked up. We continued to write each other.

Nine years later, I preached in that prison. It was very emotional and difficult for me to stand in the pulpit and see for the first time, my good friend whom I hadn't seen in twenty-nine years.

He is one of the strongest Christians I know in any prison. I told Bill one day that as Christians we are supposed to let our lights shine. We are not supposed to blind people. He has such a glow on his face that if he was in a dark cave, he would light it up.

According to the State of Florida, his EOS (end of sentence) is 99/99/9999; that is on his official papers. Bill is at peace. When God allows me to get on a plane and go see my friend in Florida, I sure enjoy our time together. He is another story of God's grace.

Tony Moreno a.k.a. Mr. T

Tony was the guy who played his own part in *Heart of Stone*, the docudrama we made of my life. He was also the one who owned Mr. Records, the head shop next door to the cathouse eighty-year-old May ran. Tony sold cocaine to the whole west side and was a big dealer in the city. He owed my partner Kenny and I some money and we had a falling out with him.

After I became a Christian and was working on the GM plant in 1987, I shared Jesus one day with one of the guys who worked for me. He told me his son was a Christian and that he went to a Bible study at Tony Moreno's house. I just knew it couldn't be the same Tony. The guy I knew was mean as a rattlesnake and would be the least likely candidate for Christ. I gave my name and phone number to this plumber and told him to have his son give it to Tony.

A few days later, I got a call and it was the Tony I knew. He asked me to come over to his house. I was a little apprehensive, because the last time we saw each other it wasn't a friendly meeting. I knocked on his door, and he invited me in.

"Sit down, Bill." He just stared at me and chuckled. "Don't say anything…I just want to look at you."

"I just wanna look at you too, Tony."

God had changed our hard looks so much that we both just wanted to see the change. Tony gave his heart to the Lord the same month and same year as me, April of 1983. We had no idea until now, four years later. Tony and I were both walking in the reverent fear of the Lord. Proverbs 9:10 says the fear of the Lord is the beginning of wisdom.

> *"Who is as the wise man? and who knoweth the interpretation of a thing? a man's wisdom maketh his face to shine, and the boldness of his face shall be changed."* Ecclesiastes 8:1

Tony is one of the biggest soul winners I know. He is out there every chance he gets, leading someone to Christ. He has interpreted for me in Spanish speaking churches, and witnessed in prisons with me.

One very memorable prison outreach was at the United States Disciplinary Barracks at Fort Leavenworth, Kansas. The USDB at Leavenworth has the only military death row in the United States. If a member of our armed forces does something to deserve the death penalty, they will go to death row at Leavenworth. Civilians don't go there to do ministry. Tony and I are part of a small number of nonmilitary men who have ever ministered on death row at Leavenworth USDB. We do not take that lightly, but consider ourselves blessed by God.

As Tony worked his way past the cells that day, he finally stopped where he felt the Holy Spirit told him to. The prisoner he stood in front of was from the Philippines and had murdered his whole family. Tony just stood silently in front of his cell, because God hadn't given him a verse or a word to speak yet. The inmate spoke first.

"You probably want to talk to me about God…right? See those men walking in the yard? They all know God…but it took this tiny cell for me to know the Son of God, JESUS CHRIST."

Tony about fell over. They talked about Jesus and prayed together—Tony probably got more encouraged than the inmate. That happens many times; the inmate becomes the encourager. That is okay though, because the Bible says we are to encourage one another daily.

Tony and I have remained friends over the last thirty years, but I'm sure it wouldn't have been that way minus Jesus. He and I used to be in the dope house together, now we are going to be in Heaven together. Praise the Lord!!

High School Reunion

The first time Gayle called me was to invite me to our thirty-five-year high school class reunion. I was shocked. I thought they were only for people who actually graduated. Since Christ had changed me and made me a new creation, I had lots of regrets of how I had lived my life. One thing I really wished was that I had paid attention in school and been a better student. I knew if I had used as much time studying as I did being a rebel, I could have been a brain surgeon.

"I can't Gayle, I didn't graduate, I quit."

"We don't care if you quit, we just want to see you."

This was like a healing for me; my old classmates accepted me. This was a BRIGHT LIGHT for me. I had known some of them since kindergarten. They asked each classmate to write a bio of what they had been doing since high school. I couldn't wait to write one. They posted them in a book for everyone to read. I told them I had been a dirty rotten person until I was almost forty years old, and Jesus had made me brand new.

When Gayle called me again and invited me to our fifty-year reunion, I was excited. This time they posted a different person's bio each week on the website leading up to our fifty-year reunion. The week they posted mine, Jesus got the glory.

There was no way I would have known most of my classmates, everyone changes and fifty years is a very long time. I went to school with some brilliant people; they were smart enough to put our high school picture on our name tags. When I walked up to someone, I looked at their name tag and it was like being back in high school.

My problem all night was when I looked at the picture on a name tag, and saw who wore it, I was certain they had the wrong tag on. Don't get me wrong, I am not making fun of how anyone looks as they get older. I'm the guy who sometimes, while shaving, leans forward, squinting into the mirror, and says,

"Dad… is that you?"

An even *brighter* light is that I have begun to rebuild friendships with some of my classmates. I started to kindergarten over sixty years ago with some of them and it's good to have them back in my life. I have been invited to speak in one of their churches and several of my classmates plan to attend. It has been a blast seeing them and hanging out.

Debbie and Bill Corum

Bill and his wife are in full-time prison and inner-city ministry. The prison ministry takes them all over America and abroad. They have seen men and women be deeply touched, as they have shared together the testimony of God's redeeming power in their lives. The inner-city and street ministry is in Kansas City, Missouri.

They have been married over 33 years and give all the Glory to Jesus Christ. Both agree that without Jesus there would have been no hope for their marriage. They have a heart to see damaged marriages like theirs be reconciled.

They have learned to not have their expectations in each other, but to have their expectations in Christ. It is one of the keys to a successful marriage.

Their prayer for everyone who reads this book is that they will find the peace that only HE can give.

ABOUT THE AUTHOR

Bill Corum, an ordained minister, author, and motivational speaker has been speaking in prisons, churches, high schools and colleges world wide for almost 30 years. His powerful presentations detail the consequences that are the results of making bad choices of using drugs, alcohol, pornography and living a life of crime while providing hope and inspiration to those who are wanting to find a way to change. Bill speaks from a first hand account after personally traveling over 2,500 miles in hand-cuffs, waist-chains and leg-irons while being incarcerated in 10 different states.

Since becoming a Christian in 1983, Bill's primary mission has been serving various roles in ministry including being a platform speaker for the Bill Glass ministry Champions for Life and Fellowship of Christian Athletes, the director of correctional services of The Salvation Army, and founder and director of Prison Power Ministries. Bill has shared his testimony on many television shows including twice on the 700 Club and was the first American to speak in a prison in the former East Germany. In 1996, Bill was a co-founder and President of Integrity correctional centers, a private jail that processed and held over 25,000 inmates under his leadership. In 2003, he helped co-found and became the Vice President of Metcalf Auto Plaza, until his retirement in 2012 when he felt a calling to re-enter the ministry full time. The former golden glove heavyweight boxer still packs a powerful punch when sharing his personal message of going from having the desire of obtaining money, power, and influence to finding salvation, love, and finally peace in your life.

Contact Bill at:

www.billcorum.com

www.theultimatepardon.com

P.O. Box 281, Lone Jack, MO 64070

SPECIAL NOTE TO THE INCARCERATED

Bill enjoys hearing from inmates, and reads every letter he gets personally. However due to the amount of mail he gets, he cannot correspond with those who write him. If you have asked Jesus to come into your heart and want to grow spiritually, Bill says, "Jesus saved me, but His word is what changed me." You will only be changed by applying His word to your everyday life.

You can contact the ministry below to sign up for a correspondence bible study.

ARM Prison Outreach

P.O. Box 1490

Joplin, MO 64802